The Piano on Film

ALSO BY DAVID HUCKVALE
AND FROM MCFARLAND

---

*Terrors of the Flesh: The Philosophy
of Body Horror in Film* (2020)

Dirk Bogarde: Matinee Idol, Art House Star (2019)

Movie Magick: The Occult in Film (2018)

*A Green and Pagan Land: Myth, Magic and Landscape
in British Film and Television* (2018)

Music for the Superman: Nietzsche and the Great Composers (2017)

*A Dark and Stormy Oeuvre: Crime, Magic and Power in
the Novels of Edward Bulwer-Lytton* (2016)

Hammer Films' Psychological Thrillers, 1950–1972 (2014)

Poe Evermore: The Legacy in Film, Music and Television (2014)

*The Occult Arts of Music: An Esoteric Survey
from Pythagoras to Pop Culture* (2013)

*James Bernard, Composer to Count Dracula: A Critical
Biography* (2006; paperback 2012)

*Ancient Egypt in the Popular Imagination: Building a
Fantasy in Film, Literature, Music and Art* (2012)

*Visconti and the German Dream: Romanticism, Wagner
and the Nazi Catastrophe in Film* (2012)

*Touchstones of Gothic Horror: A Film Genealogy
of Eleven Motifs and Images* (2010)

Hammer Film Scores and the Musical Avant-Garde (2008)

The Piano on Film

DAVID HUCKVALE

McFarland & Company, Inc., Publishers
Jefferson, North Carolina

ISBN (print) 978-1-4766-8634-9
ISBN (ebook) 978-1-4766-4388-5

LIBRARY OF CONGRESS AND BRITISH LIBRARY
CATALOGUING DATA ARE AVAILABLE

Library of Congress Control Number 2022004509

© 2022 David Huckvale. All rights reserved

No part of this book may be reproduced or transmitted in any form or by any means, electronic or mechanical, including photocopying or recording, or by any information storage and retrieval system, without permission in writing from the publisher.

Front cover photograph © Shutterstock/n_at

Printed in the United States of America

*McFarland & Company, Inc., Publishers
Box 611, Jefferson, North Carolina 28640
www.mcfarlandpub.com*

Table of Contents

Introduction 1

One. The Romantic Piano 7
Two. Picture Palace Pianos 35
Three. Paderewski and Liberace 64
Four. Grand Galop Cinématique 81
Five. Piano Lessons 103
Six. Practice Makes Perfect 115
Seven. Surrogate Pianos 149
Eight. Sex and Violence 158

Finale 187
Chapter Notes 191
Bibliography 195
Index 201

ALGERNON: Did you hear what I was playing, Lane?
LANE: I didn't think it polite to listen, sir.
ALGERNON: I'm sorry for that, for your sake. I don't play accurately—anyone can play accurately—but I play with wonderful expression. As far as the piano is concerned, sentiment is my forte. I keep science for Life.
LANE: Yes, sir.

—Oscar Wilde, *The Importance of Being Earnest*

Introduction

Conjure to yourself the coffin-black of a Venetian gondola, or, indeed, of the gondola black of an elegant coffin. Imagine the sheen of a luxurious black limousine, or the bittersweet taste of dark chocolates with soft centers. Alternatively, you might like to contemplate the smooth surface of a highly lacquered Chinese box: A shiny black concert grand piano reminds me of all these things. Played by a master, its strings can suggest a gondolier singing on a moonlit canal, or a throbbing threnody. A piano recital is also rather like consuming a mouth-watering assortment of chocolate treats or taking a smooth journey through breathtaking scenery. (The English comic Dudley Moore once performed a TV sketch in which he did just this: "driving" his grand piano down a motorway, dressed in white tie and tails. The faster he played, the faster he moved.) The piano is, above all, a musical box of many puzzles.

Under the hands of a master, the piano can perform miracles. It is the pre-eminent vehicle of musical virtuosity, of sonic eroticism and emotional power. Its strings can be made to vibrate with the softness of a snowflake or the thundering power of a battering ram. They can soothe with the delicacy of a falling petal and overwhelm with the majesty of Niagara Falls; but it is not just in the concert hall where this magic happens.

I have played the piano since I was nine years old, when I came home from school one day and saw, to my indescribable delight, a second-hand Collard and Collard upright being wheeled down the front path of the family home. My mother, sensing that I was drawn to her own mother's even older piano, had thoughtfully purchased the instrument for me; but I was an ill-disciplined student. I stood aloof from scales, was bored by studies and cared little for technique, believing I could learn to play through love of the piano alone. I strummed and improvised, was not diligent, and by the time some discipline had been drilled into me by several unappealing elderly ladies, and later at university, it was far too late to think of my ever being good enough seriously to consider making it a career. Besides,

I lacked the personality, the physical and emotional stamina to survive the punishing life of a concert pianist, even if I had acquired the necessary transcendental technique.

But the piano has never ceased to fascinate me. I play every day, and, for me, there is nothing so absorbing, compulsive and delightful as daily practice. Some people go to Mass. I go to my piano, where I get to know pieces from the inside, as it were. I have even managed to play through the whole of Fauré's *Ballade* Op. 19, the manuscript of which Liszt himself sent back to the composer with the single comment "Too difficult."

One does not need to know how to play the piano to make the prospect of owning one desirable in itself. Apropos of this, I was once asked to play the newly acquired Steinway grand of a 1980s yuppie, which stood on a dais in the living room of his new mansion, flanked by fake fluted columns. He couldn't play even "Chopsticks" himself, but he liked the idea of someone playing his pride and joy for him and a gathering of friends and relations. He requested the flashiest pieces I could manage and the evening was a great success, but I couldn't help feeling that he seemed to be aspiring to something he didn't really want: an aura of culture without having to bother to understand it. (Similarly, so many film sets are dressed with a grand piano, which is never actually played. And have you ever noticed how many celebrities like to be interviewed with a piano in the background?)

A few years before my yuppie concert, a hairdressing salon had also engaged my services to play the rather more battered grand piano that stood ostentatiously in the window. Whatever I played on it was of course drowned by the hair dryers surrounding it; but the point was that the piano gave the business *class*, because, by that time, part of the "classiness" of a piano was due to its redundancy. What had once been a ubiquitous object and a relatively ubiquitous skill were by then rather unusual. Playing the piano had come to be regarded as something of an eccentricity.

Films, however, are filled with pianos, far more than you might at first expect, and I have often wondered what cinematic pianos can tell us about the cultural history of this instrument. The book before you is therefore an attempt at an explanation. By the time of Hollywood's Golden Age, the piano itself had already begun to lose its long-held status as the King of Instruments. The popular Romanticism of the movies kept that status alive, but it was an afterlife like the Frankenstein Monster or the undead existence of Count Dracula. Films in fact perpetuated what was already dead or at least dying: the ideals and esthetics of Romanticism itself.

Film can sometimes invest new life into classical music, rebranding it and bringing it to audiences who might never have heard it before. The most famous example of this kind of thing might be Bo Widerberg's 1967 Romantic drama *Elvira Madigan,* which famously used the slow movement of Mozart's C-major Piano Concerto (No. 22). That piece is now almost always referred to as the "Elvira Madigan" Concerto, to the extent that no doubt some people might think this was a title Mozart himself gave to the work. But Mozart certainly never had in mind an army deserter kissing the eponymous tightrope walker while his face is still covered in shaving soap, which is how the music is introduced to us in the film.

Film also makes use of the visual impact of pianos in set decoration, as well as reimagining that archetypal Romantic form of the piano concerto. Movie concertos give only the *impression* of a concerto, just as composer biopics give only an impression (and often a very misleading one) of composers' lives.

Films have also reflected the politics of the piano. Until relatively recently, black pianists, for example, were rarely seen playing grand pianos, only humble uprights, while women, so often in the past required to play the piano if they wished successfully to enter the marriage market, are often shown in films as concert performers, but not as composers, which was traditionally the preserve of men. Film is equally concerned with piano teachers, who are often represented as tyrants or Svengalis. Cartoons and comedians have often used the piano virtuosity for comic effect, sometimes to make a serious point.

While film perpetuates the image of the piano in all its forms, the instrument has been made largely redundant in popular music by electronic keyboards. As the piano now lives an increasingly rarified existence in concert halls, it is not unreasonable to ask if the cinema is its mausoleum. Did the piano in fact die when European culture attempted suicide in 1914? Films kept it on life support throughout the first half of the twentieth century, but by the 1960s, popular culture made classical music in general and piano music in particular remote, to the extent that in recent years, both have been used to disperse juvenile delinquents on Britain's streets. It seems that we are now left with a corpse, which quietly putrefies on our TV and computer screens, awaiting a decent burial. The piano can be regarded as a microcosm of an entire culture and the manner in which it has been presented by the cinema is a fascinating way to explore its curious destiny from Mozart and Beethoven, to Liberace and Elton John.

When Beethoven composed his 32 piano sonatas around the turn of the eighteenth century, the mood they expressed about the culture from which they sprang was, as Kenneth Clarke has expressed it (albeit with regard to a different epoch), one of "heroic energy, confidence ... strength of will and intellect."[1] Indeed, one might employ these terms as the necessary ingredients for any civilization, but Beethoven's piano sonatas have these qualities ingrained in every note that forms them. Bernard Rose's 1995 Beethoven film *Immortal Beloved*, starring Gary Oldman as the great

Ludwig van (as a Beethoven admirer of him in Anthony Burgess' novel, *A Clockwork Orange*, refers to him), depicts the creation of Beethoven's famous "Moonlight" Sonata as the product of an improvisation inspired by a new Broadwood piano imported from London. This, explains Countess Giulietta Guicciardi (Valeria Gonino), to whom the work was later dedicated, is "of the latest design and is the first of its kind in Vienna. Tomorrow morning, I shall send away the servants and we shall all be out. I have done this so that you might try out this new invention undisturbed."

Beethoven arrives, unaware that the countess is secretly watching him from behind a panel. He examines the instrument, closes its lid, opens it again, plays a series of chaotic chords and then, laying his head on the folded back lid, begins to improvise the "Moonlight," which Beethoven himself identified as "Sonata quasi una fantasia"—a sonata that is almost a fantasy. In the opening movement, as the Beethoven scholar Luigi Magnani has described it, "a thrilling existential theme is dominated by the abstract but attractive demands of the composition; yet this in no way means that it loses the original vibrant feeling or ardent inventive impulse which give it life."

> It is "almost a fantasy" when Beethoven expresses the depth of his idea while appearing to give free rein to his imagination; when he reconciles the shiver of inspiration with the rational structures of form.[2]

This mixture of rhapsodic improvisation united with classical structures was conceivably made possible only by this kind of instrument, which can play both soft and loud, which has pedals to sustain the sound, and in which a single player can command both harmony and melodic aspects. The music emerges from the piano, rather than the piano playing the music after the event of its composition, and it was this aspect of improvisation and introversion which sowed the seeds for so much of the piano music that followed, for Beethoven eventually so exhausted the possibilities of sonata form that there was nowhere to go after him but into freer, more individualistic musical structures. This is made quite clear in Thomas Mann's novel about music, politics and culture, *Doctor Faustus*, in which a music teacher Wendel Kretshmar performs, and explains while he performs, Beethoven's Op. 111 Sonata. His description of the music marks it out as a pinnacle of culture:

> What now happens to this mild utterance, rhythmically, harmonically, contrapuntally, to this pensive, subdued formulation, with what its master blesses and to what condemns it, into what black nights and dazzling flashes, crystal spheres wherein coldness and heat, repose and ecstasy are one and the same, he flings it down and lifts it up, all that one may well call vast, strange, extravagantly magnificent, without thereby giving it a name, because it is quite

truly nameless; and with laboring hands Kretschmar played us all those enormous transformations, singing at the same time with the greatest violence: "Dim-dada!" and mingling his singing with shouts. "These chains of trills!" he yelled. "These flourishes and cadenzas! Do you hear the conventions that are left in? Here—the language—is no longer—purified of the flourishes—domination—the appearance—of art is thrown off—at last—art always throws off the appearance of art. Dim-dada! Do listen, how here—the melody is dragged down by the centrifugal weight of chords! It becomes static, monotonous— twice D, three times D, one after the other—the chords do it—dim-dada!" ... It had happened that the sonata had come, in the second, enormous movement, to an end, an end without any return. And when he said "the sonata," he meant not only this one in C minor, but the sonata in general, as a species, as traditional art-form; it was here at an end, brought to an end, it had fulfilled its destiny, reached its goal, beyond which there was no going.³

If, after all that, we hurtle forward in time to Liberace playing "Roll Out the Barrel" or Elton John singing the title song of Dexter Fletcher's biopic, *Rocketman* (2019), in which we find Taron Egerton as John, dressed in spangles and playing his silver grand piano to a vast, screaming audience, we begin to have some kind of idea not only of the decline of the piano but also of the decline of the idealistic culture to which it gave birth in the nineteenth century. The piano is thus a fascinating symbol of the decay of a culture, and the way in which it is presented in films is most instructive.

One

The Romantic Piano

Pianos Do Furnish a Room

It was Liszt who most impressively made the piano romantic. A Liszt recital (a term he largely invented himself) became an almost supernatural event, a musical miracle, presided over by a godlike genius with a whole world of sonic effects at his command. Of the many accounts of Liszt's playing, the reminiscences of his American pupil, Amy Fay, captures both the emotional intensity of the experience but also its visual and imagistic effect, which partly helps explain the cinema's later flirtation with the composer and his works:

> It was the first time I had heard him, and I don't know which was the most extraordinary—the Scherzo, with its wonderful lightness and swiftness, the Adagio with its depth and pathos, or the last movement, where the whole keyboard seemed to *donnern und blitzen* (thunder and lighten). There is such a vividness about everything he plays that it does not seem as if it were mere music you were listening to, but it is as if he had called up a real living *form,* and you saw it breathing before your face and eyes. It gives *me* almost a ghostly feeling to hear him, and it seems as if the air were peopled with spirits. Oh, he is a perfect wizard! It is interesting to see him as it is to hear him, for his face changes with every modulations of the piece, and he looks exactly as he is playing. He has one element that is most captivating, and that is, a sort of delicate and fitful mirth that keeps peering out at you here and there! It is most peculiar, and when he plays that way, the most bewitching little expression comes over his face.[1]

Liszt was a superstar, and largely thanks to him, the piano became a physical embodiment of music itself. On a more mundane level, the piano is also a piece of furniture, as well as a status symbol on account of its size, its beauty, its complexity and, not least, its value. This is particularly the case with a grand piano (or Flügel to use the German term), rather than the space-saving bourgeois upright (which was originally known as a piano "in the form of a console"). Just such an instrument was purchased for just such a reason by cocoa plantation owner Christopher Leiningen (Charlton Heston) in *The Naked Jungle* (dir. Byron Haskin, 1954). He admits he knows nothing about music, but would nonetheless like to hear it played before the termites get at it. "I had it brought up river 2000 miles," he explains. He has also had a wife (Eleanor Parker) brought up to him by the same route, and she proceeds to play a Chopin Prelude on it, lamentably demonstrating just how out of tune it is. (The marriage is similarly flat.) Chopin being too sad for this unhappy woman, she transfers her attention to a transcription of Mendelssohn's "On Wings of Song." But when Leiningen learns that she has been married before, he is furious. "The only condition I ever made about anything I ever brought up the river was that it be new. Worth the effort. This piano you're sitting at was never played by anyone before it came here." The wife now realizes what her role in this arrangement is to be. "You wanted an ornament. Something nice-looking to go with the rest of the furniture ... that's the kind of woman you want." Slamming the keyboard to cause an appropriate discord, she adds, "If you knew more about music, you'd realize that a good piano is better when it's played. This is not a very good piano!"—and she storms off.

Grand pianos like Leiningen's were not always black: Late Romanticism made them so, not so much in imitation of the noirs worn by Liszt and the violinist Paganini, who inspired him, but through the desire in the early twentieth century not to be distracted from musical purity by instrumental decoration. In Liszt's own time, pianos were often ornate affairs, enlivened by veneers, by ormolu and by intricate carvings. Sometimes they were even painted or inlaid with marquetry. (Films, not surprisingly, often favor the most decorative examples. Katharine Hepburn as Clara Schumann, for example, sits at a keyboard flanked by winged cherubs in *Song of Love* [dir. Clarence Brown, 1947].) The black piano is the musical equivalent of Vienna's streamlined Looshaus, completed in 1911, which was so modern that Emperor Franz Joseph instructed his coachman to take a different route home to avoid him having to look at it. Adolf Loos, the architect of this "house without eyebrows," as the Viennese like to call it, believed that "ornament is crime." Pianos followed suit, and concert grands are still black. However, in the wake of showmen like Liberace, who revived the esthetic of Liszt and turned it into super-kitsch, they have since been covered in mirrors, sprayed silver, and even, in the film *Pal Joey* (dir. George Sidney, 1957), painted scarlet (along with the piano stool) for Frank Sinatra to sit at and strum as he sings "That's Why the Lady Is a Tramp."

One would expect films about composers to feature pianos, and many of the interiors of Tony Palmer's 1983 film *Wagner* are furnished with them. But they are not all owned by professional musicians. Because of pianos' high status, aristocratic drawing rooms always required musical instruments as part of their furnishings. In the nineteenth century, a grand piano was considered a mark of culture and good taste, even in the most unmusical of families. In grander homes, the presence of a grand piano offered the possibility of private musical gatherings, and such salon soirées have often been recreated in films, particularly the two versions of Patrick Hamilton's play *Gaslight*. The first, directed by Thorold Dickinson in 1940, stars Anton Walbrook and Diana Wynyard, who play a husband and wife: Paul Mallen is intent on driving his wife Bella insane as part of his plan to recover some valuable jewels, which he was unable to retrieve after having murdered a woman for them in the neighboring house some years before. Midway through the film, Paul and Bella attend a piano recital given at an upper-class social gathering, which resembles the kind of environment captured by James Tissot in his society paintings of such events, particularly "Hush" aka "The Concert" from 1875, in which elegantly attired members of the upper class gather on the staircase, clustered around the door and beneath the chandelier of an equally elegant salon to hear a violinist, accompanied by the inevitable grand piano. The pianist in *Gaslight* is in fact the English player Angus Morrison, and this is the only recording of his playing in existence. He performs a Lanner Waltz, arranged by the film's musical director Richard Addinsell. During the performance, Mallen looks for but cannot find his watch. In fact, he has deliberately planted it in his wife's handbag, to convince her that she is losing her mind, Mallen having previously accused her of such kleptomania. Bella breaks down under the accusation, starts sobbing and interrupts the recital. This causes an embarrassing scene. The pianist stops playing, annoyed by the disturbance, while Paul leads the tearful Bella out of the room.

The story was recapitulated, with a few alterations, in an MGM remake, directed by Charles Vidor in 1944, with Charles Boyer and Ingrid Bergman in the leading roles. Boyer's character is now professional musician Gregory Anton, whom Bergman's Paula meets while taking singing lessons in Italy. At one stage, Gregory plays a Strauss Waltz to his new wife on his own piano. "Don't you think this is charming?" he asks. "It's from the new operetta at the Gaiety. I wish I could write tunes like Strauss." The grander piano recital scene takes place in a much larger environment than the earlier film—in fact, a large wrought-iron conservatory—and the pianist this time is the Polish Jakob Gimpel, who went on to perform Liszt's music for the soundtrack of director Paul Wendkos' *The Mephisto Waltz* (1970). In *Gaslight*, he plays the beginning of Beethoven's "Pathètique" Sonata and a longer extract from Chopin's Ballade No. 1 (Op. 23). The music is different from the 1940 version but the scene plays out much as before, with embarrassment all round.

Boyer had already experienced this kind of environment in *The Constant Nymph* (dir. Edmund Goulding, 1943), in which he plays a composer who performs his own discordant piano piece (specially written for the film by Erich Wolfgang Korngold). Sitting at interlocking grands, he and Max Rabinowitz launch into what is not to everyone's taste. "It's beyond a wonder to me any reasonable piano can stand up under such a pounding!" blusters one member of the audience (Charles Coburn). "Maybe that's why they have two pianos," observes a more tolerant guest.

A more intimate (and melodic) version of this kind of musical occasion occurs in *Gosford Park* (dir. Robert Altman, 2002), in which Jeremy Northam impersonates Ivor Novello, one of the guests at a weekend house party who sings for his supper with a rendering of "The Land of Might-Have-Been" to his own piano accompaniment. He sits at the keyboard while the other guests and the rest of the family entertain themselves with cards, drink and conversation. "It seems to be much more than background music," complains Dame Maggie Smith's Constance Trentham. Indeed, background music is exactly what was required in such a situation. No doubt the Gosford Park piano was quite unused to Brahms Sonatas and Liszt Fantasies, despite the fact that the constantly tippling guests who listen to Novello are all somewhat "Brahms and Liszt" themselves (to employ musical Cockney rhyming slang). The piano is merely a status symbol in *Gosford Park*—what one ought to have in a drawing room just as a library should be filled with books, which no one actually bothers to read. Eric Idle, imitating Noël Coward in *Monty Python's The Meaning of Life* (dir. Terry Jones, 1983), had a more responsive audience for his rendition (at another grand) of the "Penis Song." "What a frightfully witty song," says one of the elegantly dressed restaurant diners whom Idle serenades with all the different names for this particular organ, thus exposing the absurdity of genteel manners in general. When someone breaks wind, everyone is appalled, but a woman's announcement that she is about to have her period goes unnoticed.

One scene in Robin Hardy's *The Wicker Man* (1973) similarly inverts the respectable connotation of the domestic piano. Lord Summerisle (Christopher Lee) presides over a neo-pagan community of apple growers, who still indulge in human sacrifices to ensure their harvest. He lives in a suitably grand dwelling, rather like Gosford Park, so one would expect the drawing room to be furnished with a grand piano. But the song he sings to his own accompaniment with the local schoolteacher, Miss Rose (Diane Cilento), is far from respectable. "The Tinker of Rye" is overflowing with sexual innuendo, which shocks Edward Woodwood's Christian policeman,

Sgt. Howie, when he interrupts the entertainment. The piano falls silent, mid-phrase, along with the singing.

> The piano is the social instrument par excellence. It is a drawing-room furniture, a sign of bourgeois prosperity, the most massive of the devices by which the young are tortured in the name of education and the grown-up in the name of entertainment.[2]

But far more humble homes across the globe also had their uprights, later to be replaced by radios, record players, CDs and now the instant accessibility of everything on the Internet. In D.H. Lawrence's play *A Collier's Friday Night,* for example, even the home of a Nottingham miner has its cultural corner. "The Maiden's Prayer" and "Anitra's Dance" from Grieg's *Peer Gynt* Suite are duly played upon the parlor piano. Lawrence explained that the piano represented

> a blind reaching out for beauty. To the woman it is a possession and a piece of furniture and something to feel superior about. But see the elderly colliers trying to learn to play, see them listening with queer alert faces to their daughter's execution of "The Maiden's Prayer," and you will see a blind, unsatisfied craving for beauty. It is far more deep in the men than in the women. The women want show. The men want beauty, and still want it."[3]

It was indeed the lack of twentieth-century technology that made the piano indispensable. It was not so much for its particular sound but for its ability to suggest an entire orchestra that made it so ubiquitous. In a time without mechanical reproduction, pianos were essential. Wagner even took under his wing a "house pianist" in the person of the Jewish Josef Rubinstein, who transcribed the composer's *Siegfried Idyll* for piano and, acting as a kind of human gramophone, was "switched on" by Wagner whenever he wanted to be entertained. In the twentieth century, Adolf Hitler similarly used the services of his friend Ernst "Putzi" Hanfstaengl, another accomplished piano player, to entertain him with bleeding chunks from Wagner's *oeuvre* in the small hours of the morning.

> Often towards midnight, tired after a day of speech and meetings with local Gauleiters, Hitler would suddenly demand he [Hanfstaengl] play something on the piano. Putzi never had time to practice these days but would expertly busk for an hour or more, starting perhaps with some Bach or Chopin or some of his own marches, but always finishing with *Tristan und Isolde* and *Meistersinger.* Putzi tried to introduce more modern works, such as Rachmaninoff's Second Piano Concerto, but it was too adventurous for the Nazi strongman. Hitler did, however, develop an unexpected passion for the work of Irving Berlin and made Putzi play his arrangement of a Russian lullaby over and over again. Putzi did not have the heart to tell him that Berlin was Jewish. While Putzi played, Hitler would sit in a half doze, literally gurgling with delight, and his entourage would not dare to interrupt.[4]

Biopics

In Ken Russell's Tchaikovsky biopic *The Music Lovers* (1971), we see Anton Rubinstein (Max Adrian) performing the same function as Putzi Hanfstaengle and (the unrelated) Josef Rubinstein. He entertains the reclusive Nadezhda von Meck (Izabella Telezynska) with Tchaikovsky's *Romeo and Juliet* Overture in his own piano arrangement; but von Meck does not wish Tchaikovsky to prostitute himself in this manner. He must remain heard but not seen, as was actually the case during von Meck's eccentric patronage of the composer: The two never met. Richard Chamberlain, who plays Tchaikovsky, is shown at the keyboard, performing the famous B-flat minor Piano Concerto, which is abridged to form a kind of "potted concerto." Chamberlain sweats his way through the scales and arpeggios, virtually impregnating the instrument, only to be mercilessly taunted immediately afterwards by Rubinstein, who mocks his composition as "woman's stuff," no doubt intended as a reference to Tchaikovsky's homosexuality. Here the concerto as a metaphor of the tortured hero against society reaches its peak. "It's the best thing I've ever written, and I will not change a single note!" Tchaikovsky rages, but as everyone knows, he ultimately lost his battle against the prejudice of society. Even today in Russia, there are those who would deny Tchaikovsky's personal reality. Russell's piano concerto scene perfectly symbolizes this struggle.

Cinematically speaking, struggles of one sort or another were central to the biopic genre. George Gershwin, as portrayed in *Rhapsody in Blue*, is another kind of outsider, this time a Jew from humble origins. ("A Boy from the Sidewalks of New York Who Captured the Heart of a Nation" as the trailer put it.) He triumphs of course, the film reaching its peak in a beautifully staged performance of the piece that gives the film its title. Whereas Oscar Levant's performance of Gershwin's Concerto in F in *An American in Paris* (dir. Vincente Minnelli, 1951) is the ultimate musical ego trip (see below), Robert Alda's impersonation of Gershwin playing this work in *Rhapsody in Blue* emphasizes the vulnerability of the composer. Twice he stumbles over passagework during this performance, covering his tracks with a frown. This, of course, increases the tension but also humanizes Gershwin as a specifically American hero. The implication, for the American audiences who originally watched this hagiography, is that "Gershwin is one of us." The film is a long way away from Liberace kitsch, though it is there implicitly (this is Hollywood, after all). The manner in which the orchestra is filmed is, as one might expect, particularly cinematic. No concert hall (before Liberace came on the scene) would have presented its orchestra in this way, spotlighting individual players who stand apart for their solos. The mood lighting, which enhances the different section of the

Reflections in black: Robert Alda as George Gershwin in *Rhapsody in Blue*.

music, the art deco design of the set, and the geometric placing of the players create a completely different esthetic. Gershwin's piano in the "Rhapsody in Blue" segment even has a Liberace-style mirrored piano lid, which reflects Alda's fingers. (It is Levant we hear on the soundtrack. He also appears as himself in the action.)

The various pianos that are used in the performances also symbolize Gershwin's rise to wealth and fame. He begins his career playing uprights, which suit Tin Pan Alley rather better than Carnegie Hall. There is also a considerable amount of what would now be called cultural appropriation in Gershwin's music: the influence of Negro music, reconstituted in a post–Lisztian mold of bourgeois virtuosity. This is now a contentious area, especially among black musicologists, and it is easy to decode what's going on in purely visual terms: The black concert grand piano is, ironically, an instrument for white performers. Black players invariably had to make do with an upright. That kind of piano, designed for domestic use, is problematic when it comes to public performance, for the soloist is placed in the position of sitting at a bureau, which is something one only does in an office or a parlor. Indeed, uprights came to prominence when space in less wealthy homes became limited; hence they were born with an inferiority complex. Placed against a wall while playing to oneself or a small group of guests is one thing, but when pushed out onto a stage, an upright lacks status, not to mention sonic power. The height of the instrument also overshadows the player and screens him or her from half the audience at least, while less tall uprights look merely puny. However, these disadvantages make the upright appropriate for more egalitarian contexts.

What is perfectly respectable in a grand piano (raising its swan-like lid to reveal the gilded iron frame and discreet mechanism) has a somewhat seedier connotation in an upright. An upright's mechanism, when revealed, is not only clumsier and more obviously mechanical, it is also much more visible, when the front panel is removed, which perhaps explains its proletarian signification. (The bourgeois, of course, is always keen to cover up the piano's secrets along with its legs.) It would seem that uprights are bourgeois in private and proletarian in public. Just as music has always been codified along class lines, instruments also carry their connotations of class, depending of course upon context. Popular pianists like to reveal the mechanism of their uprights. The white British Russ Conway and black Trinidian Winifred Atwell often did this. So too did the highly gifted black American Thomas "Fats" Waller. (He was also a keen player of J.S. Bach, but the bad temper of racial prejudice at the time forbade him the opportunity to play the well-tempered klavier in public. Like Liberace, Waller had been deeply impressed by Paderewski, but Waller could never have been a Liberace, for Liberace promoted a specifically "white" brand of kitsch. In fact, it's hard to say if Black kitsch can really be said to exit, as kitsch is always an appropriation, and Black culture, having been historically the underdog, never appropriated anything: It was too busy maintaining its own identity. Dominant cultures, however, feed not only on others but also on themselves, and kitsch is so often the result.) We can observe Waller's exposed piano in *Stormy Weather* (dir. Andrew L. Stone, 1943), in which he plays wearing his trademark bowler hat with cigarette drooping from his lips. (Such a relaxed night club environment is also shared by François Truffaut's *Shoot the Piano Player* from 1960 [see below], the main titles of which roll over shots of a revealed upright action.)

Piano Appeal

Coupled with his musical miracles, Liszt's undeniable sex appeal made him truly godlike. In his youth, he was graced with good looks, a slim figure and elegant bearing. Although such things have nothing to do with what audiences heard, they had an immense effect on the experience of his performances in general. The piano itself is the most aristocratic of instruments in that there is no blowing or scraping involved. Very few orchestral instruments have the glamor and sex appeal required by the movies, not so much in themselves (though that is an important factor) but more so in what they require from their players. With the exception of the silvery flute, virtually the entire wind and brass section can be eliminated as candidates for screen stardom; the features of a face contorted by blowing is nowhere near photogenic enough. An oboist, for example, must purse his or her lips in a miserly fashion and inevitably frown with the strain of forcing so much air through an oboe's mouthpiece. Clarinets pose a similar esthetic problem, with the added disadvantage of the lips having to negotiate a wider, broader mouthpiece, which suggest sucking on an ice cream. Trumpets, trombones and horns require so much puff that the cheeks bulge out like a clown's, undermining whatever sublimities of sound such swollen cheeks may be summoning.

Percussion is reminiscent of the kindergarten. Harps, however, are an exception to which we will return. They have a glamor and grace of their own, which is related to that of the piano, sharing, as they do, a similar structure, if a differing mode of attack. But—and this is crucial—they have long-standing *feminine* and angelic connotations. Consequently, they lack phallic power. Even when conventionally feminine performers play the piano, the phallic is always with them; this is not the case with the harp, however much one might resist this now somewhat politically incorrect observation.

The cello requires splayed legs from the performer, thus exposing the genital area in both sexes. This fact was not lost on Sir Thomas Beacham, who reputedly retorted to an unfortunate (female) cellist in the orchestra he was rehearsing at the time, "Madam, you have between your legs an instrument capable of giving pleasure to thousands and all you can do is scratch it." That story may be apocryphal, but there is no disputing that cellists are visually ungainly and, if erotic, not glamorously so. The cello entirely lacks the phallic power of the guitar, so much exploited by rock and pop musicians, of course, who have always slung them as low as possible over their own genitals. The advantage here is that the guitar can be moved and thrust into the air in a way the cello cannot, and a bow is not required, allowing the fingers to touch the strings directly over the crotch in a much more suggestive manner.

Double basses are visually absurd, like bassoons and tubas, which really only leaves the violins and violas. Violas being slightly larger and mellower in tone, unfortunately lack the dynamism, energy and élan of the violin, which has thus become more successful on the cinema's casting couch; but none of these instruments can match the erotic power, glamor and authority of the grand piano, an instrument from which rich harmonies can be summoned from the fingertips alone, without anatomical distortion or facial grimacing. (That said, some pianists unfortunately cannot resist indulging in this for expressive purposes.) Whereas all the other instruments require that both hands are always fully engaged, the piano, having legs and not requiring to be *held,* allows opportunities for the pianist to raise and wave his or her hands between passages, suggesting the gestures of a magus at a rite. Indeed, this is exactly how Vincent Price presented his demonic organist Dr. Anton Phibes in the two films he made featuring that character in the 1970s. The piano thus permits the performer greater physical freedom of expression, and the effect on audiences can be rapturous if not hysterical.

Audiences today do not kiss the hem of the Versace creations worn by the virtuoso pianist Yuja Wang, but they certainly wanted to touch Liberace's spectacular outfits and admire his rings. Liberace was the Elvis of the piano, but an Elvis who looked to Liszt, that prototype of the modern pop star, for his inspiration. Whereas fans would later throw their underwear at pop singer Tom Jones, Liszt's female fans reached out to clutch his legs, and then fight each other to grab his discarded cigar butts as souvenirs. Foreshadowing the flamboyant costumes of Liberace and Elton John, Liszt would stride on stage wearing the ceremonial sword he had been presented by the Hungarian government, his chest sporting additional honorary medals. Liszt would then peel off his gloves, hurling them at his feet as if issuing a challenge to the audience. All these aspects of Liszt's stage persona were recreated in Ken Russell's Liszt biopic *Lisztomania,* but from within a 1970s glam-rock context, with Roger Daltrey of The Who in the title role. ("Lisztomania" was a term coined at the height of Liszt's incandescent fame as a performer.)

All this helps to explain why more films have been made about pianos and pianists than any other instrument or performer. There are notable exceptions, of course. In *The Magic Bow* (dir. Bernard Knowles, 1946), Stewart Granger starred as the virtuoso violinist Paganini; and in *Intermezzo* (dir. Gregory Ratoff, 1939), Leslie Howard played the fictional violin virtuoso Holger Brandt, who falls in love with his daughter's piano teacher (Ingrid Bergman). A similar kind of story formed the basis of *Humoresque* (dir. Jean Negulesco, 1946) in which Joan Crawford's society hostess Helen Wright falls in love with John Garfield's violinist Paul Boret. But this film equally featured Oscar Levant as the pianist Sid Jeffers, who plays the Liszt transcription of the "Liebestod" from Wagner's *Tristan und Isolde,* a Chopin Waltz and a Chopin Étude, part of Tchaikovsky's First Piano Concerto and several pieces by Gershwin, as well as accompanying Boret in the "Humoresque" of Dvořák, which lends the film its title, along with Rimsky-Korsakoff's "Flight of the Bumblebee."

There are also films featuring the cello. Paul Henreid mimes to the cello "concerto" specially written by Bernard Herrmann for *Deception* (dir. Irving Rapper, 1946). There is also Annand Tucker's *Hilary and Jackie* (1998), a biopic about the cellist Jacqueline du Pré, who was struck down in her prime by multiple sclerosis, thus making her ideal movie material. Peter Firth starred as a flautist who uses music to save the world in Jamil Dehlavi's *Born of Fire* (1987), while Roy Castle played his trumpet in *Dr. Terror's House of Horrors* (dir. Freddie Francis, 1965); but a film about an oboist? A melodrama about a bassoonist? The trials and tribulations of a xylophone player? The sheer ungainliness and absurdity of so many orchestral instruments is one of the reasons why Wagner decided to put the entire orchestra under the stage of his Festspielhaus in Bayreuth: It was just too distracting.

Many films feature big bands, jazz and pop music, as these forms of music are already estheticized in a way that classical music never was. The world of classical music is, in fact, extraordinarily unglamorous from a visual point of view. Orchestral musicians are not selected for their physical appearance, and the environments in which they work are usually abstract or cavernous with little direct visual appeal. Big bands and dance bands have always been more presentable with their white tuxedos, the personalized music stands (usually featuring stylish art deco designs in their 1930s heyday), the saxophones grouped together like marionettes, all choreographed in ways quite alien to a symphony orchestra in which no one stands up to play their solo. In the twentieth century, the sex appeal of pianists like Liszt was transferred to popular music, while classical music as a whole became increasingly cerebral to differentiate itself from the commercial forces that continually threaten to overwhelm it. This is not to say that classical music itself is not erotic (*Tristan und Isolde* demonstrates graphically that it was), but orchestral concerts in the twentieth century lagged far behind pop concerts in terms of visual sophistication. It was not until the cinema began to stage concerts for the screen that the shortcomings of the concert hall became apparent, and directors began to do something about it.

Walt Disney famously arranged the orchestra in *Fantasia* (1941) to make it far more *visually* appealing. As the film opens, we see silhouettes of the players and their instruments, which considerably increases their mystery. Colored lights bring them further life in a way that would have delighted the pioneers of synesthesia, such as Alexander Scriabin in the early years of the twentieth century. Such light shows are now, of course, an indispensible element of rock concerts. The way in which Disney's players are arranged on the platform also departs from tradition. Players are situated on tiered steps to enhance their visual harmony. The example of *Fantasia* was not lost on Herbert von Karajan when he made his carefully choreographed, artfully lit and expertly edited films featuring the Berlin Philharmonic Orchestra. His own performance on the podium also echoes that of the God-like Leopold Stokowski in Disney's film, and Karajan's habit of conducting the orchestra with this his eyes closed suggests that he too found the grotesqueries of musical manufacture distracting and unappealing.

Concert promoters, worried about declining audiences, could have learned much from the movies, though they have always had difficulty overcoming a general resistance to "visual distraction." However, before the advent of commercialized pop music, classical music had never been afraid of visual distraction, as we have seen with the sex appeal of Liszt, the demonic persona of Paganini and, for good measure, the waltzing that always surrounded Johann Strauss—not to mention the Gesamtkunstwerk of Wagnerian music drama and opera in general. Being as much a visual as a musical experience, and one dependent upon popular taste, the film industry fully realized what the classical music establishment of the twentieth century found so hard to accept in its pursuit of musical "purity."

Berlioz's descriptions of Liszt became a kind of blueprint for Liberace, who in his Frankenstein-like revival of Romanticism created such immensely compelling kitsch. (Kitsch is always the elaborately masked face of death.) But Liberace lived his undead existence to perhaps even greater acclaim that his progenitors.

A Brief History of the Piano

The piano has a long history, and with any long history, development characterizes it. The word "pianoforte" is merely a description of what this instrument can do, which is to sound both loud and soft, something the earlier harpsichords could never achieve because they pluck the strings, whereas pianos hit them with hammers. Clavichords also hit the strings, but with much smaller hammers (called tangents), made of brass. Consequently, they made a very different kind of sound from the heavier, felt-covered hammers of a piano: metal on metal is nowhere near as mellifluous, but at the time of the clavichord's popularity (around the middle of the eighteenth century), they achieved greater expressivity than had been possible before. Carl Philip Emmanuel Bach was particularly partial to this instrument for this reason, and he even wrote a treatise (*The True Art of Playing Keyboard Instruments,* 1753) about how to exploit it to its best effect. The sound of a clavichord is much more intimate than a piano, however, as the mechanism cannot generate what later technical developments achieved, and C.P.E. Bach's style of playing consequently characterized what was known as the *Empfindsamkeit* ("tender" or "sensitive") school.

As time moved on, the limitations of the clavichord consequently required re-thinking. In fact, they had already been re-thought during the heyday of the clavichord, but for various reasons, the new "pianoforte" didn't immediately catch on. This once novel coinage goes back to one Scipione Maffei, who published an article in 1711 about the "gravicembalo col piano e forte" ("harpsichord with loud and sound"). But Maffei was in fact only describing what had actually been invented, if only in prototype, as early as 1700 by Bartolomeo Cristofori, the keeper of the musical instruments at the Medici court in Florence. It was, however, a very different instrument from the concert grand of today, even though the basic principle was the same. Over the years, there have been square pianos, "giraffe" pianos (grands upended to save space), fortepianos and pianofortes, pianinos, cabinet pianos, "Euphonicons," uprights, baby grands, boudoir grands and honkytonks. What they all share are hammers covered in felt (or, early on, in leather) to hit the strings, and dampers to muffle their vibrations. The pedals are important too, the sustaining pedal in particular as it permits effects impossible to achieve on harpsichords and clavichords. This pedal sustains the resonance of the vibrating strings by lifting all the dampers, thus also setting in motion sympathetic vibrations from the other strings, which in the nineteenth century gave composers the illusion that they were imitating orchestral effects. Over time, strings became thicker, iron frames were introduced to permit greater tension, and sound-boards became bigger and consequently produced a much greater volume and richness of tone. With the invention, by Sébastien Érard in 1821, of the double escapement mechanism, which separated the key from the hammers, the hammers were able to move up and down much more quickly, allowing for the rapid repetition of notes. This was an effect Liszt could never resist, particularly because of its illusory qualities, as his biographer Alan Walker points out with regard to the Tarantella from the *Venezia e Napoli* supplement to book two of the *Années de pèlerinage*: "Liszt here produces a magical illusion. Like some latter-day Merlin, mixing potions and casting spells across the keyboard, the wizard deludes us into thinking that the piano has been metamorphosed into a sustaining instrument of radiant beauty."[5]

As the social historian of the piano, Dieter Hildebrandt, points out, by 1900 "the world was full of pianos—just as today it is full of cars."[6] The popularity of the piano crossed the globe:

> This hero conquered more of Europe than Napoleon and has occupied it much more permanently. It triumphed in the American civil war—on both sides—and rode out with the keenest of the pioneers to claim the Wild West. It united Germany long before Bismarck. It was a peaceful conqueror but often a tyrannical occupying force, exacting strict discipline with its loud commands. It soon terrorized whole cities, an omnipresent early Big Brother. No other general that century took so many prisoners. Over ten thousand young people

were condemned to "solitary confinement at the piano," children were chained to the instrument, and for young women in particular it was a pitiless chaperone. Some young people it frustrated in the worse sense of the word, for our hero was also a tempter, promising earthly fame and a route to immortality.[7]

In St. Petersburg, one factory built more than 11,000 pianos throughout the nineteenth century. Even in Siberia, the demand was great. "In these new towns of the expanding Empire, the piano played an even more important social role than it did in a Moscow drawing room. A piano was a 'highly respectableising piece of furniture,' observed a British musicologist of the nineteenth century, to affirm one's European education."[8]

There are still pianos in the world, and even more recordings of pianists playing them, but the piano is no longer ubiquitous. It has become increasingly professionalized, and because of that, amateur piano playing is nowhere near as commonplace as it was in the nineteenth or even the first half of the twentieth century. Many things occurred to cause this—not least two world wars and the social changes they brought, along with technological "advances" such as electronic keyboards and synthesizers. Pop still occasionally employs the piano, but it has never been an instrument suitable for busking. Bulk and weight prevent that, along with the piano's essentially bourgeois connotations. The semiotician Roland Barthes was very much aware of this change in the piano's fortunes:

> The music one plays comes from an activity that is very little auditory, being above all manual (and thus in a way much more sensual). It is the music which you or I can play, along or among friends, with no other audience than its participants (that is, with all risk of theatre, all temptation of hysteria removed); a muscular music in which the part taken by the sense of hearing is only one of ratification, as though the body was hearing—and not "the soul." ... This music has disappeared; initially the province of the idle (aristocratic) class, it lapsed into an insipid social rite with the coming of the democracy of the bourgeoisie (the piano, the young ladies, the drawing room, the nocturne) and then faded out altogether (who plays the piano today?). To find practical music in the West, one has now to look to another public, another repertoire, another instrument (the young generation, vocal music, the guitar). Concurrently, passive, receptive music, sound music, has become *the* music (that of concert, festival, record, radio): playing has ceased to exist.[9]

Transcriptions

With the decline of "musica practica," the kind of piano music we now listen to has changed quite radically. Vast quantities of "salon" music have been silenced, along with the many piano transcriptions of orchestral and operatic works which provided, in an age before recording technology, the only effective substitute for the real thing. Attending concerts and operas was (indeed, still is) expensive, but unlike today, they were once the only way to hear orchestral and operatic performances. Playing a transcription at home was the nineteenth-century equivalent of playing a CD, but in many ways more educational, as one was forced to experience the music from inside out, rather than as a merely passive listener. It was for this reason (but also, of course, for performance reasons of his own) that Liszt made his series of piano transcriptions, "reminiscences" and fantasies based on works originally written for other forces. (Many lesser-known composers also labored at this genre throughout the nineteenth century.) Beethoven's nine symphonies were among Liszt's prodigious output of transcriptions, along with his staggeringly complicated one of Berlioz's *Symphonie fantastique,* part of which he once heroically played immediately after Berlioz had conducted the orchestral version of its fourth movement, "Marche au supplice," in 1836. Its impact was recorded for us by Charles Hallé, who was present at the occasion:

> Such marvels of executive skill and power I could never have imagined.... The power he drew from his instrument was such as I have never heard since, but never harsh, never suggesting "thumping." His daring was as extraordinary as his talent. At an orchestral concert given by him and conducted by Berlioz, the "Marche au supplice," from the latter's "Symphonie fantastique," that most gorgeously instrumented piece, was performed, at the conclusion of which Liszt sat down and played his own arrangement, for the piano alone, of the same movement, with an effect even surpassing that of the full orchestra, and creating an indescribable furore. The feat had been duly announced in the programme beforehand, a proof of his indomitable courage.[10]

Virtuosic stunt though this was, Liszt's main aim was an educational one to further appreciation of new symphonic music. It is important to realize that, for better or worse, the majority of people at this time would have gotten to know orchestral works through piano transcriptions of one sort or another. Berlioz (who could not, in fact, play the instrument) envied Liszt's ability to create these orchestral effects with just fingers and thumbs. In a letter to Liszt, which Berlioz sent while on tour in Germany conducting his own works, he wrote:

> It is of small interest to you whether the town that you propose to pass through has a decent musical establishment, whether the theatre is open, the intendant willing to let you use it, etc. etc. Why should all that information concern you? You can confidently say, adapting Louis XIV:
> I am the orchestra! I am the chorus and the conductor as well. My piano sings, broods, flashes, thunders. It rivals the keenest bows in swiftness; it has its own brazen harmonies and can conjure on the evening air its veiled

enchantment of insubstantial hoards and fairy melodies, just as the orchestra can and without all the paraphernalia. I need no theatre, no special scenery, no vast construction of tiers and ramps. I don't have to wear myself out taking interminable rehearsals. I don't require a hundred musicians or even twenty—I don't require any at all. I don't even require any music. A large room with a grand piano in it, and I have an audience at my command. I simply appear, amid applause, and sit down. My memory awakens. At once, dazzling inventions spring to life beneath my fingers and rapturous exclamations greet them in response. I play Schubert's "Ave Maria" and Beethoven's "Adelaide," and all hearts reach out to me as one. No one breathes; a passionate silence reigns, a deep, still hush of wonder. Then come the explosions, the glittery set-piece that crowns the firework display, the cheers of the audience, the hail of flowers and bouquets raining round the high priest of music, rapt and quivering on his tripod, the lovely girls in their holy frenzy kissing the hem of his garment and moistening it with their tears.[11]

It was via Hans von Bülow's piano transcription of *Tristan und Isolde* that Friedrich Nietzsche first got to know Wagner's music, as he acknowledged in his autobiography *Ecce Homo*: "From the moment there was a piano score of Tristan—my compliments, Herr von Bülow!—I was a Wagnerian."[12] Similarly, in Thomas Mann's first novel *Buddenbrooks*, Gerda Buddenbrook demonstrates her passion for Wagner's music by playing a piano transcription at home, much to the displeasure of her teacher, Herr Pfühl:

Gerda Buddenbrook was an impassioned Wagnerite. But Herr Pfühl was an equally impassioned opponent—so much so that in the beginning she had despaired of winning him over.

On the day when she first laid some piano arrangements from *Tristan* on the music-rack, he played some 25 beats and then sprang up from the music-stool to stride up and down the room with disgust painted upon his face.

"I cannot play that, my dear lady! I am your most devoted servant—but I cannot. That is not music—believe me! I have always flattered myself that I knew something about music—but this is chaos! This is demagogy, blasphemy, insanity, madness! It is a perfumed fog, shot through with lightning!"[13]

Similarly, the lovers in Mann's short story "Tristan" become quite delirious with enthusiasm for Wagner's opera simply by playing it on a piano:

He sat beside her, bent forward, his hands between his knees, his head bowed. She played the beginning with exaggerated and tormenting slowness, with painfully long pauses between the single figures. The *Sehnsuchtsmotiv*, roving lost and forlorn like a voice in the night, lifted its trembling question. Then silence, a waiting. And lo, an answer: the same timorous, lonely notes, only clearer, only tenderer. Silence again. And then, with that marvelous muted *sforzando,* like mounting passion, the love-motif came in; reared and soared and yearned ecstatically upward to its consummation, and back, was resolved; the cellos taking up the melody to carry on with their deep, heavy notes of rapture and despair.

Except it is not cellos at all, but simply a piano, which can so often suggest an entire orchestra of different instruments playing together:

> Not unsuccessfully did the player seek to suggest the orchestral effects upon the poor instrument at her command. The violin runs of the great climax rang out with brilliant precision. She played with a fastidious reverence, lingering on each note, bringing out each detail, with the self-forgotten concentration of the priest who lifts the Host above his head.[14]

Marcel Proust was also fully aware of the orchestral and transcendental possibilities of the piano, about which he wrote at length in *À la recherche du temps perdu*. His descriptions of the effect it has upon M. Swann in this regard are among the most poetic to be found anywhere:

> He had suddenly become aware of the mass of the piano-part beginning to surge upward in plashing waves of sound, multiform but invisible, smooth yet restless, like the deep blue tumult of the sea, silvered and charmed into a minor key by the moonlight. But then at a certain moment, without being able to distinguish any clear outline, or to give a name to what was pleasing him, suddenly enraptured, he had tried to grasp the phrase or harmony—he did not know which—that had just been played and that had opened and expanded his soul, as the fragrance of certain roses, wafted upon the moist air of evening, has the power of dilating one's nostrils. Perhaps it was owing to his ignorance of music that he had received so confused an impression, one of those that are nonetheless the only purely musical impressions, limited in their extent, of entirely original, and irreducible to any other kind.[15]

Mme. Verdurin subsequently remarks, "You never dreamed, did you, that a piano could be made to express all that? Upon my word, you'd think it was everything but the piano! I'm caught out every time I hear it; I think I'm listening to an orchestra. Though it's better, really, than an orchestra, more complete."[16]

Romanticism as a whole was largely concerned with the inspired individual at odds with a philistine society, which was why the piano concerto became such an important form during that period. The pianist represented the hero—Faust, Byron's Manfred, Caspar David Friedrich's Wanderer Above a Sea of Mist, and even the Devil himself—*opposed* to society and its restricting conventions, and usually triumphing over it. Robert Schumann founded a secret musical society to fulfill these aims: the Davidsbündler, or Society of David, which stood against the perceived philistinism of the world's dunderheaded Goliaths. The desire to dominate the concert as an artist hero was eventually fully visualized in the popular Romanticism of *An American in Paris*, in which Oscar Levant not only plays the virtuoso solo part of Gershwin's Concerto in F but also conducts, plays all the other instruments in the orchestra, and even forms the audience, cheering himself on at the end. The sequence is Berlioz's dream come true by means of trick photography.

The Merchant Ivory film adaptation of E.M. Forster's *Howard's End* (1992) amusingly demonstrates the "orchestral" piano in the scene that also introduces the audience to the unfortunate Mr. Bast (Samuel West), who is attending a lecture on Beethoven's Fifth Symphony. On the stage of the Queen's Hall in London, a lecturer (Simon Callow) is discussing "Music and Meaning." To illustrate his theme, he plays an extract from Beethoven's masterpiece on the piano, assisted by his mother. His "explanation" of what is going on in the music gives Forster and the screenwriter Ruth Prawer Jhabvala an opportunity to lampoon the woolly approach to musical analysis that became popular in the nineteenth century:

> Beethoven's Fifth Symphony is the most sublime noise ever to have penetrated the ear of man; but what does it mean? You can hardly fail to recognize in this music a mighty drama, the struggle of a hero beset by perils, riding to magnificent victory and ultimate triumph.

A further extract then identifies "the goblins," which "signify the spirit of negation." It is a short scene but one that usefully reminds us of the importance of piano transcriptions in an age before CDs were available to demonstrate one's interpretative theories, no matter how absurd they may be. The vast library of piano transcriptions built up during the nineteenth century is largely redundant and un-played these days, apart from by those with a recherché interest in such matters, or who put to good use the still necessary skills of a piano *répétiteur* for ballet and opera rehearsals (an activity to which we will return later). Even more neglected is the immense library of "salon" music, specifically designed for domestic consumption. Because it never formed part of the concert repertoire, it has now been consigned to oblivion. A vast amount of musical history has thus been sidelined thanks to the professionalization of music. The back pages of many nineteenth-century editions of printed music present us with a ghostly gallery of forgotten names and silenced compositions. For example, the advertisements at the back of Novello's edition of Mendelssohn's oratorio, *The First Walpurgis Night*, announce pieces by Rudolf Altschul, Dudley Buck, Battison Haynes, Siegfried Jacoby, Oliver King, Ippolito Ragghianti, Fritz Spindler, Berthold Tours and Hermann Wollenhaupt, their piano "Sketches" "Morceaux de Salon," "Characteristic Pieces" and assorted dances advertised alongside Bach, Handel, Mendelssohn, Gounod and even Corelli. It is not so much that the music isn't good enough to have survived (though doubtless that is surely the case in many instances) but more that the social function it served—the arena in which it thrived—has vanished.

Anthony Burgess' novel *The Pianoplayers*, which describes pre-war piano playing in the north of England, includes several lists of the kind of thing one could find under piano stools in the old days. Strummed out during a piano-playing marathon ("NONSTOP PIANO PLAYING FOR THIRTY DAYS AND NIGHTS CAN HE DO IT?"), such a repertoire strikingly demonstrates the *integration* of popular music with what we now term classical music, before the advent of rock and roll and the electric guitar changed everything—even if we didn't always know how to spell the foreign titles:

> Avalon, Mountain Greenery, California Here I Come, Carolina In The Morning, Happy Days and Lonely Nights, Chopin's Nockturne in E Flat, Beethoven's Mignonette in G, Paderooski's Mignonette simplified, O Shinanacky Da He Play De Guitar Outside De Bazaar Haha Haha, You Were Meant For Me, Sonny Boy, Für Elise, the slow movement of Tchaikovsky's (thank you Rolf) Fifth Symphony, a piece by my dad made up as he went along for the left hand only, the same piece shoved up for the right hand only, Handel's Lager, Mendelssohn's Spring Song, In a Monastery Garden with whistling obbligato, In a Persian Market, The Sanctuary of the Heart, Handel's Water Music (selection), bits of Eine Kleine Something (Mozart), the Intermezzo from calvary Rusticano, On with the Motley from Pagliacci *not* Pally Archie, One Fine Day from Madam Butterfly, the Pilgrim's Chorus from Tan Houser, Tortoises from the Carnival of the Animals (a very good piece when you're tired, it is the Can Can from Refuse in the Underground played as slow as you like).[17]

As for "nature's call": Burgess' narrator points out that the pianist had to rely on a rubber tube attached to his penis; the tube led down to a petrol can under the piano.

A Box of Tricks

It is appropriate that the piano should have spent so much of its time pretending to be an orchestra, as it is inherently something of a charlatan. All its strings are cunningly tuned to equal temperament. Not all pianos were tuned to equal temperament to begin with (British pianos in particular lagged behind the general European trend, which began with Bach's "Well-Tempered Clavier" collection of 48 Preludes and Fugues). But if one wishes to play in all 24 major and minor keys, the layout of the keyboard requires all the notes within an octave to be tuned enharmonically. Strictly speaking, F-sharp, one of the piano's black notes, is not precisely the same pitch as its enharmonic equivalent of G-flat. A violinist would play very slightly different pitches in each case, but on the piano they are played by the same key. To create a keyboard with keys for F-sharps and G-flats, and all the other enharmonic equivalents (A-sharp and B-flat, C-sharp and D-flat, for example), would be quite impractical, the human frame being what it is. To mitigate this problem, every note on the piano is in fact slightly out of tune, even though most ears would never be able to hear it. David Rudkin's television drama *Artemis 81* (dir. Alastair Reid, 1981) elegantly expresses the idea of enharmonic equivalents. As they drive to an audition with the world-famous organist Dr. Albrecht von Drachenfels (Dan O'Herlihy), Gideon Harlax (Hywel Bennett) and Gwen Meredith (Dinah Stabb) discuss the nature of the note B-double-flat:

> "B-double-flat. Why not A?" Gideon asks.
> "A B-flat's value is depressed," Gwen explains.
> "You touch the A key," Gideon insists.
> "Mechanical coincidence," Gwen insists.

Bernard Richardson has provided us with a more technical explanation:

> On a piano keyboard, seven octaves is equivalent to twelve fifths. According to "harmonic" theory, however, seven octaves is a frequency ratio of 2:1 to the power seven—that is, 128:1—whilst twelve fifths is a frequency radio of 3:2 to the power twelve, about 129,75:1. The musical consequence of this mathematical diversion is that the circle of fifths ends up being about a quarter of a semitone sharp. The outcome is that fifths must be deliberately tuned slightly flat if we demand enharmonic equivalence....
> Tuning a piano to an equal-tempered scale is a skilled operation. It basically involves deliberate mis-tuning.[18]

Another of the piano's tricks, and the basis of the entire nineteenth-century repertoire for the instrument, is its pretention to legato. Legato is actually impossible on an instrument that creates sounds by hammers hitting strings, the vibrations of which immediately begin to decay; but through the use of the sustaining pedal, and, more importantly, the correct use of the fingers, the *illusion* of legato can be suggested. (Liszt's rival Sigismond Thalberg, was once famous for his *legato cantabile* style.) The piano is thus a musical illusionist par excellence, and consequently the pre-eminent icon of the nineteenth-century Romantic movement. Romantic pianists performed musical miracles. As we have seen, the rapid repetition of notes made possible by the double escapement of Érard quickly became one of Liszt's pianistic tricks. Others, like Alexander Dreyschock, specialized in octaves. (His most famous stunt was to play the rapid left hand line of Chopin's "Revolutionary" Étude in octaves, and he was apparently so loud, Heinrich Heine once wrote of him, "One does not seem to hear one pianist Dreyschock but *drei Schock* [three-score] of pianists."[19]) Liszt also became famous for his pounding octaves. Thalberg created the "three-handed" effect by splitting the melody between the thumbs of the left and right hands, surrounding them with cascading arpeggios played by the other eight fingers—a technique Liszt was to borrow and immortalize in his "Un sospiro" Concert Étude. Liszt outdid all competitors, as Berlioz reported in 1836:

> There were broad and simple melodies, sustained and perfectly linked phrases, and whole sheaves of notes hurled in some cases with extreme violence, yet without coarseness and losing nothing of their harmonic luxuriousness. There were melodic progressions in minor thirds, and diatonic embellishments in the bass and mid-range of the instrument (where, as is well known, the vibrations continue the longest) executed with the most incredible rapidity in staccato, such that each note produced only a flat sound, extinguished as soon as it had been emitted, absolutely detached from those that preceded in embellishments of this nature were they executed with the heel of the bow on an excellent bass-viol by a steam-engine.[20]

Paul Metzner, who quotes this passage in his book dedicated to technical virtuosity in general, goes on to explain the nature of Liszt's appeal:

> Great technicians had a strong sense of their own might and felt little need to appeal to God. Others redirected their admiration from God to great technicians. In a world conceived of in material terms, God seemed to be less important and further away from everyday life. At the same time, individuals with great ability to manipulate the material world seemed to be more important and more imminent. God was gradually replaced in the veneration of the public by individuals with great technical skill, in biology, chemistry and physics, in government, finance and war, in all sorts of performance arts, and, naturally, in machinery.[21]

Ubiquity

There was once a time when being able to play the piano was nowhere near as unusual as it is today. All sorts of people could play, from the pub pianist to the middle-class professionals. Films attest to this. Period dramas often reflect the fact that keyboard accomplishments were essential if music in the home was to be enjoyed. In Joseph L. Mankiewicz's Gothic romance *Dragonwyck* (1946), for example, the aristocratic Nicholas van Ryn (Vincent Price) attempts to entertain his cousin Miranda Wells (Gene Tierney) by somewhat inappropriately playing the second movement of Beethoven's highly pianistic "Moonlight Sonata" on a harpsichord, an instrument described by van Ryn's wife Joanna (Vivienne Osborne) as an

Harpsi-discord: Vincent Price and Gene Tierney in *Dragonwyck*.

ugly eyesore: "The servants have to be driven to dust it. They think it was going to bite them!" Beethoven obviously having failed to delight Miranda, Nicholas adds, "I think I have some new music that will please you more than Beethoven, Cousin Miranda. You can sing as I play." But Miranda chooses instead to declaim the words of Michael Balfe's setting of "I Dreamt I Dwelt in Marble Halls." The piano as an accompaniment to singing was, of course, one of its primary drawing room functions at this time; and if, like Miranda, one couldn't sing, composers came to the rescue with "musical recitations." Liszt and Schumann composed several of these, and lesser names also contributed to the field, most famous of all being Cuthbert Clarke's piano accompaniment to J. Milton Hayes' "The Green Eye of the Yellow God" in 1911.

With the advent of recorded music in the Edwardian period, the ability to play became less important, but many twentieth-century films attest to the persistence of the old ways. In *Swing Time* (dir. George Stevens, 1936) Fred Astaire accompanies his rendition of Jerome Kern's "The Way You Look Tonight" on a boudoir grand—appropriately so, as the piano is in Ginger Rogers' bedroom. He plays while she washes her hair in the bathroom. Their respective characters have had an argument, and the song helps bring them together. The piano and the song itself are thus perfectly contextualized in such a domestic setting, the charm of which later, less intimate interpretations by Frank Sinatra, Tony Bennett and Rod Stewart significantly reduce. In *Watch on the Rhine* (dir. Herman Schumlin, 1943), German engineer Kurt Muller (Paul Lukas) plays Schumann during his wife Sara's (Bette Davis) conversation with a Romanian diplomat (George

Coulouris). The diplomat is spying for the Nazis and suspects that Muller is working for the Resistance as an anti–Fascist. When the wife discovers that her husband's belongings (including his gun) have been disturbed, she alerts him at the piano. The news causes him to stop playing, but his wife continues the melody to cover their whispers. Later, the engineer sings an anti–Fascist song to his own accompaniment.

In the same year's *I Walked with a Zombie* (dir. Jacques Tourneur), a sugar plantation owner (Tom Conway) entertains himself at the piano with a rendition of Chopin's E major Étude (Op.10, No. 3). In another Val Lewton horror classic, *The Seventh Victim* (dir. Mark Robson, 1943), an understated story of devil worshippers in New York, the famous Brahms A-flat Waltz accompanies a social gathering of Satanists, which helps identify the veneer of culture and sophistication of people who are in fact all quite depraved. In *All About Eve* (dir. Joseph L. Mankiewicz, 1950), Bette Davis' Margo Channing famously lashes out at Liszt's "Liebestraum No. 3" by turning it off on a car radio with the line, "I detest cheap sentimentality." Piano music also helps to suggest the trouble she is about to cause during the film's famous party scene. Having warned her guests "Fasten your seat belts: it's going to be a bumpy night," we hear a lounge piano appropriately playing "Stormy Weather" in the background.

In "The Verger," the first of the three Somerset Maugham stories adapted for the screen in *Trio* (dir. Ken Annakin, 1950), a wedding engagement party is celebrated in a boarding house with a sing-song accompanied by a loudly strummed upright. Its female pianist strikes up with Mendelssohn's Wedding March when the happy couple announces their plans. In *The Angel Who Pawned Her Harp* (dir. Alan Bromly, 1954), a police sergeant (Edward Evans) is also a great music lover. He admires in particular Rimsky-Korsakoff's *Schéhérazade* and Tchaikovsky's *Swan Lake* ("'course the dancing's a bit much, but the music…!"). He also plays a compact little square piano in his living room, on which he later plays a waltz from his favorite ballet. Similarly, about 20 minutes into *Village of the Damned*, Wolf Rilla's 1960 adaptation of John Wyndham's *The Midwich Cuckoos*, George Sanders' Professor Zellaby is shown playing his grand piano to himself, his faithful hound lying at his feet. It is only a short scene, but splendid evidence that even up to the 1960s, home entertainment was still homespun— and that it wasn't just elegant young ladies who amused themselves at the keyboard. Three years later, in *Girl in the Headlines* (dir. Michael Truman, 1963), Ian Hendry plays another musical policeman, this time investigating a murder case. Foreshadowing Colin Dexter's Inspector Morse, he is not only an opera fan ("Policemen are also members of the human race," he explains), but he also plays the piano, the small upright in his living room eloquently indicating his policeman's income.

Films also attest to the popularity of pub pianos. Terence Fisher's *Stolen Face* (1952) stars Lizabeth Scott as a concert pianist who, while recovering from a bad cold, entertains the customers on a honkytonk piano in a country pub, starting with Beethoven's "Pathétique" Sonata before giving them what they really want with "Rolling Home," to which they all sing along. In 1952, this sort of thing was unremarkable, even if beginning to wane, and even though juke boxes were rapidly replacing public pianos throughout the 1960s, Michael Armstrong's *The Haunted House of Horror* (1969) still has a group of apparently trendy young men entertaining a husband-to-be on his stag night in a pub with a rendition of a little ditty called "Responsibility." They are accompanied with a honkytonk Bentley upright, appropriately decked with beer glasses. (We immediately cut to a somewhat "trendier" party, where the musical entertainment is of course on disc.) The year 1969 was definitely towards the tail end of this particular form of pub music, which had had its military equivalent in NAAFI bars during the Second World War. Many British war films feature at least the sound if not the sight of a NAAFI piano. Philip Leacock's 1953 *Appointment in London* with Dirk Bogarde is a good example.

The "Wild West" bar piano has, of course, a mythic status, having been immortalized in Oscar Wilde's quip, inspired by the experience of his American tour, "Please do not shoot the pianist; he is doing his best" (a quotation to which Truffaut, of course, referred in the title of his film *Shoot the Piano Player*). Movie Westerns have featured many pianos, their honkytonk tuning in many ways defining the genre, especially when it stops as the bad guy enters through the batwing doors. It became such a cliché that it was *de rigueur* in *Carry On Cowboy* (dir. Gerald Thomas, 1965), and the instrument itself actually forms part of the action during a fight scene. (Drinkers are crushed behind it.) In another scene, Kenneth Williams' Judge Burke calls the pianist "Russ"—an obvious reference to Russ Conway. This "Russ" is also required to Mickey-Mouse Joan Sims' "Ding-Dong" Belle walk down the stairs, gun in hand, before she slinks towards Sid James' Johnny Finger to confiscate his weapon. ("My, but you've got a big one," she smirks. "I'm from Texas, ma'am," Johnny explains. "We've all got big ones down there.")

Even funnier is the use of the upright that accompanies two of the *Three Amigos!* (one of them plays it) in a gloriously camp rendition of "My Little Buttercup" to an audience of grim and grimy gringos in John Landis' 1986 Western satire. Mel Brooks had inverted this trope much earlier in *Blazing Saddles* (1974), in which Richard Pryor's trendy, Gucci-clad sheriff rides past Count Basie and his Orchestra in a desert, Basie resplendent at an immaculate white concert grand.

Decline

Eventually, perhaps inevitably, the piano became the victim of its own success, and its supremacy was eventually challenged in the twentieth century. Impatient with its legato legacy, some, like Bela Bartók, attempted to make the piano more "honest" by exploiting its percussive quality. Others, like Dmitri Shostakovitch, demoted it to a "mere" orchestral instrument (as in his Fifth Symphony). So too did Korngold, in the cello concerto he wrote for *Deception*. John Cage ultimately silenced it completely in his "piece" 4'33" in which the pianist simply opens the lid of the instrument and then sits quietly on the piano stool for four minutes and 33 seconds, before closing the lid and walking off stage.

Being pre-eminently a symbol of bourgeois culture (it is the only instrument, apart from the "sacred" organ, that did not begin its life in folk music), the piano has often been the focus of political conflict. Even as far back as 1863, Russian troops defenestrated the piano on which the youthful Chopin had played, thus symbolically expressing their outrage at a failed assassination attempt of the Russian governor of Poland. Sophy Roberts records that during the later Russian revolution, the poet Vladimir Mayakovsky, in an attempt to democratize culture, urged the masses to "Drag pianos out onto the street. Beat them until they fall to pieces."[22] She adds:

> Mao Zedong's widow, who was fond of piano music, didn't quite manage to save the instrument from its unpalatable Western reputation. "During China's Cultural Revolution," writes one leading historian, "the piano was likened to a coffin, in which notes rattled about like the bones of the bourgeoisie." In 1966, Mao's Red Guards smashed instruments to pieces, raided music schools, and locked keyboards shut. Their campaign of terror drove soloists to suicide.[23]

By the 1970s, the piano was under the same sort of attack that Victoriana in general had found itself in the previous two decades. The revulsion felt for Victorian architecture in the 1950s, and its widespread demolition throughout the Britain of the 1960s, was a manifestation of the impatience with Empire, and the austerity that had resulted from the wars fought in the name of Empire. Even though there was also a nostalgia for this vanishing past, as demonstrated by the success of Hammer horror films with their lovingly recreated Victorian interiors, nothing could stop the "white heat of technology," the increasing dominance of youth culture, and the burgeoning of satire. One thinks of the Establishment comedy club in London and *That Was the Week That Was* on television. The latter often featured Tom Lehrer, who accompanied his risqué songs on a grand, thus mocking the bourgeois heritage of the piano in the process.

But fusty suburban parlors, filled with the remains of what had once been Victoriana, were usually dominated by an upright piano—the "very altar of the home, and a second hearth to people,"[24] as Sir Edward Burne-Jones so morally described it. The upright piano became a symbol of everything that was now considered outmoded, undesirable and, in so many lamentable cases, musically useless, for as Charles Rosen informs us, pianos deteriorate with age if they are not looked after:

> Parts of the action have to be constantly replaced. Not only the strings break, but also the hammers. The metal pins no longer hold the strings tightly enough to remain in tune. The felt on the hammers wears down. The springs of the action lose their tension, the little pieces of cloth and leather that regulate the repetition of the keys wear out, the joints become loose. In too dry an atmosphere, the piano begins to crack and crumble. With an old instrument, we can never be sure that we know what the original sonority was like. In its complexity, the piano is one of the most fragile of instruments. The increased tonal beauty of age is always threatened by imminent decay.[25]

Visually, also, old pianos loose their charm. The keys become yellowed with age, and whereas a new grand can look sumptuous, a battered, dusty brownwood upright can look very unappealing. The many uncared-for uprights, which had entertained (or not) their parlor audiences, especially if they had candlestick holders creaking and sagging on their front panels, became increasingly grotesque to the postwar generation, especially if the honkytonk sounds that emerged from them made them useless as musical instruments. Appalling though the spectacle was, even at the time, it is not surprising that piano-smashing contests took place on British TV shows such as *It's a Knockout* in the 1970s. To smash a piano was a symbolic way of smashing the past (and appropriate for a country that the Germans used to call "das Land ohne Musik"—the land without music). The rejection of Victoriana was depressingly widespread, and had been since the Luftwaffe started the process during the Second World War. Postwar planners, designers and architects doubtless were far more destructive than Hitler had been, and this impatience with the past, the cult of youth, and the dominance of pop and rock music over the classical tradition so typified by the piano, are all powerfully expressed in Bill Bain's 1972 thriller *Whatever Became of Jack and Jill?* Even though there are no pianos in this Amicus production, everything else is in place: a dark and grubby Victorian suburban terraced house, an elderly granny (Mona Washbourne), stained glass in the panels of the front door, ceramic tiles around the fireplace—even three flying pottery ducks on the wall in time-honored fashion. The lack of a piano is a pity, but it is hardly necessary. Against all this antiquated bric-a-brac, John Tallent (Paul Daniels) wears a floral shirt, listens to Carl Davis' approximations of rock music, meets his girlfriend Jill beneath a marble angel in a Victorian cemetery, and with her help he plans the death of Granny, which will bring him a considerable inheritance. He terrorizes Granny with alarming stories of a terrorist group called Youth Power, which aims to kill off the over-eighties. The film in so many ways foreshadows the ageism of millennials in the twenty-first century, who, unable to afford a home of their own, are resentful of more fortunate Baby Boomers. Taking advantage of a noisy student rag, which harmlessly ambles down Acacia Avenue where he and Granny live, John whips up Granny's anxiety until she suffers a heart attack. Alas, a codicil to Granny's will prevents him from inheriting her estate if he marries Jill, and in his frustration on learning this unwelcome news, he smashes up the parlor, much as contestants on *It's a Knockout* wielded crowbars over clapped-out pianos.

Recorded music has made the labor of learning how to play the piano redundant; and there is no denying that the rituals of piano culture have not always been appealing. Practice has so often been a form of torture for thousands of not particularly musical people and something of a slog even for the more talented. The unappealing volumes of studies by Czerny, not even alleviated by poetic titles, but languishing instead under oppressive opus numbers, manuals of mechanical scales and arpeggios, intimidating technical difficulties on pages filled with so many notes, are not always pleasure prospects. By the mid–1970s, piano playing had become an eccentric pastime, even somewhat suspect. Thus, it is appropriate that James Bond villain Hugo Drax (Michael Lonsdale) in *Moonraker* (dir. Lewis Gilbert, 1979) plays Chopin's "Raindrop" Prelude on the grand piano in the mansion he has had transported to America, stone by stone, from France. In Ian Fleming's original story, he fakes the performance, relying on a pianola (thus making him even more untrustworthy).

If piano-smashing wasn't bad enough, piano burning is still an unfortunate ritual in the RAF and USAF, apparently a reaction to misguided attempts to improve the culture and refinement of pilots during the Second World War by arranging for them to take unwanted piano lessons. Some contemporary composers have also asked for pianos to be burned as part of their compositions for them. Annea Lockwood's 1968 "happening," *Piano Burning* does exactly that, though does at least specify the destruction of an upright beyond repair rather than a serviceable grand. Michael Hannan's *Burning Questions* (2003) not only sets fire to a piano but also appears to immolate the classical musical canon, by starting off with a performance of Beethoven's "Moonlight" Sonata, before the piano is sent up in flames. (Significantly, Barry Conyngham, another composer present at Hannan's premiere, was heard to remark that he found "burning a perfectly good microphone more sacrilegious than burning a piano.")

If these "pieces" were expressions of frustration with the piano's dominance of Western culture, Douglas Gordon's 2012 video installation *The End of Civilisation,* which features another burning grand, is at least an acknowledgment of its status as "the ultimate symbol of western civilization. Not only is it an instrument, it's a beautiful object that works as a sculpture but it has another function entirely."[26]

Two

Picture Palace Pianos

Silent Pianos

So-called "silent" films were never silent; quite the opposite, in fact, as they were accompanied with music from beginning to end. When the Lumière brothers' screened the very first public presentation of a film in 1896, they chose *The Arrival of a Train at La Ciotat Station,* which caused the audience to panic, fearing the advancing locomotive might run them over. For this unique occasion, the Lumières hired a saxophone quartet to accompany the performance, but pianos soon took over for smaller theaters unable to afford an ensemble let alone an orchestra.

The piano, like the steam locomotive, has always fascinated filmmakers. Both are concerned with speed, mounting excitement and erotic power: steam pistons, virtuosity and screen idols seem to go together. As we shall see later, *Brief Encounter* (dir. David Lean, 1945) made Rachmaninoff's Second Piano Concerto and locomotives appear almost synonymous, while *Mr. Soft Touch* (dir. Gordon Douglas and Henry Levin, 1949), which opens with a shot of a train advancing towards us, also involves pianos.

Sound films have often celebrated the way in which their "silent" ancestors were presented. The murder mystery *The Spiral Staircase* (dir. Robert Siodmak, 1946) opens with the screening, in an inn, of the silent movie *The Kiss.* The pianist, watching the screen carefully, first plays a Chopin Waltz, followed by the introduction from the first movement of Beethoven's "Pathétique" Sonata. Eleven years later, in *The Smallest Show on Earth* (dir. Basil Dearden, 1957), Margaret Rutherford's Mrs. Fazackerlee accompanies silent weepies on an antediluvian upright to an audience of two in the faded flea-pit grandeur of the Bijou Cinema, which conveys exactly the mood captured by Graham Greene in his short story "A Little Place Off the Edgware Road":

> Craven stopped and read—there were still optimists it appeared, even in 1939, for nobody but the blindest optimist could hope to make money out of the

place as "The Home of the Silent Film." The first season of "primitives" was announced (a high-brow phrase): there would never be a second. Well, the seats were cheap, and it was perhaps worth a shilling to him, now that he was tired, to get in somewhere out of the rain. Craven bought a ticket and went in to the darkness of the stalls.

In the dead darkness a piano tinkled something monotonously recalling Mendelssohn: he sat down in the gangway seat, and could immediately feel the emptiness all round him. No, there would never be another season. On the screen a large woman in a kind of toga wrung her hands, then wobbled with curious jerky movements towards a couch. There she sat and stared out like a sheep-dog distractedly through her loose and black and stringy hair.

… Craven began at last to see—a dim waste of stalls. There were not twenty people in the place. … They lay about at intervals like corpses.…

The "Spring Song" tinkled ineptly on, and the screen flickered like indigestion.[1]

The use of a solo piano in Brian Easedale's score for Michael Powell's *Peeping Tom* (1960) is a specific reference to the musical accompaniment of silent cinema. Powell's film is an anatomy of the cinema itself, along similar lines to Hitchcock's *Rear Window* (1954), but perhaps even more intensely: Scopophilia, or "the morbid urge to gaze" as Martin Miller's Dr. Rosen puts it in *Peeping Tom*, is what the cinema is all about. In this respect, we are all peeping Toms. Everyone enjoys watching murderers at work in the movies, and all Carl Boehm's Martin Lewis does in the film is take this morbid urge to its logical conclusion by actually killing women as he films them. Ironically, the only person who can "see" what is going on is the blind Helen Stephens (Maxine Audley). We are all blinded by our compulsion to gaze that we often fail to recognize the moral ambiguity of what we are doing.

Easedale's piano is not just a reference to silent film accompaniment. It also provides a driving sense of Martin's compulsion through the use of ostinati and motoric rhythms, while the subtle echoes of Scriabin's mature piano style (particularly the finale of the Fifth Sonata with its ecstatically wide leaps in the right hand) also suggest the demonic eroticism of Martin's obsession. The music perfectly counterpoints both the surface action of the film and its meta-text, *Peeping Tom* being one of the few "sound" films to restrict its underscore largely to solo piano.

Hitchcock exploited piano music for similar reasons in *Rope* (1948). Here, Farley Granger is shown playing the first of Francis Poulenc's *Mouvements Perpetuelles*, while being questioned by James Stewart's Rupert Cadell. The obsessive rhythmic drive of Poulenc's piece is less intense than Easedale or Scriabin, but no less persistent, and the charm of the melody is only superficially innocent. As such, it is the perfect music for a pianist who has murdered his friend and hidden his body in the trunk on which he serves a buffet to his guests. Granger's outward serenity hides a repressed

Two. Picture Palace Pianos

Perpetual motion: Farley Granger (left) and James Stewart in *Rope*.

turmoil of anxiety, which is exactly the mood of Poulenc's piece. As his questioning becomes more intrusive, Cadell increases the speed of the metronome, forcing Granger's Phillip Morgan to play faster, increasing the dramatic tension. Hitchcock also filmed everything in single ten-minute takes, which used up an entire roll of film. This self-referential method of production, which is almost narcissistically technical, again refers us to the nature of the medium itself, which is subtly enhanced by the sparing, diagetic use of piano music.

There are various theories about the need for music in silent film presentation. Some have argued that the noise of the cranking mechanism was so loud, musical sounds were needed to drown them out; but the real reason is that movement without sound is inherently "uncanny." We have always associated movement with sound of some sort. In the early days, the exhibitor might have declaimed the dialogue himself, standing beside the screen. Later, unless an orchestral score had been specially composed, he would rely on the improvisatory skills of a pianist. Such pianists might also have recourse to the various libraries of incidental music, which existed in both piano solo and orchestral versions.

The most famous of these was the cinema music library of Giuseppe Becce, which first appeared in Berlin in 1919. (He had previously played

Richard Wagner in Carl Fröhlich's 1913 biopic of that formative influence on film music technique.) Becce's cues were categorized according to mood and situation: "Emotional Conflict (Sostenuto)," "Battle-Tumult-Blaze (Allegro Agitato)," "Tragic Moments (Andante)," "Agony of the Soul (Tragedia dell'Anima)," "Mob-Rule (Agitato)," "Fanatic Dervish Dance," "Lynch-Law (Agitato)," "Sinister Agitato," "Semi Oriental Maestoso," "Threatening Danger (Andante Dramatic)," "Happy Ending (Andante Largo)," "Infatuation (Andante Largo)," "Witchcraft (Semi Mysterious Andante)," "Anticipation of Danger," etc. John Huntley explains:

> Every conceivable type of music was called into service to provide material for the [silent] film orchestras—opera, the classics, light music, symphonies, musical comedy, jazz, everything—all arranged and orchestrated, published and labeled so that it could be ordered from a catalogue depending on what type of effect was required.[2]

Huntley also recalls how silent pianists often introduced audiences to classical repertoire they might now have previously encountered:

> I suppose in those days the themes from opera, ballet, concert hall, were very strong indeed. There are many, many letters, when you look back on the old magazines like the *Picturegoer* and *Cinema Weekly, Picturegoer Weekly, Picture Show*, over and over again in the 1920s you get letters from people saying, "We have a lovely pianist and he's played so many interesting things I've never heard of before, and the other night he played a thing from something called *Aida*, and he played it against a scene from an old Cecil B. DeMille silent movies, I think it was *Ten Commandments* or something." Over and over again you get these letters with people responding to it.[3]

Many famous names worked as silent film pianists. Shostakovitch is said to have laughed so much during his accompaniment of a Buster Keaton movie, he was sacked. Delius' amanuensis, Eric Fenby, also worked as a film pianist-organist; as did the father of the novelist Anthony Burgess, who recorded his memories, in lightly fictionalized guise, in *The Pianoplayers*:

> "Here's a chord you can't do without," he said, "if you're a picture-palace piano-player. You use it for fights, burst dams, thunderstorms, the voice of the Lord God, a wife telling her old man to bugger off out of the house and not come back never no more." And he showed me: G, E-flat, G-flat, A-flat. "Always the same like dangerous sound," he said, "as if something terrible's going to happen: soft for 'going to happen,' loud for 'happening.' And you can play whole strings of these chords, each one based on a different white or black note at the bottom. And you can arpeggio them to make them like very mysterious. Here's just one more chord," he said, "very, very mysterious. I see the buggers are starting to come in, so I'll have to show you quick. It's this one: C, E, G-sharp. Make it on any note. Good for ghost music, *Frankenstein*, that sort of thing."[4]

Two. Picture Palace Pianos

The ubiquity of the piano throughout the silent film era no doubt influenced its appearance in comedy shorts, in which its sheer bulk and weight are exploited for laughs. Charlie Chaplin's 1914 film *His Musical Career* casts him as a deliveryman. Mr. Rich (Fritz Schade) visits the piano showroom where Chaplin works and buys one of the instruments on display. Then Mr. Poor (Frank Hayes) appears, unable to pay his installments on a piano he bought earlier. It is now Chaplin's job to help deliver Mr. Rich's upright to the unintentionally demonic address of 666 Prospect Street, and bring back a piano from Mr. Poor, who lives in 999 Prospect Street. Confusion is thus guaranteed. Mr. Rich's piano is loaded onto a cart, pushed along sidewalks, hauled up stairs (down which it inevitably falls) and is eventually delivered to the wrong address, where Mr. Poor resides in the kind of Victorian parlor that would obviously be incomplete without a piano. He now has two. The framed embroidery of "God Bless Our Home" hanging on the wall is significant, as is Mr. Poor's hairstyle, which is reminiscent of the elder Liszt, indicating that he is a true music lover.

Chaplin and his workmate now make their way to the establishment of Mr. Rich and remove the piano he already has, the film reaching a kind of a locomotive finale as the piano rolls down a sloping road not unlike a steam train before falling into a pond, which may have given accompanists the opportunity to play a bar or two of Handel's Water Music to finish the film with a flourish.

His Musical Career inspired Laurel and Hardy's *The Music Box* (dir. James Parrott, 1932), by which time the pictures had learned to talk, but to all intents and purposes, this film could just as well be silent. This time, the piano is delivered to the right address, but the man for whom it has been bought (by his wife) detests pianos, and he promptly begins to smash it. (How can the wife be ignorant of his prejudice against the instrument?) It is surprising that the piano did not arrive already smashed up, given that it has been pushed up and fallen down an immense flight of steps, as well as rolling off of its own accord down slopes. The packing case in which it is secured no doubt helped protect it, and this, of course, conceals the piano itself from the viewer, transforming it into just a bulk to be humped.

An echo of this sort of thing can be found in *Superman Returns* (Bryan Singer, 2006). Here, the immense bulk of a grand piano is spectacularly humped by Jason (Tristan Lake Leabu), infant son of Superman and Lois Lane. Jason has inherited his father's superpowers, so when Lois is attacked by one of Lex Luther's henchmen, the boy hurls the shiny black grand at the tattooed menace, smashing both the piano and attacker in one blow.

Scoring with Pianos

Ironically, with the arrival of the movie soundtrack, the sound of the piano was heard far less in feature films that weren't specifically about pianists. Apart from using it to reference its silent era heritage, as discussed above, the sound of the piano came to signify specific qualities. Franz Waxman's main title cue for *The Philadelphia Story* (dir. George Cukor, 1940), for example, begins with a concertante piano. Towards the end of the cue, this becomes increasingly agitated, fluttering around in the upper regions like a percussive firework. The effect returns for the end title, effectively encapsulating this high-society comedy in which we observe, as James Stewart's George puts it, "the privileged classes enjoying its privileges." The piano writing here is unnecessarily virtuosic—extravagant, indeed, to match the world in which the action takes place. Hence, the sound of the piano is a signifier of status and sophistication.

Four years later, David Raksin used the piano to alienating effect in Otto Preminger's *Laura*. In the famous apartment scene in which Dana Andrews' policeman, Mark McPherson, searches for clues that might help explain the disappearance of the title character, Raksin adopted a then novel approach by using fragments of the film's one and only theme (the score is strikingly monothematic) to reflect Mark's state of mind. This helps to convey that he is falling in love with the idea of the missing woman. Much has been said about the inventiveness of Raksin's approach, but what is of most concern to us here is his manipulation of the timbre of the piano. At first, the piano plays the "Laura" theme quite normally, but later, the score specifies that the piano be "Lenatoned"—a term coined by Raksin and his sound engineer Harry Leonard to describe the effect of a wavering distortion of the sound. To create this, the playback capstan of a tape player was milled into an oval shape, which altered the pressure of the tape against the playback head. As George Burt describes it, "The result proved to be absolutely appropriate for this scene, which shows Mark's discomfort with his own emotions."[5] The effect returns at the end of the scene as Mark falls asleep in a chair, this time the piano playing a chord: "The pianist struck the chord while the microphones were turned off. A beat later, the microphones were turned on, catching only the sustained and decay characteristics of the sound. What is recorded, then, is the interplay of the partials without the attack and initial drop. This, treated by the 'Len-a-toned' device, created a special echoing sound,"[6] which suggests the experience of Mark losing consciousness just before the real-life Laura walks into the apartment.

Richard Rodney Bennett employed more than just one piano in his score for Ken Russell's *Billion Dollar Brain* (1968):

> It's fun in films to be able to use orchestras which you wouldn't actually use in the concert hall because they'd be impractical. [In *Billion Dollar Brain*], I used an orchestra of three pianos, 11 brass, four percussion and ondes martenot (a beautiful electronic instrument which I've used a lot), just to get a very hard, almost an inhuman sound which was in keeping with the film. And of course in the concert hall you couldn't usefully write for three pianos and 11 brass, because it wouldn't get played. But it was nice in the context of the film.[7]

Not only the "inhuman" sound but the three pianos also reflect and amplify the extravagance of Russell's interpretation of this last of the three Harry Palmer spy films starring Michael Caine. Bennett also includef the piano in his score for *Murder on the Orient Express* (dir. Sidney Lumet, 1974), which echoes Waxman's concertante use of the instrument in *The Philadelphia Story*. The passengers on Agatha Christie's famous train, who are all involved in the murder of Richard Widmark's Ratchett, are indeed mostly upper-class sophisticates, but Bennett's piano also suggests the ambience of the cocktail lounge and palm court orchestra, which so strongly evokes the 1920s setting of the movie.

Throughout the 1970s, a different kind of piano writing began to swell from cinema soundtracks. Much of it was composed by Henry Mancini, Francis Lai, Michel Legrande and Claude Bolling, who were all accomplished jazz pianists. Their approach to scoring for film often took the form of self-contained jazz "pieces" rather than synchronized cues in the Max Steiner sense. Consequently, these scores work well in their own terms apart from the film. A excellent example of this approach is Legrande's score for Norman Jewison's *The Thomas Crown Affair* (1968) where the piano, with one or two concertante exceptions, forms part of the overall orchestration, along with a harpsichord and harp. The reprise of the film's theme song, "Windmills of Your Mind," is notably scored for accompanied harpsichord rather than piano; but Legrande's theme for *Summer of '42* (dir. Robert Mulligan, 1971) is a kind of jazz "Warsaw Concerto" (see below), in which an orchestra later joins the piano solo. Similarly, Francis Lai's theme for *Love Story* (dir. Arthur Hiller, 1970) features a solo piano and orchestra along similar lines to *The Thomas Crown Affair*.

One of Mancini's most appealing uses of the piano in this style occurs in three cues for Blake Edwards' *The Return of the Pink Panther* (1975) and *The Revenge of the Pink Panther* (1978): "Dreamy" from the former, and "Simone" and "After the Shower" from the latter. In "Dreamy," Mancini's effortless "lounge" piano alternates with an accordion (nicely connoting the French setting). In the latter two cues, the piano is paired with a languid steel guitar, electric piano, vibraphone and Mancini's idiosyncratic use of solo flute, all set against an understated cushion of strings, with everything lightly propelled by a gentle rhythm section. All these pieces obviously match the mood of the scenes for which they were written, but are far less integral to the action, following their own musical logic. They are all examples of background music which, ironically, are much more easily foregrounded than more integral writing, when removed from their original context.

Claude Bolling brought jazz piano further to the fore in his score for *California Suite* (dir. Herbert Ross, 1978), which combines a flute and piano, sometimes with, sometimes without rhythm, bass and classical guitar in support. The transparent textures are a universe away from the tradition of Hollywood film scoring, and the score could easily be performed and enjoyed without modification or even any knowledge of the film for which it was composed. Then, in 1985, John Barry featured the piano in a highly effective but extremely pared-down score for the courtroom drama *Jagged Edge* (dir. Richard Marquand). If Erik Satie had lived long enough to work in film, it might have sounded a little like Barry's simple, understated themes for piano and flute, which quietly support this story of betrayed trust. Glenn Close plays a lawyer who defends a man (Jeff Bridges) suspected of murdering his wife. He convinces her that he is innocent, only in the end to be revealed as having been the murderer all along. For the murder scenes, which top and tail the film, Barry exploits his famous "Bond" chord by electronic means, but the piano was still the obvious instrument of choice for more romantically emotional moments, and it would continue to be used (quite anachronistically) in Abel Korzeniowki's score for Carlo Carlei's costume drama approach to *Romeo and Juliet* (2013).

Concertomania

In 1941, a rather plodding melodrama opened at the Regal Cinema, Marble Arch, in London. It was called *Dangerous Moonlight* (dir. Brian Desmond Hurst). While he had been listening to a piano concerto on the radio during the Second World War, the screenwriter, Terence Young, had an idea about a Polish concert pianist who becomes an airman to fight the Nazis.[8] Though the film was fairly standard fare—a love story set against the uncertainties of war—the music it called for created a positive sensation. Richard Addinsell was commissioned to provide not only the background underscore but also the impression of a three-movement piano concerto, in the style of Rachmaninoff, which was to stand in for the film's hero's "Warsaw Concerto." That hero, Stefan Radetsky, was played by Austrian actor Adolf Wohlbrück (who, after moving to England to escape the Nazis, changed his name to Anton Walbrook). In this film, Walbrook seems quite unable to play the piano, as the shots of him clumsily pawing the keyboard as though wiping dough off his fingers rather hilariously demonstrate to anyone who has ever bothered to learn how to play a C-major scale. Films are, of course, littered with this sort of clumsiness, which demonstrates a startling unawareness about music in general. For many people, especially since the advent of recording, music is simply "there." Its technicalities are as remote as the moon, much as they no doubt admire both music and the moon. Amusing examples of absurdly inaccurate piano miming can be found in *The Hideous Sun Demon* (dir. Robert Clarke, 1958), in which Nan Peterson serenades Robert Clarke, singing and lifting her hands over the keyboard as though her arms are being operated by a puppeteer. The absurd anti-drug propaganda film *Reefer Madness* (dir. Louis J. Gasnier, 1936), voted one of the worst films ever made, has some of the worst piano miming, though Gasnier sensibly refrains from showing the actual keyboard. "You want me to play something for you?" asks Blanche (Lillian Miles), who promptly plays an arpeggio in the wrong direction. "Faster!" insists Ralph (Dave O'Brien), as high on drugs as Blanche. "Play it faster!" Silly though all this is, it continues usefully to demonstrate how pervasive the piano once was. It is very hard indeed to imagine an anti-drug film being made today, of whatever quality, which features piano playing—even the badly mimed variety.

In *Dangerous Moonlight*, Stefan Radetsky can also play fast but, unlike Blanche, he is both a first-rate concert pianist and an accomplished composer. Walbrook's poor piano miming in the role is perplexing when one considers how well he appears to play a little waltz in Thorold Dickinson's *Gaslight*, made the previous year. His fingering in *Gaslight* is perfectly convincing, so he could obviously manage the rudiments of playing, if not the more complex parts of the Warsaw Concerto. One possible explanation for his poor miming could be that Addinsell had not completed the cue until after the scene was shot, so Walbrook may have had nothing to mime to. Whatever the reason, the result is no less unintentionally comic than the piano playing in *Reefer Madness* and *The Hideous Sun Demon*.

Radetsky conceives his Warsaw Concerto during an assault on that city, after having spent nine hours in the air fighting the Luftwaffe. Finding a bombed-out apartment with a grand piano, he strums out his inspiration, which is enhanced when American journalist Carole (Sally Gray) appears, attracted by the music. "It's not safe to be out when the moon is so bright," Radetsky says, simultaneously explaining the title of the film. He continues to play the piano as the bombs fall, with the kind of deadpan sangfroid that would later be satirized in *Carry on Up the Khyber* (dir. Gerald Thomas, 1968), in which Sid James and the usual suspects continue their elegant dinner party amid the turmoil of an Afghan attack.

A new theme now occurs to Radetsky, which he calls Carole's melody:

"You gave it to me. ... This music is you and me." So, it is inevitable that when they meet again, in America, they get married. On their honeymoon, Stefan plays her Liszt's Liebestraum No. 3 (Carole is no Margo Channing), but what we're really waiting for is the Warsaw Concerto itself, fragments of which have already found their way onto the soundtrack at regular intervals. At the film's culminating concert, Radetsky is shown first playing part of Beethoven's "Emperor" Concerto, before the camera pans down over the program held in Carole's trembling fingers, resting at last on the Warsaw Concerto. This, like the Beethoven before it, is meant to consist of the traditional three movements: "Allegro con spirito," "Romanza" and an "Allegro Moderato—Presto." Of course, there is not time to hear the whole thing even if it had existed. What was required from Addinsell was a condensed concerto, giving the impression of three movements in a single cue. Purists were of course dismayed, as the Warsaw Concerto was no such thing. As John Huntley opined, "The mere act of combining a piano with an orchestra does not make a concerto."[9] Muir Mathieson, the musical director in charge of the recording, explained what happened:

> What we really needed was a miniature concerto of exactly seven minutes which included an introduction, a first tune and a second tune (or a first subject and a second subject), the feeling of cadenzas and a very, very exciting ending, so that the whole thing was a potted concerto in a way. But I think it was an absolutely magnificently conceived potted concerto.[10]

Obviously it is not Walbrook's playing we hear on the soundtrack but that of Louis Kentner, who agreed to do the job providing he was not credited. (In those days, this kind of "session" work was regarded as distinctly *infra dig* for a concert pianist.) The success of Addinsell's pastiche, modeled on the style of Rachmaninoff, took the film producers by surprise. No one had anticipated the huge public interest in the music. No recordings had been pressed, no sheet music prepared; but this was soon remedied, and the "Warsaw Concerto" was soon being played everywhere. Huntley recalls the sheet music selling "in thousands of copies, it was heard almost daily on the radio, it made a tremendous hit in the United States, and during the war years whenever a pianist sat down in a NAAFI bar, in a pub, or in the quiet of the family circle, there would come before long the request for the 'Warsaw Concerto.'"[11] This was, in fact, a fairly tall order, as it is not a particularly easy piece to play, demonstrating, incidentally, how much more musically educated the general public was at this time, when so many more people could play the piano. Anthony Burgess supports Huntley here, recalling that during his own time in the army, "[m]usic, what there was of it for me, was mostly playing the mock–Rachmaninoff of the Warsaw Concerto."[12] Addinsell grew to resent the success of his piece, feeling it obliterated everything else he had done, but it remains the case, as Huntley points out, that the Warsaw Concerto is "perhaps the most remarkable piece of film background music ever written."[13] It is certainly one of the most often performed and in our post-modern times it has now even entered the repertoire of concert pianists, who regularly perform what Louis Kentner was too ashamed to admit to at the time.

The success of this music did not go unnoticed by rival film producers, with the inevitable consequence of a veritable craze for films featuring piano concertos. But there was a deeper underlying social reality behind this wartime cinematic phenomenon. When war with Germany was declared in 1939, all the art treasures of London's National Gallery were sent to safe locations for the duration of hostilities. This left the Gallery denuded, and caused its director, Kenneth Clarke, to feel profoundly depressed; but his mood lifted when concert pianist Myra Hess suggested to him that she might give recitals in the Gallery to boost morale and keep the arts alive amid such an atmosphere of besieged austerity. Despite the unfortunate connotations of her surname (calling to mind Hitler's principal henchman, Rudolf Hess), Myra Hess was English. Even worse, her first name was later shared by the infamous Moors murderer Myra Hindley, whom James Brady, Hindley's boyfriend and fellow murderer, used to refer as "Hessie." Thus has her name been twice defiled by the evils she was so passionately trying to defeat through her music.

Her first recital took place on October 10, 1939, in the Gallery's Octagonal Room 36 on a specially provided Steinway grand. She and Clarke were very surprised to see a queue of some 1000 people on the day of the first concert. In fact, many people had to be turned away as there simply wasn't room to accommodate them all. Hess played Sonatas by Scarlatti, two Bach Preludes and Fugues, Beethoven's "Appassionata" Sonata, a group of Schubert's Dances, a Waltz and Nocturne by Chopin and three Brahms Intermezzi, then finished with her own famous arrangement of Bach's "Jesu, Joy of Man's Desiring," which became a kind of anthem in defense of the German culture Nazism was destroying. The concerts continued five days a week for six years, and though they were not always given by Hess, she is the one who is remembered most in association with them. "The moment when she played the opening bars of Beethoven's Appassionata will always remain for me one of the great experiences of my life," Clarke later stated. "It was an assurance that all our sufferings were not in vain."[14]

These hugely significant cultural occasions were commemorated on film in Thorold Dickinson's *Men of Two Worlds* (1946), which opens with shots of London purporting to be in 1944. The camera pans across Trafalgar Square towards the National Gallery with its poster advertising the Gallery concerts. Myra Hess is the first attraction, but below her on the same poster, the hero of Dickinson's film is listed. This is Kisenga (Robert Adams), an African, educated in the West. He has composed a piece for piano and orchestra, with male voices singing a text in Swahili called "Baraza."

The camera follows audience members inside where crowds have filled the galleries for the concert. Sandbags remind us that the war is still on, as do several men in uniform. The mini-concerto, which we hear as we advance towards the octagonal Room 36, was composed by Sir Arthur Bliss, who, in Huntley's words, translates "African rhythms and colour to a Western style."[15] "Baraza" means a noisy African council meeting, and Bliss' piece is certainly indicative of such an event, with plenty of his own characteristically percussive rhythms. Eileen Joyce played the solo piano part for the soundtrack, having previously worked on *The Seventh Veil* (dir. Compton Bennett, 1945), and performed Hubert Bath's "Cornish Rhapsody" for *Love Story* (dir. Leslie Arliss, 1944). The choir is made up of entirely white singers, and the orchestral players are white, making the sight of Kisenga at the Steinway Grand all the more striking. This is certainly an exception to the general rule at that time that black pianists were confined to upright pianos. The piece is a great success with the wartime audience in the film, and it also enjoyed a life of its own beyond the film, being recorded by Decca, again with Mathieson and Joyce, as part of a series of "Incidental Music from British Films" in 1946.

After these opening shots, the action transfers to Africa: Kisgena has returned to take up a position as a teacher, much to the dismay of his English fans. There is consequently little further reference to his musical career, apart from a scene in which he hammers away at another, slightly less grand piano, disappointed by the rejection of his fellow Africans, who feel that he has betrayed his country by allowing himself to be educated by the hated colonial white man.

The wartime movie concerto craze was predominantly a British affair, though Hollywood's *The Great Lie* (dir. Edmund Goulding, 1941) featured Mary Astor playing Tchaikovsky's First Piano Concerto (and a Chopin Waltz). Coincidentally, that film, like *Dangerous Moonlight*, links aviation with pianos, though not in the same role. The lie of the title concerns the identity of the mother of pilot Peter Van Allen's (George Brent) child. He thinks the mother is the woman he eventually marries (Bette Davis) instead of Astor's Sandra. In fact, the mother is Sandra—all of which has very little to do with Tchaikovsky, but that doesn't stop composer Max Steiner from having some fun at Tchaikovsky's expense in the opening scenes, having a somewhat boozy saxophone play around with the big theme to suggest the morning after the night before (in which the child was conceived).

The British film industry responded to *Dangerous Moonlight*'s success with *The Common Touch* (dir. John Baxter, 1941). The story concerns a down-and-out pianist (Mark Hambourg) who recalls the scenes of his former triumphs across Europe while playing Tchaikovsky's famous work. In 1944, *Love Story* called for another potted concerto. This time, however, it was called, more properly, a rhapsody. As the film was set in Cornwall, the piece was therefore marketed as "Cornish Rhapsody," and this time sheet music and recordings were prepared well in advance.

Margaret Lockwood plays terminally ill concert pianist Lissa Campbell, who is inspired by the sound of surf and seagulls during a final holiday before she dies. She also falls in love with Stewart Granger's Kit and, as Huntley describes it, "her feeling of freedom underneath the Cornish skies, the emotion inspired in her by the grandeur of the rocky cost and the sea, the sadness that her life may be ended just as she has found love"[16] are all poured into the Rhapsody. Life curiously imitated art when Hubert Bath died the year after he composed his most famous piece.

Love Story is another wartime romance, in which the piano continues its role an icon of the cultural values for which the war is being fought. Absurdities such as the appearance of a Steinway concert grand in an outdoor theater on a Cornish cliff edge serve only to emphasize the determination to fight against all the odds in defense of civilization. The final scenes set in the Royal Albert Hall have Lockwood convincingly miming Joyce's soundtrack performance at the keyboard. The whole thing obviously informed the postwar *While I Live* (dir. John Harlow, 1947). Also set in Cornwall, it concerns the accidental death of another female pianist composer, who dies in a sleepwalking accident before completing "The Dream of Olwen," her piece for piano and orchestra (in fact composed by Charles Williams). Later in the film, it seems as though she has been reincarnated, much to the relief of her guilt-ridden sister, who was partly responsible for the sleepwalking accident. Williams' piece became immensely popular and, like the other potted concertos of the time, went on to have a long life of its own far longer than the reputation of the film itself. Although the war had been over for two years when *While I Live* was released, the story's concern with death, loss and resurrection resonated strongly with the experience of recent events, and once again, it was the piano that mediated these emotions, inspiring hopes of better things.

The same year, the Canadian crime thriller *Whispering City* (dir. Fedor Ozep) featured André Mathieu's "Québec" Concerto, which the composer had begun a few years earlier as a bona fide concerto, but which here masquerades as the work of the film's composer hero, Michel Lacoste (Helmut Dantine). Though it was not originally a potted concerto like the Warsaw Concerto, the fact that it appeared in a film, had a city in its title and was in late–Romantic Rachmaninoff style made the comparison hard to resist.

It was also marketed as a movie concerto with a solo piano arrangement of "The Theme from the Quebec Concerto," drawn from the second movement, and advertised by Toronto's Southern publishers as "From the Film *Whispering City*." Actually, the concerto plays a very minor part in the film. There is a rehearsal scene (with absurd lines such as "Can we have a little more expression in the strings?"), an argument between the composer and his sick wife (she complains, "It doesn't matter than I'm going to die—you have to finish your concerto!") and an almost incidental performance scene in which we hardly see the piano or the pianist. The story—a murder mystery involving double-crossing and subterfuge—has nothing to do with the concerto, but one can see where Ozep, his screenwriters Rian James and Leonard Lee and, perhaps more to the point, the music publishers were coming from. They may have been in Quebec (or Toronto) but they were looking over their shoulders back to Warsaw.

Rachmaninoff's influence over all these film concertos made the appearance of a genuine Rachmaninoff concerto almost inevitable, and this occurred in Lean's *Brief Encounter*. Muir Mathieson was very much against using so famous a piece in the context of a cinematic underscore:

> That has always been my argument against using music that's known, because if you suddenly bring in one of the standard classics at a highly emotional moment, somebody is bound to say, "What's that music? I know that," and the moment of tension is gone. That's why I've always maintained that it's much, much better to have a score specially written for a film. There are occasions, of course, when you can use "a standard classic," so long as you establish that that is what the work is.[17]

Huntley was in full agreement here:

> I think it was a mistake to use the Rachmaninoff Piano Concerto No. 2 in this particular case. I like the Rachmaninoff No. 2 far too well to be able to follow a first-class film at the same time which is largely unrelated in any way to the music....
>
> One of the loveliest railway shots ever is amplified by those first eight chords of the No. 2 Concerto and as we swing into the main theme, up comes the titling. However, as soon as the story begins to unfold, we are continually distracted from the fascinating plot to listen to Eileen Joyce, with Muir Mathieson and the National Symphony Orchestra, in a brilliant rendering of a work which, despite many hearings, still requires my full attention. It cannot be done. Either listen to Rachmaninoff or Coward, but they have so little in common that you cannot listen to both.[18]

But "Rach. 2" was Noël Coward's favorite piece of music and, though he had not included it in the original play on which the film is based, he insisted it should be used, against the advice of not only Mathieson but also Lean. Huntley explained to Kevin Brownlow what happened next:

Noël Coward said, "No, no, no. She listens to Rachmaninov on the radio, she borrows her books from the Boots Library and she eats at the Kardomah."

Muir said, "I will only do it if you show her switching on the radio and if you respect the original music."

Coward was happy to play fast and loose with the music, but if you listen to it you'll hear that it begins with the first eight piano chords and ends with the last part of the third movement of the concerto.

As the last bars of Rachmaninov were played, everyone dissolved into tears in the audience and even Muir admitted that no specially composed score could have been quite so effective as that Rachmaninov.[19]

In fact, the film ends with an especially composed ending, truncating Rachmaninoff's original, which would have been inappropriately elaborate; but the material does indeed derive from the last part of the concerto. What is often overlooked in *Brief Encounter*'s music is the masterly manner in which Mathieson extracted and subtly manipulated sections from the Rachmaninoff score to fit the mood and momentum of the scenes they accompany. From the opening chords during the main titles, after a train screeches past, the selections are by no means arbitrary. The sound of trains and their banshee-like whistles are also treated as significant sonic events, hence a whistle from a train traveling toward the camera introduces the famous opening of the concerto, and subsequent whistles emphasize the fatalistic mood of the station itself as a place of departure and loneliness. A little later, when Laura (Celia Johnson) hears a distant train whistle after her return home, it reminds her of her final parting with Alec (Trevor Howard), and she has to pull herself together in front of her husband.

A little earlier, during the conversation between Laura and Dolly (Everley Gregg), Rachmaninoff's solo horn perfectly expresses Laura's mood. Then, during her soliloquy "This can't last. This misery can't last," we hear perhaps the saddest piece of music ever written: those final bars of the slow movement with their chromatically altered chords in the piano, the strings extending the melody with sustained notes, and the flutes murmuring in triplets above. In her subsequent soliloquy, while listening to the concerto on the radio, it is the same solo horn passage that introduces her voice-over.

At other times, the more lively sections help transitions between scenes: As Lean cuts from the station to a street scene following Laura walking, the piano's more active passage helps establish normality, as Laura picks up a book from Boots, at which point the music is cut off at a naturally occurring cadence.

The big theme from the third movement underscores the growing affection between Laura and Alec in the refreshment room as Alec discusses his medical passions. After his departure, Laura wanders along the platform lost in thought, as the piano commences its ruminative meandering in the "Meno mosso" section of the third movement. This aptly accompanies both the action and the thoughts of Laura as she imagines Alec "getting out at Churley, giving up his ticket, walking back through the streets, letting himself in his house with his latchkey. His wife, Madeline, would probably be in the hall to meet him, or perhaps upstairs in her room, not feeling very well...." The "Meno mosso" section ends, perfectly timed to coincide with Laura's "the first awful feeling of danger swept over me," when escaping steam from a train changes the mood.

After an attempt to put Alec out of her mind, Laura is once again on the platform and suddenly realizes that she is panic-stricken "at the thought of not seeing him again." At this moment, Alec runs up the slope of what is actually Carnforth Station, beneath the now world-famous clock, and again Mathieson chooses an appropriately rising passage from the concerto, which not only mirrors the action of ascent but also the growing excitement as Laura and Alec reunite. The section is taken from the "Allegro scherzando" finale of the third movement, and Alec's appearance on the slope is perfectly timed to begin as the piano enters "poco a poco accelerando" in its scalic ascent. We move into the "Agitato" section with the piano's arpeggios, the mood of excitement and delight growing all the time as the station master's whistle blows, increasing the sense of exhilaration. "Quickly, quickly, the whistle's gone!" Laura shouts. They agree to meet again next Thursday, as Alec catches his train with only seconds to spare, and here Mathieson holds on to the big *fff* C major chord to which all this leads. By cutting what follows in Rachmaninoff's score, he brings the "cue" to a hugely optimistic conclusion, as Laura stares, wild-eyed with delight, at the departing train.

Mathieson went on to conduct Bernard Stevens' score for Brian Desmond Hurst's melodrama *The Mark of Cain* (1947). Eric Portman is Richard Howard, a scheming, suave, vengeful, sinister, cultured and musical villain, who poisons his own brother and then frames his brother's wife (Sally Gray). His musicality is demonstrated in a short scene in which he accompanies his sister-in-law in one of the Songs of the Auvergne; but Richard is merely a dilettante, and his artistic interests only confirm the audience's distrust of such a character. It is left to a professional to play Rachmaninoff in a concert scene midway through the film. Instead of reprising the Second Concerto so soon after *Brief Encounter*, Mathieson chose an extract from the less often performed First Concerto, which had been premiered in 1893, five years before the date in which the film is set. The bona fide professional, Albert Ferber, performs here with a cameo appearance on the rostrum from John Hollingsworth, later to be music supervisor on most of Hammer Films' early Gothic horrors. As Hollingsworth never appeared in any of his Hammer films, it is doubly interesting to see him at work here, and Ferber's screen presence is the complete opposite of the tormented souls so often portrayed by actors in cinematic concerts. He's upright, clean-cut, his features in Rachmaninoff-like repose, all the emotion concentrated in his fingers. The First Concerto, however, isn't anywhere near as melodically sensational as the Second, and *The Mark of Cain* demonstrates the vital importance of the Second to the success of *Brief Encounter*.

Brief Encounter is set in the 1930s and so makes no reference to the Second World War, even though it was filmed during the closing stages of that conflict. (Carnforth station was chosen as the main location rather than one in London because it was so much safer.[20]) But audiences at the time could not have been completely immune to the wartime connotation of trains, stations and departures summoned by the film. It is therefore appropriate to regard it as yet another cinematic child of the Myra Hess concerts. So too is the much more obviously wartime and immediately postwar setting of *The Glass Mountain* (dir. Henry Cass, 1949). As was the case with Anton Walbrook's Stefan Radetsky, Michael Dennison's Richard Wilder is a musical member of the RAF, who is shot down over Italy's Dolomite Mountains and rescued by Valentina Cortesa's Alida. She tells him the Legend of the Glass Mountain, concerning a ghost that lures her faithless partner over the precipice of the mountain in question. The story inspires Richard to compose an opera, which also somewhat reflects his own situation, for although he is already married to someone else, he becomes romantically involved with Alida. After the war, his opera is staged at the Fenice Opera House in Venice, and Richard's wife flies in to attend. Alas, her plane crashes into the very same Glass Mountain, but fortunately she survives, and Richard, who realizes he has been rather too romantically involved with Alida, returns home to live happily ever after, as one might expect.

The plot has much in common with *Brief Encounter*, and it even uses a train to separate the lovers midway through the proceedings. Admittedly, Nino Rota was no Rachmaninoff, and Henry Cass no David Lean, but the similarities nonetheless remain, especially in the light of the tremendous success of Rota's "Legend of the Glass Mountain." That concertante piece for piano and orchestra does not in fact feature on the soundtrack, though the themes it employs do, in a different guise. Rota obviously realized that he might have a considerable hit on his hands if he dressed up his material as a kind of Warsaw Concerto. So successful was it that a host of light music maestros from Mantovani to Geoff Love have since covered it, enshrining the work as a movie potted concerto, which technically speaking it is not. (The same approach was taken when marketing Edward Ward's "Lullaby of the Bells" from Arthur Lubin's 1943 *Phantom of the Opera*. In the film, the piece is a song with piano accompaniment, but in its incarnation as sheet music, it was re-arranged for solo piano and given the title of "Piano Concerto." The main melody is given a dramatic *ff* introduction, chiming bells are imitated by fifths, and two cadenzas give sufficient virtuosity to the affair to satisfy many of its admirers that this is what a concerto is. It is not.)

In *The Glass Mountain*, there are certain justifications for Rota's concerto transformation, for although Richard is composing an opera rather than a concerto, he does compose at a piano, and also plays excerpts of his work on the piano. When he runs through the opera with Tito Gobbi at La Fenice, he performs on an elaborately decorated grand, but we also find Richard seated before an upright during rehearsals. Earlier in the film, when Richard and his wife enter an empty house and imagine how it would look if they moved in, Richard imagines a "decorative Bechstein" grand, which promptly materializes in his imagination (and on screen).

The popularity of the Warsaw Concerto did not fail to make an impression on Miklós Rózsa when he reworked material from his score for Hitchcock's *Spellbound* (1946). Hitchcock's psychological thriller has absolutely nothing to do with pianos, but that didn't stop Rózsa from transforming his score into another concertante piece for piano and orchestra. Shostakovitch followed suit in 1951 when he scored Mikheil Chiaureli's *The Unforgettable Year 1919*, the most celebrated cue of which has long been mistranslated as "The Assault on Beautiful Gorky." In fact, the piece has nothing to do with the city of Nizhny Novgorod, which used to be known as Gorky. The title should more correctly be translated as "The Storming of Red Hill Fort," which is what "Krasnaya Gorka" means. But the inappropriate title has stuck, as has the music, which is more than can be said for the film for which it was written. *The Unforgettable Year 1919* is perhaps Soviet Russia's most inflated and artificial piece of political propaganda in praise of Stalin's involvement in that year's Russian Civil War. "This fantastic picture naturally had nothing to do with reality," remarked Shostakovitch in his *Testimony*,[21] and he was under no illusions about the film or his contribution to it, listing it among his "shameful enterprises."[22] He also claimed that Chiaureli couldn't tell "a piano from a toilet bowl,"[23] but the "The Storming of Red Hill Fort" is far more elaborate than the film deserves and is highly effective in its own terms with its fountain-like piano arpeggios and "big" tune. However, there are so many explosions, so much gunfire and general military mayhem in the section of film for which it was originally intended, it is just as well that the music has managed to establish itself as a piece in its own right, otherwise no one would really have been able to hear it.

Hollywood also had its own flirtation with Rachmaninoff's Second Piano Concerto, beginning with a film made the year after *Brief Encounter*:

Two. Picture Palace Pianos

Frank Borzage's florid classical musical comedy *I've Always Loved You* (1946) includes more of Rachmaninoff's concerto than any other feature film, not only "in rehearsal" but also in two sizable concert scenes. None other than Artur Rubinstein played the concerto for the soundtrack recording, along with a variety of popular classics, while various individuals mimed to this high-status repertoire, including a youthful André Previn who auditions to become a pupil of Philip Dorn's virtuoso, Leopold Goronoff. Goronoff is an impossibly selfish, arrogant and quixotic concert pianist, whose first name suggests that of the most famous American conductor of the day, Leopold Stokowski, while his surname echoes that of Rachmaninoff. The sets for this, the most expensive film Republic ever made, are so grand that the opening credits refer to "architecture" rather than set design. Vast structures are decorated with statues, busts, columns, flower arrangements in immense vases, expensive furniture and a great deal of swagging. The grand piano used during the opening audition is elaborately gilded with paintings in cartouches. Asked to play Bach, Previn's character says he is "more in tune with Debussy," but he is overruled by the maestro. He begins to play Bach's D-minor Toccata, only to be interrupted to make way for other hopefuls. One girl plays Mendelssohn, another plays the famous Rachmaninoff Prelude in C-sharp minor; but then the heroine of the film, Catherine McLeod's Myra Hassman, comes forward. She plays Beethoven's "Appassionata" Sonata (her miming to Rubinstein is very convincing), and finally Goronoff is impressed. Myra Hassman (a name that echoes Myra Hess) stops halfway through the first movement, explaining, "It goes on and on..." which is an oddly philistine thing to say during an audition that's going so well. Goronoff responds by asking for the Presto, and agrees to take Myra on as his student.

We cut to Myra and her father playing Rachmaninoff's concerto back on the Pennsylvania farm where they live. Unusually for a farmhouse, there are two pianos on which to perform. When Goronoff arrives with his usual flamboyance, he plays the orchestral part with Myra, but they are interrupted by the sound of a tractor, driven by bare-chested farmhand George Sampter (Bill Carter). George represents the unsophisticated, homespun authenticity of Americans, as opposed to the elaborate, arty, well-dressed self-indulgence of Europeans. Even so, Goronoff gives up his European tour to stay at the farm and nurture Myra's talent. He takes her through Rachmaninoff's cadenza, urging her to be "crisp, like icicles breaking off a roof."

Enter Maria Ouspenskaya as Goronoff's mother. Ouspenskaya had encountered the piano in 1941's *Kings Row*, but her connection with it here is more intimate, for she will decide if Goronoff is hearing Myra "with his ears or his eyes." She determines that it is the former, and Myra, having passed the test, is allowed to enter the family business, so to speak.

Goronov's grand: Catherine McLeod, Felix Bressart and Philip Dorn (right) in *I've Always Loved You*.

Another immensely elaborate set now represents Goronoff's New York apartment. He and Myra again rehearse Rach. 2. Goronoff, dressed in a gray velvet smoking jacket with quilted silk lapels, plays on a decorated grand; Myra plays her part on a black Steinway. Then Goronoff goes on tour. We hear of his triumph with Chopin's and Schumann's concerti (Rubinstein obliges with brief extracts), and then Myra and her mentor find themselves in another grandiose setting in Rio de Janeiro. They go through Rach. 2 yet again, this time with even more meaningless and certainly more misogynistic "interpretations" from Goronoff:

> GORONOFF: This is the female theme. And now the male theme. I am the man. I am the man. I am the man.
> MYRA: And I am the woman. And I love you.
> GORONOFF: So. It should be so. A concerto is like that. There is a beginning, a blossoming at which we call the exposition; then in the end, like a man who has lived, you see the result of his life.
> MYRA: But the woman, maestro.
> GORONOFF: There is no woman in music.

The maestro next decides to seduce a blonde creature who has come into his purview, and he asks Myra to play Liszt's transcription of Wagner's

Liebestod from *Tristan und Isolde* during the seduction. But this situation not being at all to Myra's liking, she plays with increasing force, thus deliberately ruining the mood. At this stage, she thinks she is in love with Goronoff, a possibility that Goronoff, in his selfish way, hasn't considered. He is, in truth, rather more in thrall to his mother, in a relationship that strongly resembles Liberace's domestic arrangements.

At last, Goronoff decides Myra is ready for her debut concert at Carnegie Hall, the vast proscenium of which provides another cinematic spectacle. Goronoff asks Myra if she is nervous, which she is. "Cabbages!" Goronoff replies. The audience to him is merely "rows of cabbages. Cabbages can't hurt you." He warms the cabbages up by conducting an overture, after which stagehands in their shirt sleeves wheel on the Steinway, somehow managing to hoist it up onto its raised dais. And once more, but this time in its full orchestral guise, Rach. 2 is wheeled out after it. During the famous opening chords of the concerto, the camera zooms from a long shot, which takes in the whole proscenium, towards Myra at the piano dressed in a shell-pink gown. Thus is created the perfect cinematic picture of pianistic eroticism.

But all is not well, as Myra's exquisite playing makes Goronoff jealous. The music thus "expresses" emotional conflict, just as it does in *Brief Encounter*. During the third movement, as Myra grows increasingly disturbed by the situation, the camera sits directly behind the keyboard, which lies firmly along the bottom of the screen, its tooth-like imagery almost devouring the pianist as she plays. Negulesco's *Humoresque* from the same year features the same effect, which we can trace back to a nineteenth-century caricature of Liszt by Klic., where the keyboard similarly runs along the bottom of the picture. (Note, also, how one of the pianist's fans even imitates Liszt's famous hairstyle!)

After a blazing row back in the opulent flat, Myra returns to the farm and plays Chopin to herself—but also in synchronization with Goronoff, who plays the same piece in his Carnegie Hall recitals. They thus almost telepathically communicate with each other through music, as Madame Goronoff explains in the mystical manner Ouspenskaya had already perfected as Maleva the gypsy in *The Wolf Man* (dir. George Waggner, 1941). When farmhand George interrupts Maya and she stops playing, so too does Goronoff all those miles away.

Myra now realizes it is George she has always loved, not Goronoff, and she marries him, which is just as well. "Music," Madame Goronoff adds, by way of confirmation, "is Goronoff's mistress," and the final scene, set several years later, provides yet another performance by Myra and Goronoff of Rach. 2, with Carnegie Hall decorated with immense Corinthian columns at the back of the stage. As the final bars resound, the camera zooms back

Franz before Bugs: A nineteenth-century cartoon of Liszt by Klic.

over the audience to provide a long shot of the entire proscenium, and the screen at last announces THE END.

In 1948, Hollywood gave another composer and a different piano concerto a break in John Cromwell's *Night Song*. Dana Andrews is Dan Evans, a blind pianist who wins a prize to have his concerto played by Artur Rubinstein with Eugene Ormandy on the podium. Socialite Cathy Mallory (Merle Oberon) falls for Evans, who rejects her (his blindness has understandably embittered him and has also made him suspicious of pity). Undeterred, Cathy disguises herself as another woman and pretends to be blind herself. This time she succeeds, and manages to persuade Evans to complete his concerto, which wins the competition. In the lengthy concert scene that follows, Rubinstein does indeed perform his concerto, though in fact this was composed by the real-life American composer, Leith Stevens. Evans uses his prize money to have his sight restored by means of an expensive operation, and eventually discovers that Mary and Cathy are the same person, leading to a happy ending. Rubinstein's appearance lends the film huge prestige, as does Steven's concerto, despite the fact that the film itself can't really return the compliment. When the concert begins, and Rubinstein strides out to his grand piano, we might expect something like Rachmaninoff to ensue, but Stevens' style is more jazz-influenced, even though it is appropriately brooding and heroic in its accessibly tonal language. While Rubinstein plays, the screen visualizes Evans' reminiscences of walking by the sea hand in hand with Cathy-Mary (whose face is suitably blurred whenever Evans is shown thinking about her).

The Stevens concerto is a worthy piece, and rather more memorable than the bubblegum pop songs composed by William Sylvester's blind pianist Paul in Lance Comfort's *Blind Corner* (1964). As well as being similarly embittered, this pianist has an unfaithful wife (Barbara Shelley). Unlike Merle Oberon, Shelley's Lady Macbeth doesn't love her pianist husband at all and pretends to fall in love with an artist, whom she then persuades to murder her husband, thus leaving the field clear for her to inherit his fortune and go off with the man she *really* loves: her husband's manager (Mark Eden).

It is significant that it was pop music rather than piano concertos that this pianist is more interested in composing. By the 1960s, the piano movie was beginning its decline; but throughout the 1950s, the ubiquitous Second Concerto had managed to maintain its Hollywood appeal. William Dieterle's *September Affair* (1950) has Joan Fontaine as the pianist Marianne Stuart in a loose replay of the plot of *The Glass Mountain*. While in Italy, she falls in love with a married man (Joseph Cotten). When his wife is reported dead in a plane crash, the lovers carry on living in Florence until the wife comes looking for her husband. In a Florence café, Marianne plays "September Song" on an upright, hence the film's title. She later mixes the song with Rach. 2 on a grand. It mixes rather well. Then we watch her rehearsing a sizable portion of the concerto, with Françoise Rosay playing the orchestral part on the second of the two grands at their disposal. Rosay, who had only two years previously demolished Dirk Bogarde's aspiring pianist George Bland in *Quartet* (see below), plays much the same role of music pedagogue, though here she is rather more complimentary: "For the first time in your life, you have played as a mature artist," she congratulates Marianne.

Marianne has no desire to continue being a concert pianist, but a concert scene eventually materializes. It is not quite as lavish as the one in *I've Always Loved You*, but it does contain another large chunk of Rach. 2. Fontaine, in a fulsome gown, pearls and diamond earrings, again demonstrates the erotic appeal of both the piano and the "ultimate" concerto.

Rather more glamor wrapped itself around the piece four years later in Charles Vidor's Rachmaninoff-fest, *Rhapsody* (1954). The opening chords of Rach. 2 introduce the main titles, which sweep past against the familiar brooding intensity of the opening bars of the first movement. Here,

Grand passion: Joseph Cotten and Joan Fontaine in *September Affair*.

Elizabeth Taylor plays Louise Durant, an untalented pianist in love with a violinist (Vittorio Gassman). She follows him to the conservatoire in Zürich, hoping to enroll as a student there so as to remain with him, but her audition doesn't go well. She launches into Liszt's "Liebestraum No. 3" but stops after making several clumsy mistakes. "It's not very good, is it?" she asks Michael Chekhov's sympathetic professor. Louise admits her ulterior motive for wanting to take lessons, and the professor pulls a few strings. She can stay; but she then attracts the attention of a handsome pianist (John Ericson). And, as is so often the case in films that feature Rach. 2, a love triangle forms the plot, such as it is.

We are treated to another lengthy rehearsal scene of the slow movement, and a lengthy concert scene, almost matching the Rachmaninoff quotient of *I've Always Loved You*, and this is because *Rhapsody*'s *raison d'être* is to juxtapose the yearning melancholy of the concerto with incredibly glamorous shots of Elizabeth Taylor in her prime, lavishly dressed, adorned with jewels and also emoting yearning melancholy. During the culminating concert scene, she looks on in white fur and silk, in long-held close-ups, as the music surges forth, epitomizing what many have always felt music to be about: the expression of passion, which in this case is quite understandable. Taylor is much more glamorous than Celia Johnson, but both do much the same job of staring wistfully, with tears in their eyes, as Rachmaninoff thunders all around them. Despite the movie's title, there are no actual rhapsodies in *Rhapsody*—let alone Rachmaninoff's *Rhapsody on a Theme of Paganini*. (*Rhapsody* is rather more concerned with "rapture," which does sound similar, it has to be said.)

Rachmaninoff's Paganini Rhapsody appeared in the portmanteau film *The Story of Three Loves* (dir. Gottfried Reinhardt and Vincente Minnelli, 1953). In "The Jealous Lover," the first of its three stories, James Mason, recapitulating the kind of character he had played in *The Seventh Veil*, stars as a gruff and only seemingly terrifying impresario, Charles Coutray. He persuades Moira Shearer's Paula Woodward to resume her ballet career, which ill health had forced her to abandon. She improvises elegantly to Rachmaninoff in Coutray's studio, inspiring him with plans to re-work his ballet around her. But the strain proves too much for Paula, who collapses and dies when she returns home to her aunt (Agnes Moorhead). Milkós Rózsa, who was in charge of the underscore of the film, allows Rachmaninoff to speak for himself during these lengthy scenes, but then takes Rachmaninoff's material and subjects it to his own personal treatment. This sets the musical tone for the rest of the film, which brought the Paganini Rhapsody to new audiences, its success even inspiring pop pianist Winifred Atwell to record her own version. Atwell had trained classically before moving onto honkytonk hits. In bringing Rachmaninoff to the charts she accredits herself well, though it is Rózsa rather than Rachmaninoff who is credited as the composer on the record label! However, musical culture at that time being weaponized to such an extent in the power struggle between commercialism and the avant-garde, that having a black, female pop pianist perform a late–Romantic work deemed by the establishment to be out of date and irrelevant did nothing to help restore Rachmaninoff's reputation among the modernist elite.

Rachmaninoff had now almost become a film composer himself, so pervasive had his music become on so many soundtracks, and cinematic exposure was doing a great deal of harm to his reputation in the concert hall. His late Romantic style, tainted by association with the likes of Elizabeth Taylor, Joan Fontaine *et al.*, sent his reputation plummeting. The 1954 entry for Rachmaninoff in the *Grove Dictionary of Music* reflected this, attacking him for the very thing that makes his music so remarkable: the miraculous ability to create sustained and seemingly self-generating melodies:

> As a composer he can hardly be said to have belonged to his time at all. His music is well constructed and effective, but monotonous in texture, which consists in essence mainly of artificial and gushing tunes accompanied by a variety

of figures derived from arpeggios. The enormous popular success some few of Rachmaninoff's works had in his lifetime is not likely to last, and musicians never regarded it with much favor.

Even the film industry began to think that Rachmaninoff was suffering from over-exposure, and in 1955, Billy Wilder provided some much-needed satire with *The Seven Year Itch*. Tom Ewell plays a New York businessman, Richard Sherman, who is enjoying some free time with his family away for the summer. He listens to a recording of "good old Rachmaninoff. The Second Piano Concerto," adding, "It never misses." He then imagines himself playing the great Sergei's masterpiece on his own piano. He even looks a little like Goronoff in *I've Always Loved You*, complete with a cod Russian accent and a red silk dressing gown. As the familiar themes roll out, Marilyn Monroe appears as "The Girl" and sits on his lap. "Every time I hear that, I go to pieces," she groans in a mock swoon. "It shakes me. It quakes me. It makes me feel goose-pimply all over. I don't know where I am or what I am or what I'm doing. Don't stop! Don't stop! Don't ever stop."

He stops.

"Why did you stop?"

"Why? Because now I'm going to take you in my arms and kiss you very quickly and very hard."

Rachmaninoff gradually became less pervasive as the 1960s dawned, but he continued to make his presence felt in *The World of Henry Orient*

Floored by Rachmaninoff: Tom Ewell and Marilyn Monroe in *The Seven Year Itch*.

(dir. George Ray Hill, 1964), in which two lonely schoolgirls befriend each other. One of them, Valerie (Tippy Walker) plays Rach. 2 on the piano, and then puts on a recording while she and her friend Marian (Merrie Spaeth) discuss their problematic private lives. Marian's parents are divorced, but as Rachmaninoff moodily underscores their conversation, Valerie insists with suitably Romantic idealism, "He's got to go back to his one true love. And then he'd take her in his arms and rain kisses on her upturned face and they'd just love each other right there on the front door."

This is touching, though it is obviously not to be taken as seriously as the same sentiments expressed by adult characters in movies from the 1940s and '50s. Henry Orient (Peter Sellers) is a concert pianist specializing in the avant-garde. (The character is loosely based on Oscar Levant, hence his unusual name.) The two girls keep encountering him on his amorous escapades and the coincidences convince him that they have been sent out to spy on him. Elmer Bernstein, who scored the film, nicely characterizes Orient on the first of these encounters with the kind of avant-garde music for which Orient is known, making all need for dialogue redundant.

Being a music lover, Valerie is excited about hearing Orient perform, and goes along with her mother, grandmother and Marian to his next concert. For this scene, Bernstein composed a "modernist" Warsaw Concerto of his own. Its discords and rhythmic irregularities cause Valerie's grandmother to exclaim, "If this is music, what's that stuff Cole Porter writes?" Another audience member turns off his hearing aid and smiles contentedly, while the orchestra's double bass players indulge in a game of draughts during Orient's lengthy solo passage. Lost in his meandering cadenza, Orient looks up to observe his exasperated conductor mouth the words "B-flat" to bring him back to the right tonality for the orchestra to carry on playing. A percussionist dutifully counts, counts, counts until it is time for him to blow a steam whistle. Despite these modernist credentials, Orient is not above using the piano in its old-fashioned role as an instrument of seduction, during which he too assumes a fake foreign accent.

The film industry's Rachmaninoff mania does beg the question why the Second Concerto became such an incredibly popular piece. The story of its genesis is well known: Suffering from profound depression after the fiasco of his first symphony, Rachmaninoff took psychotherapy from a Dr. Dahl, to whom the concerto is dedicated. Rachmaninoff himself described what happened:

> I heard the same hypnotic formula repeated day after day while I lay half asleep in an armchair in Dahl's study. "You will begin to write your Concerto— You will work with great facility—The Concerto will be of excellent quality." It was always the same, without interruption. Although it may sound incredible, this cure really helped me. Already at the beginning of the summer I began

again to compose. The material grew in bulk and new musical ideas began to stir within me—far more than I needed for my concerto. I felt that Dr. Dahl's treatment had strengthened my nervous system to a miraculous degree.[24]

Of course, Rachmaninoff's concerto is a masterpiece of technical accomplishment, but it is primarily a construction of very long melodies, and it is this that creates so much of its immense appeal. So irresistible are these melodies that popular songwriters have long raided them along with those from other works by Rachmaninoff, popularizing his tunes but damaging his reputation in the process by turning them into disposable kitsch. By the 1940s, Rach. 2 had become *the* concerto, not only in its own terms, but also because Rachmaninoff himself had so often performed it. His biographer Geoffrey Norris summed it up as being "notable for its conciseness and for its lyrical themes, which are just sufficiently contrasted to ensure that they are not spoilt by over-abundance or over-exposure."[25] But by the mid-twentieth century, the commercial exploitation and over-exposure of the work as a whole had had a devastatingly deleterious effect: Rachmaninoff became the victim of his own success, as well as of changing fashion. Consequently, when *Brief Encounter* was disastrously remade in 1974 with Sophia Loren and Richard Burton, Rachmaninoff was nowhere to be heard. The closest we get to any piano music is when Loren's character sits briefly on the stool of the humble upright in her living room and strums two or three notes, which don't even form a recognizable tune. The British Rail diesel trains, which hurtle back and forth at regular intervals, also lack the magic of steam, and Loren and Burton, hopelessly miscast as ordinary English people, seem absurd, as Rachmaninoff would have sounded in such an unconvincing context.

But Rachmaninoff has survived and his music has continued to fertilize popular culture. Two years after the *Brief Encounter* remake, Eric Carmen combined the famous theme of the Second Concerto's second movement with the big theme from the Adagio of Rachmaninoff's Second Symphony for his million-selling hit song "All by Myself." Towards the end, he included a lengthy instrumental passage for piano and orchestra as a tribute to his inspiration. Many fans thought it was all his own work, but the royalties he had to pay to Rachmaninoff's estate made clear that it was not. Then in 1980, the famous eighteenth variation of the Paganini Rhapsody returned as the love theme of Jeannot Szwarc's *Somewhere in Time* starring Christopher Reeve and Jane Seymour. Subsequently, the Second Concerto has found itself consistently in the top three of Classic FM radio's "Ultimate Hall of Fame." Rachmaninoff is as unstoppable as the steam trains with which he is now forever associated, and there is nothing wrong with that. It is, however, sadly the case that the success of the

Second Concerto in the modern world is largely because it flies in the face of our contemporary sensibilities. The world's most popular piano concerto is so very popular because Hollywood has turned it into the kitsch of popular Romanticism. The world from which it comes no longer exists, but films like *I've Always Loved You, Rhapsody* and *September Affair* want us to believe that it still does.

Three

Paderewski and Liberace

Post-Romanticism

The crisis in which Western Romantic culture found itself after the First World War had many consequences, most of which lie far beyond the confines of this book. However, what *is* relevant here is the decline of piano as *the* musical instrument of Western culture. After the catastrophe of 1914, only memories of its former confidence and glory remained. These, however, were immensely powerful memories for the public at large, even though they were persistently rejected by the avant-garde: Dadaism, Futurism, Neo-classicism, Neue Sachlichkeit, Modernism, Serialism and a host of other new esthetics, which decreed that Romantic culture was dead, *and* that it had been responsible for the First World War, with its cult of heroism, nationalism, egoism and irrationalism. The brave new world of postwar Europe trampled upon the legacy of Liszt and the monolith of the concert grand, and insisted that the esthetic they represented was now irrelevant—a spent force, unsuitable for more streamlined, rational times. The arrival of electronic instruments compounded this opinion.

But memories and nostalgia are powerful forces which no amount of intellectual finger-wagging can dispel, particularly when they are harnessed to a consumer society with technological means at its disposal. Schoenberg may have hoped that the creation of serialism would ensure the supremacy of German music for the next hundred years (a rather unfortunate turn of phrase, given the pretensions of German "kultur" under the Nazis' "Thousand Year Reich"), but the ultimate musical victor was not serialism, fascinating though that experiment had been. It was, rather, the very tonality Schoenberg considered to have been exhausted by Richard Wagner, whose music Schoenberg regarded as being so chromatic that it had destabilized the principles of tonality for good. (Such an interpretation overlooks the fact that Wagner opens his music drama *Das Rheingold* with an extensive rumination on the notes of an E-flat major chord and brings his final drama

Parsifal to a radiant conclusion of D-flat major.) While concert composers labored under Schoenberg's tyranny, commercial music (show tunes, film music, dance music) carried on using major and minor keys. As technology improved, a form of popular Romanticism emerged triumphant: what is now called pop music. Pop music is the highly commercialized descendent of what used to be known as folk music, which the Romantic composers Chopin, Liszt and Dvořák had explored so productively. In many ways, pop music was the logical descendent of Schubert's Lieder and Chopin's short Waltzes and Mazurkas. That Barry Manilow adapted Chopin's C minor Prelude for his hit song "Could It Be Magic" should not surprise us.

This is perhaps the most obvious of the connections between commercial pop culture and the Romantic composers of nineteenth-century culture. Popular Romanticism is a kind of after-life—even a radioactive half-life. Radioactivity causes mutations, and as we have seen with Eric Carmen's "All by Myself," popular culture voraciously feeds upon and transforms the dead culture of Romanticism. Pop music is now the commander-in-chief, and the musical culture that gave it life is today used to disperse delinquent youths like a kind of acoustic tear gas.

Kitsch

Kitsch misunderstands (either willfully or unknowingly) the historical model it attempts to imitate. It is sometimes flippant. Nineteenth-century Romantic music is often wholly serious in intent but regarded as kitsch by later purists. Mendelssohn's Fugue in E minor is a supreme example of religious kitsch, which exploits the idiom of Bach, turning it into the world's first concert fugue, with flashy Lisztian effects. All together, these effects combine to evoke a pious feeling without the inconvenience of having to go to church, or even of requiring any faith. In Charles Rosen's words:

> This is kitsch insofar as it substitutes for religion itself the emotional shell of religion. It evades all aspects of controversy, of dramatic conflict. It does not comfort, but only makes us comfortable. Virtuosity and religion have a reciprocal display in Mendelssohn's fugue: the religious atmosphere makes the virtuoso display seem less trivial, more deeply serious, while the virtuosity makes the feeling of being in church more effective, passionate and interesting. Religion is drained of all content and has become powerfully sensuous, a purely aesthetic form of the sublime.

The E Minor Fugue is, as I have said, unequivocally a masterpiece.[1]

Gounod's "Ave Maria," which assumes that Bach's C minor Prelude from Book One of the 38 Preludes and Fugues, is really only an accompaniment waiting for a melody, is somewhat less of a kitsch masterpiece because it is an adaptation of an existing work rather than a highly original pastiche like Mendelssohn's. For all that, both pieces are imitative, sentimentalized, commercialized, somewhat pretentious and retrogressive theatrical misunderstandings of Bach; but the world would be a poorer place without them. Tchaikovsky's *Mozartiana* (which sentimentalizes Mozart's *Ave verum*) and his kitschification of the melody of Mozart's K503 piano concerto in the rococo divertissement of his opera *The Queen of Spades*, are also masterpieces of kitsch. Like all kitsch adaptations, they falsify their models, reviving what is dead in an attempt to escape reality.

By resurrecting the past and misinterpreting it, kitsch creates a cultural vacuum which will absorb any amount of influences. Loving the past, no matter how carefully considered, implies a psychological resistance to the present as well as a fear of the future. Kitsch pickles the past while disguising the modern technologies that make it possible. King Ludwig's fantasy medieval *Neuschwanstein* castle, for example, sports hot and cold running water, was constructed with the help of one of the world's first steam cranes and superimposes an antique architectural style on modern building techniques, including a cast-iron framework in the throne room to support the massive dome. Ironically, the more industrialized a country becomes, the more kitsch it produces. As Nietzsche pointed out in the second of his *Untimely Meditations* on "The Uses and Disadvantages of History for Life":

> The oversaturation of an age with history ... leads an age into a dangerous mood of irony in regard to itself and subsequently into the even more dangerous mood of cynicism: in this mood, however, it develops more and more a prudent radical egoism through which the forces of life are paralyzed and at last destroyed.[2]

Thanks to industrialization, we are able to resurrect the past as never before. Industrialization repackages the past, falsifies it, glamorizes it, suggests that it a better place than the present. Why do we continue to perform the music of the past? Who listens to the music of the past? *In* the past, only what was *contemporary* was considered relevant. That the lifeblood of classical music has stopped pumping is only too evident in the fact that no modern opera has ever attracted the audience of a television soap opera. Classical music is now a ghetto, and the piano has become a shrine at which outcasts worship what has been lost. Custodians of the past certainly have energy, but the very act of attempting to conserve the past implies a sneaking sense of their own impotence and irrelevance.

Post-modernism is inevitably a kitsch state of affairs. Never before has the past been so accessible, never before has technology permitted us to manipulate and exploit the past as we can now. To be post-modern is to suffer a singularly terminal condition, where we can only suffocate in a cultural vacuum of kitsch. Surrounded by versions of the past and fantasies of the future, we increasingly find it difficult to define the present. The present is always taken for granted in pre-industrial societies. Even the lover of minimalism and the ultra-modern is responding to (by rejecting) the kitsch that surrounds him. He is also the victim of kitsch. Kitsch is the hidden meaning of capitalism, and it is appropriate that kitsch didn't really get going until the industrial nineteenth century. Kitsch is the monarch of a counterfeit kingdom, which, like capitalism itself, promises everything for a price but is morally bankrupt.

It is significant that Liberace was cast as a mortician in Tony Richardson's 1965 film adaptation of Evelyn Waugh's novella *The Loved One*. The grotesque resurrection of Liszt that was Liberace is not so far removed from Boris Karloff's Frankenstein Monster. Liberace was nothing if not a reanimated assemblage of long-dead cultural body parts: a curious figure wearing a pantomimic fantasy of period dress who anachronistically performed Chopin and boogie-woogie while flashing his teeth like a benevolent vampire.

In Stephen Soderbergh's 2019 Liberace biopic *Behind the Candelabra*, Liberace's Ludwigian taste in interior design—an example of conspicuous consumption if ever there was one—is carefully recreated. "Lee thinks he's King Ludwig II," says the friend who introduces Matt Damon's Scott Thorson to the great man. Scott asks, "Who's he?"

"The Liberace of Bavaria," the friend explains.

In fact, Ludwig himself, according to his piano teacher, was the most un-musical of men, despite being the impassioned champion of Richard Wagner. The teacher claimed that Ludwig couldn't tell a Strauss waltz from a Beethoven sonata,[3] and Wagner soon realized that his patron responded more to his ideas, poetry and stage spectacle than to the music, which washed over him without any real effect. Though it is doubtful that Liberace ever played any of Wagner's music, there is no denying that Liberace was extremely musical, and we of course see some very decorous pianos in *Beyond the Candelabra*, but *Behind the Candelabra* is in fact much less about pianos and Liberace's act and much more about the destructive effect of Liberace's corrosively possessive personality on lamb-to-the-slaughter Scott.

The hypnotic effect Liberace had on audiences is quickly established in an early scene in which Scott first encounters him at a live performance in the 1970s. The act was the same as it always was, including the boogie-woogie number with the ladies, and then the "fellas" shouting out "Hey" in the "boogie-woogie break." Liberace's ability to engage his audience was the secret of his success, far more so than his virtuosity (though that was important too). It was the power of his personality that made him a star, not the power of his musicality. With it, he was able to demolish the barriers erected by the musical establishment, opening up the classics to a much wider audience. By his so doing, the classics became increasingly kitschified. He made a fetish of the past, while simultaneously emphasizing its irrelevance to the present (which is one way of defining kitsch in general). Liszt, Chopin and the rest were juxtaposed with popular songs, film music and his own dance routines; and the elaborate pianos, dancing fountains and increasingly theatrical costumes paved the way for the similarly gay Elton John (*née* Reginald Dwight), who modified Liberace's approach, jettisoning the classical music and writing his own songs instead. There had been other popular piano players before him (Winifred Atwell, Mrs. Mills, Russ Conway), but none of them had the theatricality of Liberace or Elton John. Liberace demonstrated that musical performance is popularly perceived as an accompaniment to an image. After all, when fans reminisce about Abba, the first thing that is usually mentioned is what they used to wear. At one point, when Elton John is about to go on stage in an outrageously camp costume, his lyricist Bernie Taupin asks, "Don't you want just to go out there and sing without this ridiculous paraphernalia? Just be yourself, Reggie."

"Why the fuck would I want that, Bernie?" Elton hisses. "People don't pay to see Reginald Dwight. They pay to see Elton John!" Seeing is believing, perhaps more than hearing. Only Elton John kept Liberace's candle burning in the wind, and, as such, he is the last in the line of Liszt's illegitimate offspring.

Paderewski

Władziu Valentino Liberace began his professional life with serious aspirations towards becoming a concert pianist. The great Paderewski heard him and was sufficiently impressed to claim, "Someday this boy may take my place." The great man even placed his hand on the eight-year-old's head,[4] echoing the kiss Beethoven planted on the 11-year-old Liszt's cheek.

But Liberace, highly accomplished though he was, was not cut out for a life of sober interpretation.

> I wanted to give the world *entertainment* that would be new and different to them, to introduce people, who had never been to a piano recital or a symphony concert because they thought it would bore them, to the wonderful works they'd been denying themselves.[5]

Besides, Liberace was Milwaukee, from the Midwest, and by the time he had that momentous encounter, the European Romantic tradition, of which

Paderewski was the last great representative, would soon be finished off for good by the Second World War.

Paderewski had, in fact, paved the way for the kind of "redemptive" drama of Liberace's *Sincerely Yours* (dir. Gordon Douglas, 1955, see below), by starring in a film playing both the piano and himself. *Moonlight Sonata* (dir. Lothar Mendes, 1937) is something of an oddity. John Huntley has written at some length about it in his book on British film music:

> Visitors were not allowed on the set during the time Paderewski was playing. Only the artists or technicians saw him at work, and the few weeks he spent at Denham are still remembered by the old hands from the studios. No film star ever caused such interest. The soul of courtesy, he would solemnly raise his hat to electricians and carpenters on the floor when he arrived and departed. He never started work until three o'clock in the afternoon, but came to the studios by 2:15 to see the previous day's "rushes." During the shooting of a big concert hall sequence, a crowd of 400 extras were paid a guinea a day to sit and hear Paderewski play, a privilege for which thousands would have paid five, ten and fifteen guineas themselves just to hear his performance. Needless to say, a 75-year-old master musician was pretty fussy about the recording of his music. When it was discovered that the wooden floor gave too much resonance, boards were torn up and a concrete floor substituted....
>
> And then there was the piano stool. Paderewski was accompanied on all his tours by his own piano stool which stood on the platform of every concert hall in the world at one time or another; he played in practically every leading

Starring Paderewski: Ignacy Paderewski in *Moonlight Sonata*.

city in Europe, North and South America, Australia, New Zealand and South Africa during his life, make about 20 complete tours of the United States alone. The case in which the piano stool traveled was encrusted with over a thousand labels. The stool—which was actually a chair—was leather-seated, with a long fringe, and was adjustable. It was a very heavy affair, but without it Paderewski refused to play, so it spent a number of weeks in the studios while the film was being shot. ... He appears totally unconscious of acting a part, and except for being obviously bothered by the studio lights, he is delightfully natural, like a polished and somewhat eccentric gentleman from a Russian story.[6]

The recital with which *Moonlight Sonata* begins is set in a strikingly art-deco concert hall, its style somewhat reminiscent of the Anthroposophist, Rudolf Steiner's first Goetheanum building, which is appropriate as Paderewski is definitely shown to be presiding over a sacred rite. It is Music that is being worshipped here, and Paderewski is very much presented as its elderly high priest. We hear him render those essential components of the Romantic repertoire, Chopin's A-flat Polonaise and Liszt's Second Hungarian Rhapsody.

We are introduced to one particular couple in the audience, whose child (it is tempting to think of him as the infant Liberace himself) later approaches the great man in homage. The mother requests Beethoven's "Moonlight" Sonata, which Paderewski later admits is not a normal encore piece, but it has associations for both him and the young family, whom he already knows....

A flashback takes us to a plane making an emergency landing in Sweden. One of the passengers is Paderewski, who is soon put up in the home of a wealthy Swedish aristocrat. There he meets Ingrid Hansen (Barbara Greene) and Eric Molander (Charles Farrell), the couple we saw at the concert, except that at this stage they are not married. Eric is obviously in love with Ingrid, but Ingrid finds one of the other rescued passengers more interesting. This is Eric Portman's confidence trickster, Mario de la Costa. Mario is already married, but this doesn't stop him from attempting to seduce poor Ingrid. Eventually, the truth is revealed, Ingrid and Eric are united, and their union blessed by Paderewski's rendition of the "Moonlight."

As well as being an obvious vehicle for his performances (he, of course, plays his famous Minuet) Paderewski also functions as a mediator, resolving emotional discord by means of the healing powers of music. His presence ensures that there will be a happy ending, much as Liberace's in *Sincerely Yours* dissipates negativity and brings people together. One of Paderewski's admirers, Dr. William Mason of New York, referred to the pianist's "intensity of aspiration." He also remarked on "the indefinable poetic haze with which Paderewski invests and surrounds all that he plays which renders him so unique and impressive among modern pianists."[7] Liberace may have lacked the "poetic haze," but certainly understood the power of "aspiration" (even if somewhat more materialistically than Mason's implied metaphysical meaning). It was also a quality sought, if somewhat myopically, by his target audience. Liberace's entire act was always aspirational. His act satisfied his audience's desire for the "classiness" of the European cultural tradition, while at the same time celebrating the homespun popular culture with which it felt most comfortable.

This "classy" circus style showmanship was curiously foreshadowed in a Paderewski anecdote, included in Henry Lahee's *Famous Pianists*:

> In England a circus performer took the name of Paderewski and made a contract to give performances with a dancing bear at ten pounds per week. The proprietor of the circus apparently labored under a delusion as to identity, for he wrote to the pianist Paderewski and insisted on his fulfilling the contract, until eventually he was convinced of his mistake. The performer, having been discovered and questioned as to why he had assumed the name of Paderewski, declared that he had a right to assume any name that he chose, and he added, confidentially, "It isn't worth making a fuss about,—I shall be a good advertisement for M. Paderewski."[8]

Lahee also identified Paderewski as "a drawing card," who "attracted people who could not be attracted by any other player,"[9] which, of course, helped Paderewski to make a great deal of money, though not quite as much as Liberace. Even so, he managed to pull in $7382 for a single concert in Chicago and $21,000 for two concerts in St Louis.[10] (Significantly, perhaps, Paderewski's biggest successes were in the U.S.) Paderewski also road-showed himself in a manner that Liberace would imitate and exceed. Harold Schonberg lists Paderewski's entourage as including "his private railroad car, his chef and butler, his masseur and private physician, his tuner, his wife, and *her* aides." These were not tours but "royal processions. He made an impact on women that, in hysteria and abandon, rivaled the triumphs of Liszt. Women would line up to worship the hands insured for a hundred thousand dollars. (Today they would be insured for ten million."[11]). Liberace insured his hands for an even more fabulous sum, as well as investing in real estate, which was another hobby of his idol: Paderewski owned a portfolio of properties. Schonberg tellingly sums him up as "an unparalleled showman. And so while his competitors were counting his wrong notes, he was counting his dollars"[12] and, as Liberace would later describe it, "crying all the way to the bank."

The adulation Paderewski received from his fans outstripped mere musical appreciation. Like Liberace, he was a *personality*.

> Audiences would refuse to leave the hall, and often insisted on encores on the stage and insist on shaking hands with the pianist. In Texas whole schools

traveled many miles to see him. All over America, crowds waited at railroad crossings to see his private car pass, hoping to get a glimpse of the Paderewski profile. Often crowds would line the streets from hotel to concert hall.[13]

The fact that Liberace was gay, which Paderewski was not, did not prevent his unknowing female fans from recapitulating the antics of Paderewski's a generation earlier: They "mobbed the long-suffering pianist, pressing around him, shaking his hands, giving him flowers, pestering him for autographs, and begging him in tearful voices to come back again soon."[14] Equally significant is the fact that both Liberace and Paderewski both featured in popular songs of the day. Paderewski is referenced in Irving Berlin's 1920 hit "I Love a Piano" (later heard in *Easter Parade* [dir. Charles Walters, 1948]), while Liberace had an entire song devoted to him in Bobby Gimby and Johnny Wayne's 1954 comedy number "When Liberace Winks at Me." As a mark of just how much of a household name Paderewski was, his name features briefly in Levin and Douglas' *Mr. Soft Touch.* Having accidentally destroyed the upright in a men's hostel by falling on it, Glenn Ford's Joe Miracle visits a piano showroom to buy a replacement, unaware that the showroom, filled with dusty grands, is actually a front for the gambling joint at the back. While negotiating a deal with the "owner," two gamblers stride in and blow the man's cover: "Paderewski and Rachmaninoff, hmmm?" Joe inquires.

Liberace

Liberace's meeting with Paderewski took place in 1927, nine years after the end of the First World War. The cultural environment Liberace might then have been dreaming of was light years away; and anyway, he wanted to have much more fun than the traditional concert platform offered. He also wanted to make a lot more money, and realized that the best way to achieve all these things was to inflate what pop culture was already doing, by combining the popular with the Romantic, to take the trappings of Liszt and Chopin and mix them with the "Beer Barrel Polka" and "Chopsticks." Liszt, of course, had never been averse to playing "Chopsticks," and loved to decorate his operatic transcriptions with perfumed clouds of scales and arpeggios, just as Liberace would do with big film themes, such as Alfred Newman's *Exodus*. But the difference was that Liszt was a great artist, whereas Liberace was merely a great entertainer. Liberace composed no masterpieces, nor was he anyway near as brilliant a pianist. He first became famous on television, a medium ideally suited to his intimate approach to performance (that famous Liberace wink). His TV shows brought him into thousands of ordinary homes, which lacked pianos of their own, let alone someone able to play them. Liberace made "classical" music popular by presenting it in this non-threatening but still "classy" way. As his producer Don Fedderson explained:

> Contrary to what everyone believes, when you're on television you're not playing to tens of millions of people. Your audience is really small groups; families sitting around in their living rooms, or playrooms or people in beds in hospitals. Maybe it's not a group at all. Your audience may be just one lonely person. ... [W]hile you are entertaining them, you are their guest. It's a very personal kind of thing.[15]

Fedderson called the Liberace effect "lightning in a bottle," which it surely was. For many people, before Liberace came to the rescue, the concert grand was an intimidating icon of culture only to be found in that equally intimidating temple, the concert hall, with its elite priesthood of snobs and critics. Liberace swung open the temple doors with a gracious smile and brought the piano home with his mix of the classical repertoire and the "homey." Before the transmissions began, however, Fedderson wanted Liberace to know what kind of people would be watching him: He took him on a tour of the Los Angeles suburbs, pointing out to him that it was the poor and middle-class districts that had the most TV aerials. Liberace immediately understood: "The audience was not the sophisticated, intellectual element that had a kind of snobbish attitude about all popular entertainment anyway, and so had nothing but sneers for TV. It was the solid backbone people of America. The ones who did the work, kept things going and were ready to be friendly to anyone who was friendly to them."[16] The stage was set for his new show:

> His instrument now is a standard Baldwin, a lucrative contract with that manufacturer having displaced his otherwise beloved Blüthner. A small, electrically lit candelabrum casts obscure light on the left. At the keys, the pianist sits in formal evening wear. He appears lost in the music as he plays. An unseen orchestra accompanies him. As the lights come up, the camera dollies in for a close-up, and the angle changes. He appears through the open lid of the piano now, over the strings. He looks up as he concludes the piece, shifting his concentration from the music to the camera—to "the box" at home. He smiles, revealing his trademark dimples. He welcomes you to the show in that peculiar voice with odd halts and hesitations, as if he is almost forgetting his cues. Or as if he is not acting at all. He tells you what is coming, and that, of course, varied from show to show in the 177 episodes that Guild Films produced in the two years after 1953.
>
> ... He changed costumes many times to fit the music, donning, for example, a "wild number" for "The Beer Barrel Polka" or a military uniform for his dance accompaniment to "Boogie-Woogie Bugle Boy." Sometimes the costume changes illustrated the shifts from classical to popular music. When playing his version of Tchaikovsky's Second Piano Concerto, he wore the traditional white tie and black tails of the concert stage, but when the music segued into "Tonight We Love," the ballad based on Tchaikowsky's theme, he appeared all

in white evening wear—and then went back to black when he returned to the formal composition.¹⁷

Liberace was very intelligent but by no means intellectual. Musical vampire that he was, he fed off Hollywood's image of European culture, in particular George Cukor's Chopin biopic, *A Song to Remember* (1945). A spectacular misunderstanding of historical reality, this flamboyant confection starred Cornel Wilde as Chopin, who, curiously, looked rather more like Liberace than Chopin (though Stephen Bekassy's Liszt was much more like the original). When Wilde says to Merle Oberon's George Sand, "This melody is for you, George," it is hard not to make the anachronistic comparison with Liberace addressing his own brother George, as he did on his original TV shows. Crucially, the film gave Liberace the idea of using a candelabra as a signature stage prop, and in general terms *A Song to Remember* laid the groundwork for Liberace's opulent esthetic of "palatial kitsch." We see it all in an early scene at which Chopin performs for a Russian count, who is entertaining his guests over dinner. (This again reminds one of Liberace's own professional beginnings as a pianist as New York supper clubs.) It's all there: the elaborate piano, the candelabra, the swagging, the ormolu, the carpets, the opulent excess. Another scene has Liszt introduce the young, then unknown Chopin to his own audience. Attracting the crowd's

Corny and wild: Cornel Wilde in *A Song to Remember*.

attention by announcing that he, Liszt, will play, he then asks for the lights to be dimmed, thus allowing Chopin to perform instead. When the lights go back on, Chopin duly receives his rapturous applause. This incident is actually based on a historical anecdote related by Charles Rollinat, one of George Sand's friends, in which Liszt had apparently annoyed Chopin by embellishing his music unnecessarily. "It is only Chopin who has the right to alter Chopin," Chopin is claimed to have insisted.

"Ah, my friend, you were right!" Liszt conceded. "The works of genius like you are sacred; it is a profanation to meddle with them. You are a true poet, and I am only a mountebank."

Whereupon Chopin, much to Liszt's annoyance, replied, "We have each our genre."

Five days later, at another gathering, Liszt apparently had his revenge. He asked for all the lights put out and the curtains were drawn. He then announced that Chopin was to play, but as Chopin walked to the piano, Liszt whispered in his ear, and it was Liszt who again played Chopin's own music, this time much more obediently. When Liszt struck a match at the end of the performance, everyone was amazed. Even Chopin said, "I too believed it was Chopin."

"You see," Liszt smiled, "Liszt can be Chopin when he likes; but could Chopin be Liszt?"

Chopin's biographer Frederick Niecks calls this story "improbable," as Liszt was known to be a generous performer and also had no recollection of the incident.[18] *A Song to Remember* transforms the story into a demonstration of Liszt's much more likely kindness to his rival, as does the earlier scene in which Liszt plays Chopin's A-flat major Polonaise, during which he says he wants to shake Chopin's hand, but equally doesn't want to stop playing. Chopin therefore plays the right-hand part while Liszt carries on with the left-hand, thus leaving each of them a free hand to salute one another. It's just the kind of stunt Liberace would have appreciated.

Miklós Rózsa's *Song to Remember* score also demonstrates what Diaghilev's ballet *Les Sylphides* (which employed orchestrated versions of Chopin's piano pieces) had earlier revealed: that Chopin's melodies, when orchestrated, often lose their poetry and become the worst kind of Hollywood film music. (The same, admittedly, can be said the Liszt's "Un sospiro" Concert Étude in D-flat major, which became the saccharine "theme" of the Liszt biopic *Song Without End*, also directed in part by Charles Vidor in 1960.) This is not to say that Chopin's advanced harmonies do not transfer effectively to the orchestra, as Thomas Mann understood very well:

> [T]here are quite a few things in Chopin which, not only harmonically but also in a general, psychological sense more than anticipate Wagner, indeed surpass him. Take the C-sharp minor Nocturne Op. 27, No. 2, and the duet that

begins after the enharmonic change from C-sharp minor to D-flat major. That surpasses in despairing beauty of sound all the *Tristan* orgies—even in the intimate medium of the piano, though not as a grand battle of voluptuosity; without the bullfight character of a theatrical mysticism robust in its corruption.[19]

A Song to Remember also echoes Chopin's own preference for dimmed lighting when performing in salon environments. (His intimate approach made him unwilling to play in concert halls.) Liberace was in agreement with Chopin here. Not only did he court intimacy, even when playing to a large crowd, but, as his biographer Darden Asbury Pyron observes, "He was working on particular notions about candlelight, half-light, and other partial illumination as a source of mystery, excitement, and romance."[20]

Later in Liberace's stage career, spectacular "dancing waters," infused with changing colors, would accompany his cadenzas. Liberace was "informed" by the movies, so it was logical that he would eventually appear in them. His Hollywood career was sadly short-lived but nonetheless illuminating, particularly so in his most characteristic performance in *Sincerely Yours*, which is both highly insincere (Liberace, the closeted homosexual, plays a role in which two woman fall in love with him and he ends up marrying one of them), and quintessentially what Liberace was all about. He, of course, plays himself, lightly disguised as the concert pianist Anthony Warrin, who also likes to play pop. Alex Nicol, who plays the fictional composer Howard Ferguson, delivers a line that succinctly sums up Liberace's act and the aspirations of his middle-brow audience: "He respects the classics but from a sitting position, not on his knees."

Warrin-Liberace wants to have both a popular audience of ordinary folk *and* the Carnegie Hall crowd. To achieve this, he performs a tap dancing routine after playing Tchaikovsky's Piano Concerto No. 1 (just the big tune at the beginning and the coda at the end of the final movement, sandwiched together, as Ken Russell would later repeat in *The Music Lovers*). There's also a snatch of "Tea for Two" and a sing-along to "When Irish Eyes Are Smiling." Rachmaninoff never did that. *Sincerely Yours* demonstrates that Liberace's basic act was, at least by the time the film was made, fully worked out, and it remained virtually unchanged until his death: popular classics, "Chopsticks" (mixed with Liszt's Second Hungarian Rhapsody), "The Beer Barrel Polka," Gershwin, boogie-woogie with audience participation, and songs concocted by Liberace. (Here it is "Sincerely Yours," based on Chopin's A-flat major Étude. Later it would be something like "Ciao"—as in "Never say goodbye, say 'Ciao'"—not to mention his signature tune of Sammy Fain's "I'll Be Seeing You").

The flamboyant costumes and ultra-camp came later, but the musical elements were all in place by 1954, along with the song-and-dance routines,

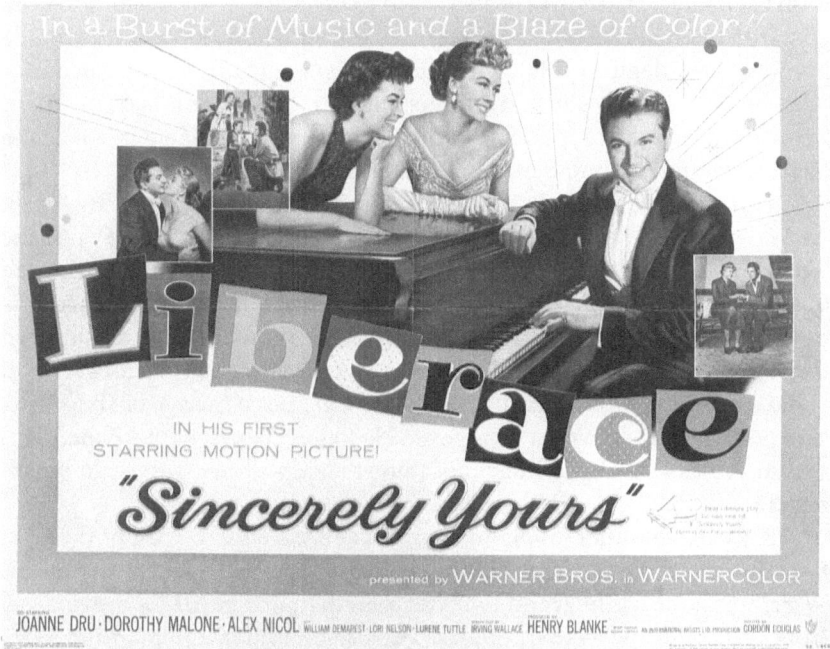

Abracandelabra: Poster for *Sincerely Yours*.

the maestro's habitual winks to his weak-kneed female fans, the good looks, which plastic surgery and age eventually mutated into a kitsch Phantom of the Opera, along with considerable, if sugar-coated charm, which very few women at the time realized were hallmarks of his homosexuality. One scene in particular exemplifies this. A group of middle-aged ladies swoon as Warrin enters a restaurant. "I almost feel I can reach out and touch you," he says. "Do you mind if I touch you?" He does so. "You wanna touch me? Go ahead. Come on." The lady strokes his leg. "A little higher, honey. About here is where I get the message." This is Lisztomania modernized—Liszt's routine of ravishment; and Liberace follows it up with his boogie-woogie, reassuring the ladies that it's quite respectable to enjoy what you like. This inspires them with confidence to tackle the classics in his company, after all, he's a concert pianist. He "knows" about Mozart, and can play him too, but he's also "one of us."

Sincerely Yours also anticipates the later Liberace Museum in a scene in which Warrin and his girlfriend Linda (Dorothy Malone) visit an exhibition of very grand grands with even grander provenances: Liszt's piano, Chopin's piano, Mozart's harpsichord. ("That's a funny-sounding piano!" Linda remarks, allowing Warrin to explain, for the audience's benefit, that it isn't actually a piano.) We're also asked to believe that the exhibition even contains the instrument on which Liberace's mentor, Paderewski, made his American debut in 1891. Liberace went on actually to own such pianos, some of which really had once belonged to Chopin and Liszt in "Paris, France" (as he liked to specify), all of which are now exhibited in what is in fact a converted shopping mall in Palm Springs, Florida.

This scene in *Sincerely Yours* turns the piano into a commodity fetish. As Warrin tries each of them out, he also begins to fall in love with the woman to whom he is playing. Desire and acquisition blend in a triumph of aspirational consumerism. This film realized that its main audience, like the woman Warrin entertains, knows very little about classical music, even though it might respect it and wish to acquire the status that goes with it. "Linda, did you know Mozart was a musical genius at the age of six?" Warrin asks. "He became a great composer. He was decorated by the Pope." And with that *Reader's Digest* nugget of knowledge, we are assumed to be left replete.

A variety of different pianos are paraded through the rest of the film. Usually, we are given the ubiquitous black grand, but at a charity event, Warrin plays a white grand, which immediately signifies a move away from the highbrow to the popular. The perspex lid of the piano in Warrin's swanky apartment goes even further, signifying that Warrin is not a fusty classical musician, out of touch with "the people." He never plays an upright, however, for they are reserved for the lower orders. Warrin is presented as a cool, well-dressed, compassionate and non-threatening kind of guy. He is obviously "a genius" but he can also have fun. The variety of pianos on display reconstitutes the European Romantic tradition into something quintessentially American, consumerist and, as always, aspirational. Warrin-Liberace plays then all, and thus he comes to represent what Liberace's biographer Pyron calls "an American Boy."

> Liberace seemed to me a kind of emblem of modern America, overflowing with both the virtues and vices of the contemporary national character. I began imagining him as the American Boy. ... It seemed that his homosexuality encouraged his campy artificiality; the campiness, in turn, encouraged the caricature, in life and art, of the American dream.[21]

The way in which *Sincerely Yours* focuses on the "big tune" of Tchaikovsky's piano concerto in the finale is also significant. Structurally, this famous introduction has very little to do with the rest of the concerto's first movement, but this is the element of the piece as a whole that lodged in the popular imagination, for the public has always preferred a big tune to a thematic cell, let alone its development. Liberace was *all* about introductions and finales. As he wrote in a *Jazz Monthly* article:

> My whole trick is to keep the tune well out in front. If I play Tchaikovsky, I play his melodies and skip his spiritual struggles. Naturally I condense. I have to know just how many notes my audience will stand for. If there's time left over, I fill in with a lot of runs up and down the keyboard.

(His *Jazz Monthly* article has been much quoted. It even appeared in the program for the original production of Peter Shaffer's play *Amadeus* in 1979, which is where I first became acquainted with it.)

Thus did Liberace deliberately tailor his act to the requirements of his audiences. They knew *of* Romantic culture and they knew that the grand piano signified the power and authority of such culture, while simultaneously not knowing much *about* it; nor were they particularly interested in so doing, but hoped some of the "classiness" would rub off on them. They respected Culture but they looked forward to joining in with "When Irish Eyes Are Smiling," which Liberace always promised as a reward for paying attention, like a musical sugar lump. In *Sincerely Yours*, an elderly lady assisting Warrin at a charity ball gets requests for two different pieces by Chopin. "Another Chopin?" she asks. "I never heard him on television. He must be on the same time as Ed Sullivan." But Warrin is no snob. He's happy to play "good old American folk music" instead of a Brahms Scherzo if that's what people want to hear, and the lady's ignorance about Chopin does not interfere with his affection for her. He has immense sympathy with ordinary people. Having gone deaf (echoes of Beethoven), Warrin spends his time in the park like a benevolent Peeping Tom, training his binoculars on people on whom he later takes pity. (The film is based on the earlier George Arliss vehicle *The Man Who Played God* [dir. John D. Adolfi, 1932], itself a remake of a 1922 silent adaptation of a short story written in 1912.) The aforementioned elderly lady is taken on a shopping trip and given a makeover. Through it all, the piano retains its power and authority, and this is its major appeal.

Warrin becomes something of a saint, much as Liberace himself had become. His audiences listen raptly, as if to a god. There is a strong feeling of religious enthusiasm here: Warrin is presented as the saint of music to whom audiences may look for guidance and enlightenment without fear of intimidation. (In the abovementioned "touching" scene, Warrin assumes the miracle-performing power of the Virgin Mary in effigy.) More than that: Warrin becomes a patron saint of democracy, bringing together classes and generations through the power of American show business. At one stage, he goes to church in search of God; he doesn't find him because in a sense, he has become God himself; and the instrument of his healing is the piano—that symbol of culture and authority, eroticism, miracle and redemption.

Liberace was not the only musical American Boy; his career and general approach were foreshadowed by a now somewhat lesser-known figure, who was also graced with his own biopic in *The Eddie Duchin Story*, directed by George Sidney one year after *Sincerely Yours*. In this, Tyrone Power plays the title role (though not the pianos, which were dubbed by Carmen Cavallaro). Duchin specialized in what used to be called "sweet" music, as opposed to jazz; it consisted of show tunes and light classics. Duchin's signature tune was a Chopin Waltz, which he played in various syncopated arrangements over the years, and his arpeggio decorations of such numbers very much resembles Liberace's style. Sidney's film contains the classic American Dream line "I know exactly what I wanted, and I got it," and it tells us how. Starting out as a pharmacy student, Duchin throws himself into New York night life, plays casinos and marries a society hostess. (Played by Kim Novak, she dies in childbirth, but not before uttering another classic line: "I fell in love with your hands before I fell in love with you.") While serving in the war, Duchin finds an abandoned honkytonk upright and tries out his old Chopin Waltz on it. This attracts the attention of a black boy, whom Duchin then teaches how to accompany him on "Chopsticks." The boy plays the alternating two notes in the bass, while Eddie elaborates. So too would Liberace.

By the time the real-life Duchin returned to civilian life, Liberace was already stretching his wings, ready to build on these significant foundations. All he had to add was the ever more elaborate and knowing kitsch. Seen from our own perspective, Duchin's performance of the Latin-American classic "Brazil" in the film might seen distinctly kitsch already, flanked as he is by maracas and bongo drums, with the piano's mirror-lid reflecting his fluttering fingers. But in the context of the time this was simply "class"—a kind of sophistication. Even when he segues into a boogie-woogie, very much as Liberace would later, we're not quite in Liberace-land, but the stage was very definitely set.

Four

Grand Galop Cinématique

Circus Stunts

Paderewski and Liberace summed up what the composer biopic was all about: passion and redemption. But Liberace included another element, which was always implicit in virtuosity, and this was comedy. Liszt was often sent up by cartoonists in his day; his posturing and highly melodramatic style of performance encouraged this. So too did his various ostentations, such as his penchant for appearing on stage with the ceremonial sword he was given by the grateful Hungarian nation, or his ceremonial peeling off of gloves. Liberace's emphasis on the democratization of culture by means of pluralism meant that it was possible both to worship at the shrine of music but also to "have fun."

As already mentioned, this approach was not alien to Liszt, though it annoyed the more serious and aristocratic Chopin. The biopic *Chopin: A Desire for Love* (dir. Jerzy Antczak, 2002) has Piotr Adamczyk's Chopin affectionately satirize Liszt's flamboyant, glissando-ridden style. "Ladies and gentlemen!" he announces to the glittering gathering, "I give you long-fingered Franz Liszt!" Michel Konarski's Liszt looks on, enjoying the joke immensely, as Chopin flicks his coattails over his face, bends over the keyboard and launches into the big tune of the ubiquitous Second Hungarian Rhapsody.

One of Liszt's greatest keyboard stunts was a kind of duel with himself in which the right hand has to keep up with the relentless pace of the left. The *Grand galop chromatique* is exactly what the title says it is. It is certainly grand, spanning virtually the entire range of the piano keyboard. A true gallop is also very fast—one of the fastest pieces in the piano repertoire. It is also chromatic, being little more, in material terms, than a harmonized chromatic scale. An alternating section, including fiendishly wide leaps for the right hand, brings in some contrast, but Liszt is not interested in anything more than the sensation he could create by technique alone. A vamping base sets up the rhythm and the chromatic scales never failed to bring the house down as the piece hurtles towards the final chord. The *Grand galop* is the musical equivalent of a circus bareback rider. Indeed, Liszt described his early career as "my traveling circus life" and this piece was his most popular stunt.

One of the first cartoons to exploit the implicit comedy of Liszt's virtuosic stunts, and in particular, the Second Hungarian Rhapsody, was the early Mickey Mouse cartoon *The Opry House* (dir. Ub Iwerks and Walt Disney, 1929). In a noisy, animal-filled vaudeville theater, an asbestos safety curtain rises over the stage to reveal Mickey walking towards a piano stool. He flicks up his tail, suggesting the soon to be much-parodied coattail of Bugs Bunny and Tom the cat, and pulls the grand piano towards him. He then runs his hands through his long, Lisztian locks (another important cliché), raises his hands like the Sorcerer's Apprentice he would later become in *Fantasia*, and launches into Rachmaninoff's famous Prelude. With each of the thundering chords, the keyboard bends like a sagging bookshelf, until a rapid arpeggio to the top of the piano causes Mickey to lose his balance and fall flat on his face. He resumes his seat, without lifting his tail again, but this time with a sheepish grin, and now the piano helps out by playing the high notes itself. (Such leaps provided much comedy in later cartoons.) Mickey whistles up a curious black blob, which then hits the final high note.

He launches into a new piece, and now the piano starts playing itself more competitively, thus introducing the next important element in piano comedy: the duel. Mickey tries to stop it, but the piano keeps playing, just as Sparky's magic piano would do later. So Mickey decides to tie the keys together into a knot before launching into the finale of the Hungarian Rhapsody. The piano and the stool start acting like donkeys, and kick Mickey off stage. They have a good laugh about this and while the stool dances a jig, the piano, standing on its hind legs, uses its front legs to play the keyboard. Mickey returns to continue his Rhapsody, but this soon degenerates into "Chopsticks" before a return of the Rachmaninoff Prelude and the final curtain.

We see here most of the significant elements in Bugs Bunny and Tom and Jerry's piano cartoons. Both poked fun at the idea of coattail-flicking and theatrical posing at the keyboard, before going on to expose the comedic appeal of the Liszt Rhapsody, which Liberace incorporated into his own version of "Chopsticks." ("I always loved the classics," he would say by way of introduction to this number. "And here is perhaps the foremost piano classic of all time." Laughter always greeted the "Chopsticks" theme after such a grand build-up, and the piece, under Liberace's fingers, is indeed a delight, especially when it metamorphoses into the Rhapsody, to which it actually has much musically in common.)

Franz before Tom: "Fantaisie Brilliante sur Liszt" from *La Vie Parisienne*, April 3, 1886.

Tom and Jerry's Oscar-winning *The Cat Concerto* (dir. William Hanna and Joseph Barbera, 1947), along with Bugs Bunny's *Rhapsody Rabbit* (dir. Fritz Freleng, 1946) and *Wideo Wabbit* (dir. Robert McKimson, 1956), provide a compendium of virtuoso effects. In the first of these, Tom the cat strides onto the stage of the Hollywood Bowl with his nose in the air,

Maestroso pomposo—Tom plays Liszt in *The Cat Concerto*.

takes his seat on the piano stool and wipes his paws with a handkerchief. During the orchestral passage that follows his introductory intonation, his starched shirtfront keels over towards the keyboard. Breaking through his serious demeanor, Tom then gives his audience a Liberacean wink of self-satisfaction as he replaces his shirtfront before the piece continues.

This awakens Jerry, who slumbers in the lower regions of the piano strings. The rapid passage works so characteristic of Liszt's virtuoso style is choreographed with shots of Jerry running back and forth under the keys. This image of the disintegration of the keyboard due to the rapidity of execution had been satirized in Liszt's own time in a cartoon that shows much the same thing happening. Rapidity was always part of a virtuoso's armory. In an age of industrialization, of steam trains and increasingly accelerated urban living, notes per second did rather equate to miles per hour. *The Cat Concerto* is merely making obvious what was always a major part of Liszt's appeal: sheer, breathtaking *skill* in velocity. There is a major set of studies by Liszt's teacher, Carl Czerny, called *The School of Velocity,* the title of which speaks volumes. Speed and seeming impossibility were the watchwords of Liszt's virtuosity. Liszt once referred to himself as a kind of jockey: "My piano is to me what his vessel is to a sailor, his horse to the Arab."[1] He was a kind of a piano centaur, and his biographer Anthony Wilkinson referred to the music he wrote to display his virtuosity as "Oats for His Horse."[2] His aim was to do for the piano what Paganini had done for the violin—to create a transcendental technique, which would achieve what had hitherto been deemed impossible. This super-human, Faustian ambition was Romanticism through and through, as Thomas Mann pointed out in his essay on Wagner: It quotes a letter from Liszt to that composer, who was at the time embarking on the composition of his monumental *Ring* cycle:

> Go to work and apply yourself with the utter singleness of mind to your task. If you need a brief, let it be the one that the cathedral chapter of Seville gave to the architect commissioned to build their new cathedral: "Build us a temple such that future generations will say the canons were mad ever to undertake such an extraordinary work." Yet there the cathedral stands!

"Now *that* is the nineteenth century!"[3] Mann adds. There is a great deal of conjuring in such an esthetic, which resembles the art of a stage illusionist. To demonstrate that the impossible *was* possible, Liszt had to work out an entirely new way of playing the piano. Whereas some of Beethoven's music (and Chopin's) is difficult because it doesn't necessarily fit under the hands, Liszt wanted to make the music sound as difficult as possible, but also make it as playable as possible. Louis Kenter, who played the Warsaw Concerto for *Dangerous Moonlight*, observed,

> Liszt's music is easier to perform than Chopin's because the latter, though he wisely limited himself almost entirely to the piano, nevertheless retained a certain abstract and idiosyncratic quality, a proud insistence that the music comes first and that the difficulties simply had to be overcome (a demand Chopin himself was not always able to fulfill), whereas Liszt obviously never wrote anything down that he at least could not play immediately.[4]

That is not to say that he avoided difficulties. On the contrary, he deliberately reworked the problems Paganini posed for the violin into the piano's own terms; and in the most virtuosic music he wrote, the pianistic problems sometimes mattered more than the music (though by no means is all of Liszt's music dictated by such concerns).

Such showmanship, such emphasis on technique, is not so far removed from circus acrobatics, and the clowns who entertain the audience in between such gymnastic "turns." It should not, therefore, be surprising that much fun has been made of Liszt's "transcendentalism." Experiencing virtuosic fireworks makes us smile with delight at the sheer audacity and skill of the performer. There is also a kind of violence at work. Piano hammers hit the strings, and the hammers are activated by the player forcefully striking the keys. The gladiatorial contests of ancient Rome are also not so far away here. The appeal is hard-wired in us, it is a sexual game—thrilling, funny, absurd, compelling.

The infamous violence of Tom and Jerry cartoons in general also makes itself felt in *The Cat Concerto*. At one stage, Jerry slams the piano lid onto Tom's fingers, which is reminiscent of something that actually happened to Liszt's piano-playing contemporary Louis Gottschalk, who had a carriage door slammed on his fingers by a jealous rival during a tour of

Spain. The same thing happens to a young man called Sebastian Valmont (Ryan Phillippe) in the teen drama *Cruel Intentions* (dir. Roger Kumble, 1999). Sebastian is introduced to his unpleasant stepsister Kathryn (Sarah Michelle Gellar), who plays Beethoven's "Moonlight" Sonata on her Steinway grand. Sebastian asks if he can play this impressive instrument, and gets a patronizing smile from Kathryn when he plays "Chopsticks." But when he launches into "The Flight of the Bumblebee," Kathryn cannot contain her jealousy and subjects her rival to Gottschalk's fate. Gottschalk apparently took 91 days to recover from this appalling injury,[5] but Tom the cat takes considerably less time to spring back into action. His next feat is to execute the rapid leaps for which this piece (and Liszt's output in general) is famous. Jerry is, however, ready with a pair of scissors to chop off the agile claw, but Tom manages to avoid them. Jerry then places a mousetrap on the keys, and this time does manage to inflict injury. The ensuing acciaccaturas, those cheeky squashed-in notes Liszt so often used for either comedic or ironic effect, are then visualized by Tom pouncing on the keys in his pursuit of his antagonist. When he starts playing the music with his feet, we enter the well-worn territory of the piano "stunt" to which so many child prodigies were subjected, and which Chico Marx made something of a specialty.

Disney's 1929 short *When the Cat's Away* features an early example of this technique. A different Tom the Cat opens the film. He's off for a day out, leaving the mice to invade the house and have a party. Two mice leap onto the piano keyboard and play "Ach, du Lieber Augustin" with their feet, while the other mice play other instruments. Then the two piano mice form another foot duet called "Listen to the Mockingbird," which also involves a cuckoo clock and a saxophone. But the mice realize the piano is also a player piano. They insert a piano roll and watch the instrument play itself, while a scrawny parrot sings along. Tom Hanks paid perhaps unconscious tribute to all these animated musical feet in *Big* (dir. Penny Marshall, 1988), in which his character, Josh, plays "Chopsticks" with Robert Loggia's Mr. MacMillan on a giant foot-operated electronic keyboard, laid out on the floor of a toy shop.

How often must pianists have wished for an extending finger like Tom's telescopic claw, which allows him to reach right up to the top of the keyboard without moving his paw! The most celebrated example of this effect can be found in Liszt's *La Campanella* (one of his Paganini transcriptions). Alan Walker, explains that the main difficulty of the notorious rapid leaps in this piece

> is not so much the distances to be traversed (at most two octaves) as the fact that the player must endure the ordeal of leaping back and forth across the void at speed for extended periods. In order to play such a passage with security, the player must feel that the piano is an extension of his own body. You do

not need your eyes to tell you that your limbs are attached to your torso. Likewise, this passage can be played blindfold by the pianist who has 'internalized' the topography of his instrument. Again, the caricaturists of the time drew truer than they knew when, inspired by Greek mythology, they depicted Liszt as a piano-centaur—half man, half piano—a unique amalgam in which the instrument and the player had become indissolubly merged."[6]

Immediately after Tom has demonstrated his extending claw, he starts to play in a more syncopated, jazzy style, again echoing what Chico Marx had been doing and what Liberace would carry on doing on TV. As the piece works towards its frantic conclusion, the piano hammers imitate golf sticks, driving Jerry up and down the strings. When they play glissandi, the hammers hurl him about on a musical tidal wave, and the piano reveals its potential as a demonic *machine*. (Ken Russell would take this aspect of the instrument even further when he turned it into a flame-throwing weapon in 1975's *Lisztomania*.) In a gesture of revenge, Jerry breaks off two of the piano's hammers and embarks on another of Romanticism's predilections: a piano duel. Liszt and Thalberg had engaged in a similar contest in Paris in 1837. The finale of these various fixtures had taken place in the salon of Princess Belgiojoso, who diplomatically resolved the contest with the words, "Thalberg is the greatest pianist in the world, but Liszt is unique."[7] There is no such diplomacy in the cartoon, however. As the Rhapsody enters its coda, Tom and Jerry's piano duel exploits velocity once more. So great is the strain on Tom that his clothing falls apart and he collapses onto the keyboard, in perfect synchronization with the Rhapsody's final notes.

Duels

Many other films exploit the comedy potential of piano duels. *Rhapsody Rabbit* (1946), which predates *The Cat Concerto*, has similar jokes but here, Bugs' adversary is, yet again, Elmer Fudd. Bugs begins with another homage to Liszt by peeling off different colored gloves, one on top of the other right down to a boxing glove on his left paw. These he lets fall to the ground, just as Liszt so often dropped the gauntlet at the beginning of his own recitals. Similarly, Bugs is performing a circus act here. Like Tom, he flicks up his coattails. Another wink in Liszt's direction occurs when he shoots a man in the audience who has an irritating cough. This makes one think of Liszt's famous retort to the Tsar or Russia, who interrupted Liszt's performance by entering late, talking to an official. Liszt immediately stopped playing. When asked why he had done so, he replied, "Music herself should be silent when the Tsar of Russia speaks." It is a tribute to the rapidly advanced status of musicians that he was not punished for such insolence. (This scene was enacted by Dirk Bogarde when he played Liszt in *Song Without End* [dir. George Cukor and Charles Vidor, 1960].)

During his opening bars, Bugs pushes back his ears (another reference to Liszt's long hair) and, after nibbling a handy carrot, launches into the main theme with another proto–Liberace wink at the audience, this time over his shoulder. Rapidly repeated notes result in tangled fingers, which even get trapped in the keys and have to be pulled apart with his feet. A phone rings, and Bugs asks who it is. "Franz Liszt?" he replies. "Never heard of him. Wrong number." His sparring partner is, like Tom's, a mouse. We have the same mousetrap joke, along with intrusion of jazz—this time a boogie-woogie initiated by the mouse. As we have seen, boogie-woogie became a well-established element in Liberace's act, and one wonders if this cartoon had influenced him. Bugs also taps his feet while playing, again foreshadowing Liberace, who did the same thing when things got particularly rhythmic. "Chopsticks" is part of the mix, when Bugs traps the mouse under the lid of the piano keyboard, before inserting a stick of dynamite.

As the "Friska" section of Liszt's (inevitable) Hungarian Rhapsody No. 2 gets underway, Bugs proudly boasts, "Look, one hand!" and then, "No hands!" as we see him playing with his toes. One of the most innovative visual jokes here is when the keyboard imitates a typewriter in perfect

Franz Liszt? Sorry, wrong number! Bugs Bunny in *Rhapsody Rabbit*.

synchronization with a staccato passage, which does indeed suggest this kind of action. Whereas Tom has a telescopic claw, Bugs uses his ears to execute wide leaps. The second great invention is having Bugs gather up groups of keys in his hand in a descending phrase, and then throw them back into place to match a rapid scale. Horrified by the complexity of the music that now confronts him, he embarks on the coda, strips off his evening dress, oils his hands and offers up a quick prayer, just as the mouse takes over and plays the final furious bars himself on a miniature, mouse-sized piano. The last three notes are then finally flung out by the dejected virtuoso.

An equivalent of this kind of thing actually took place in Moscow during the Second World War three years before *Rhapsody Rabbit* was produced. In 1943, Gregory Haimovsky, the pianist best known for having given the Moscow premiere of Messiaen's *Turangalîla Symphony* in 1971, found himself booked to play the same Hungarian Rhapsody of Liszt in a military hospital in the city. Unfortunately, the piano with which he was provided was a decrepit upright, which was missing many of its keys in the lower octaves. His biographer, Marissa Silverman, takes up the story:

> Haimovsky began to think about how he could play Liszt's Second Rhapsody. This required all the missing keys. The beginning is a slow recitative followed by a *Tempo guisto vivace* with large leaps in the left hand. While playing it, Haimovsky threw his left hand violently into the lowest and last octave in order to avoid the missing keys. Because of the intensity of the music, and his vigorous efforts, he could have accidentally severed his fingers on the metal bars under the missing keys. To avoid this injury, he lurched to the left so often and so much that he almost slipped of the chair. After finishing, he wiped sweat from his brow. Loud applause filled the hall.[8]

Rhapsody Rabbit was later referenced in *Who Killed Roger Rabbit* (dir. Robert Zemeckis, 1988) in which Daffy and Donald Duck compete with each other, Daffy on a white upright, Donald at a black grand. They play, very competitively, the Hungarian Rhapsody (association over the years has made it more cartoon music than concert piece), and Donald brings the competition to an end by firing a cannon at Daffy's piano, blasting a hole in the lid. All this is much to consternation of Bob Hoskins' Eddie Valliant, whose has never forgotten how his brother was crushed to death by a "toon" piano.

Bugs paid another tribute to Liszt in 1956, by which time Liberace had become a well-established television icon. In *Wideo Wabbit,* as had briefly been the case in *Rhapsody Rabbit,* Bugs' teeth become piano keys, in what is surely a comment on Liberace's pearly white smile. On a grand piano decked with candelabra, Bugs performs the ubiquitous Hungarian Rhapsody, his fingers again getting tangled up in their own virtuosity. He imitates Liberace's winsome manner of speech, referring to "George"

(Liberace's collaborative brother) and "Mother" (Liberace often appeared with his adored matriarch). However, one of the candelabra is armed with sticks of dynamite instead of candles and these usefully blow up Bugs' eternal adversary, Elmer Fudd.

Musical duels continued in *Amadeus* (dir. Miloš Forman, 1984), in which Tom Hulce's Mozart humiliates F. Murray Abraham's Salieri by improving the little march of welcome the latter has composed in his honor. "That doesn't really work, does it?" Mozart observes of one of Salieri's phrases. All Salieri can do is cringe in silence as Mozart, with guffaws and a habitual lack of social polish, demonstrates not only his own blazing compositional talent but also his virtuosic skill at the keyboard. In *The Legend of 1900* (dir. Guiseppe Tornatore, 1998), a pianist, known as Danny Boodman T.D. Lemon 1900 (Tim Roth) duels with jazz legend Jelly Roll Morton (Clarence Williams). So rapidly does 1900 play that Tornatore shows us four hands flickering over the keyboard, rather in the manner of the German cartoonist Wilhelm Busch, whose series of vignettes "Der Virtuos— Ein Neujahrskonzert," which first appeared in 1865, shows a pianist with four arms wrestling with a tortuous "Fuga del diavolo." After 1900's manic display of speed, the strings of the piano have become so hot that he is able to light a cigarette with them. The piano on which all this takes place is a grand, but not a black concert grand. Natural wood seems more suitable for the milieu of a duel that takes place aboard a ship, the music of which is not classical but jazz. The semiotics of a piano's appearance here is just as important as what is played on it.

Similarly, brown wood uprights feature in the piano duel featured in *Scott Joplin—The Movie* (dir. Jeremy Kagen, 1977), made in the wake of Joplin's renaissance, thanks to the use of his piece, "The Entertainer," in *The Sting* (dir. George Roy Hill, 1973). Jay Chou's 2007 *Secret* transfers the idea to a Taiwanese music school where two prodigies compete. Chopin's "Black Key" Étude is transposed onto the white keys, the steely precision of the improvisations on a Chopin Waltz are matched like for like, and the camera hurtles through the pianos' mechanisms as if in pursuit of the torrent of notes, while the girls look on in admiration.

Flirtation

Girls often look on in admiration during such virtuoso displays, for virtuosity has always been a kind of mating game, like a musical peacock's tail. In many of the films Chico Marx made with his brothers, there is usually a scene in which he plays the piano, surrounded by admiring women. In *Horse Feathers* (dir. Norman Z. McLeod, 1932), a young woman sits

Four. Grand Galop Cinématique 91

A New Year's Day concert: "Fuga del diavolo" by Wilhelm Busch.

A New Year's Day concert: "Finale furioso" by Wilhelm Busch.

decorously beside him on the piano stool. In McLeod's *Monkey Business* (1931), Chico is joined by an orchestra, with which he competes during a performance of Delibes' "Pizzicato Polka." That piece contains a famous accelerando, after the execution of which, Chico exclaims to the off-screen conductor: "Ha! I beat you that time!" Sometimes he performs duets with his normally harp-playing sibling Harpo and, again, we observe the origin of what would eventually become Liberace stunts, such as, in *A Night in Casablanca* (dir. Archie Mayo, 1946), Chico's combination of Liszt's Second Hungarian Rhapsody with "The Beer Barrel Polka" (always a popular coupling with Liberace). Chico also indulges in visual humor, such as the use of a wandering, sometimes wagging finger, which parades over the keyboard like a character in its own right. In the *Night in Casablanca* act, Chico and the fez-wearing band behind him also bounce on their seats in time with the music. Most inventive of all is the physical comedy in *Go West* (dir. Edward Buzzell, 1940), in which Harpo is about to eat an apple, but before he can bite it, Chico snatches it from him and uses it to produce glissandi by rubbing it against the keys. There were always glissandi in Chico's piano routines, but not always with an apple.

Another rather endearing duet between Harpo and Chico in *The Big Store* (dir. Charles Reisner, 1941) has them leaning together in correspondence to the "leaning" harmonies they play at cadence points, coming together as affectionate brothers in the midst of their mock piano dueling. Sometimes Harpo looks on at Chico's pyrotechnics the same way that the admiring friend of the virtuoso in Wilhelm Busch's "Der Virtuos" ogles his talented friend, finally with his eyes busting from their sockets in astonishment.

Lisztomania

By the time Ken Russell made *Lisztomania* in 1975, it would have been hard to avoid Liberace's influence, even if Russell had wanted to. He fully embraced the kitsch element that had always been part of Liszt's esthetic, and elaborated it by presenting Liszt's superstar lifestyle from the perspective of '70s glam-rock. The film was conceived as a kind of sequel to Russell's previous film *Tommy,* which starred Roger Daltrey of The Who in the title role, and Elton John as the Pinball Wizard. Elton does not appear in *Lisztomania,* but he is nonetheless Liberace's (and therefore Liszt's) ultimate descendent, renowned for equally outrageous costumes, a camp, gay persona and, of course, dexterity at the keyboard. Elton is probably the last of the popular piano players who thrived in the wake of Liberace's success: names such as Russ Conway, Winifred Atwell and, earlier, the pre–Liberace

Four. Grand Galop Cinématique

Franz the who? Roger Daltrey as Liszt in *Lisztomania*.

maestro of the piano medley, Charlie Kunz. Of all these, only Liberace sang. ("I don't sing well," he told his rapt audiences, "but I sing sexy," an epithet that could be applied to Elton John as well.) In the biopic of John's autobiography, *Rocketman*, Taron Egerton's Elton performs on a variety of Liberace-esque grand pianos—one sprayed silver, another white, several traditionally black. It is a kind of swan song to the memory of this once ubiquitous instrument.

The pop parallels of *Lisztomania* were clear to Russell from the start: "Liszt was the first pop star of them all—idolized by the fans."[9] But it was really the producer David Puttnam who steered the film in the direction it eventually took. "What really intrigued me," Russell confessed in his autobiography, "was [Liszt's] strange relationship with Richard Wagner. However, that had little appeal to Puttnam, who was more at home at a pop concert than in the concert hall."

> He threw out my first script for being too straight and urged me to write another emphasizing the pop element. We had many discussions on the subject, sometimes at his place, sometimes at mine—frequently over dinner. I

soon counted him as a friend and although we had little in common but our enthusiasm for movies and music, that alone was enough to prevent the conversation flagging. I'd enthuse about Scriabin and Sibelius, he'd rave on about Keith Emerson and Rick Wakeman. I don't know who was the more receptive; I just know that the script became less and less classical—and more and more pop-orientated until it was to Puttnam's satisfaction.[10]

Daltrey, who approximated Liszt's bone structure, also had the ability actually to play Liszt's music on the piano, so he got the job. Russell's wife Shirley Kingston adorned him with a dressing gown with piano-key decoration on its flamboyant collar. This complemented the Liberacean piano-key motifs decorating Liszt's accommodation. One of Philip Harrison's spectacular sets places a gold piano on a stepped dais, itself decorated with piano keys. The inside of the piano lid is mirrored, while piano-key motifs in quilted silk adorn six alcoves behind it. Even the fireplace has a piano-key frieze over the hearth. All this is deliberately resonant of Liberace's famous piano-shaped swimming pool in Palm Springs, along with his penchant for piano-key decoration in general.

Reversing history, Russell filters Liszt's character through the influence of both glam rock, cartoons and Liberace. In the opening concert, "Chopsticks" continually interrupts Liszt's transcription of Wagner's *Rienzi Overture*. The bonneted girls in the audience join in with a "la-la" song, just as Liberace's elderly female adorers enjoyed humming along to "I Will Always Love You." Like Bugs Bunny, Daltrey's maestro pulls off a pair of green gloves, the index finger of which is phallically long. "I hope you like it!" he smiles, as he wiggles it suggestively. Later, Daltrey performs a Cossack dance on the lid of his mirrored grand against a silver fringe curtain, which is not only a reference to Liszt's promotion of Hungarian culture but also to the tap-dancing routines Liberace often inserted after his flamboyant medleys. Liszt later turns up wearing his Hungarian costume complete with ceremonial sword. Russell's satirical conflation of periods and styles simultaneously provides us with Liszt's biography and his reception history.

During a flashback scene depicting Liszt's romance with Countess Marie d'Agoult (Fiona Lewis), Russell chose the silent film style of Charlie Chaplin, whom Daltrey impersonates while sitting at a humble upright, singing a rock version of "Liebestraum No. 3." He later plays "Funerailles" on an up-to-date white grand, before the finale of the film has him exorcising Paul Daniels' vampiric Richard Wagner by performing his own "*Totentanz*" on the aforementioned revolving and then flame-throwing grand with its perspex lid (another homage to Liberace's klavier collection). The transformation of Wagner into a vampire is a truly inspired visual joke, Wagner having fed on Liszt's musical invention on many occasions. The film ends with an update of *The Phantom of the Opera*, Liszt having

Four. Grand Galop Cinématique

assembled all the women in his life to stand in the pipes of his celestial organ, which swoops down on earth to destroy the Nazified Wagner, now a kind of Frankenstein Monster toting a machine-gun guitar. "Love has won," the lyrics of the song insist, and for the Catholic Ken, so too had the Abbé Liszt. All the facts of Liszt's biography are left intact behind the glam-rock surface. Even the line, "Oh, piss off, Brahms," spat out early on by the Hungarian maestro, is historically justified, as Brahms was the only composer Liszt failed to champion, due largely to the fact that Brahms signed a letter attacking the "New German School" of composing, of which Liszt and Wagner were the leading lights.

One of the things Liszt most definitely did not have in common with Liberace was a homosexual orientation. All the camp exaggeration here has nothing gay about it, which is important to point out, I think, as it demonstrates quite clearly that a camp esthetic is by no means the sole property of homosexuals. However, when Dirk Bogarde played the role in *Song Without End,* not only was its director George Cukor gay, but so too was Bogarde, whose performance as Liszt has all the highly strung, somewhat tetchy mannerisms he brought to his other roles. He also looks rather more like Cliff Richard than the wizard from Hungary (but it is hard to say if

Dirk Bogarde as Liszt (with Genevieve Page) in *Song Without End.*

this is significant, as no one is quite sure if Cliff Richard is gay or not). In Russell's film, Sarah Kestelman plays Princess Carolyne Wittgenstein (the second of Liszt's great loves) with robust *joi de vivre*, whereas Bogarde's Liszt falls in love with the much more refined and immobile Carolyn of Capucine. (Bogarde later attempted to replicate this relationship in real life, professing to have "fallen in love" with the model-cum-actress in an entirely unrealistic attempt to hide his far more meaningful relationship with Anthony Forward.) While Cukor took a much more overtly serious approach to the subject than Russell, the result was unintentionally satirical, and failed to penetrate the reality of Liszt's "traveling circus life." Russell's version is undoubtedly much more revealing and actually closer to the truth.

Unlike Daltrey, Bogarde could not play the piano, and consequently suffered many painful hours of coaching by Victor Aller, who helpfully explained, "You got 85 minutes of fucking music in this production. Eighty-five minutes of music not including conducting Les Préludes and the Rákóczy March." Aller had coached Cornel Wilde to be Chopin in *A Song to Remember*, but as Aller pointed out, "Cornel Wilde could play tennis" and therefore had some sort of coordination; Bogarde did not: "He can't even play 'Happy Families.'"[11] Bogarde was dismayed by the studio's insistence that he learn to play the instrument, but in the end, almost as if by a miracle, he managed to create a reasonably convincing mime of Liszt's complex fingering, faking

> the major chunk of [Concerto] No. 1 in E flat with the entire orchestra in the Cuvillies Theatre, Munich, accurately enough and with some degree of Lisztian panache; it brought the house to its feet voluntarily, and the orchestra applauded, beaming brightly. Aller turned his back and burst into tears. I had no retreat without valour; and although I frequently choked to death on the dialogue, I almost began to enjoy my steady walk to the piano in every palace, church, concert hall and drawing room from Bayreuth to the Hungarian border.[12]

It was this walk to the instrument that mattered most, for Bogarde had been hired to humanize high art for his fan base. Bogarde could walk the walk even if he couldn't play the piano, and that was really what people had come to see. Such fans had much in common with those of Liberace's (another gay artist adored by so many unsuspecting female fans who no doubt had rather less inspiring husbands waiting for them at home).

"You look cute," said Charles Vidor, the production's original director. Bogarde confessed to feeling ridiculous.

> You look great, kid! I like the hair. You look just like him ... like the pictures we got up in the office ... you seen them? You look just like him. Claude-Pierre

said so too and he should know. Claude-Pierre is French from France and he's done all your costooms and he KNOWS.[13]

Twelve years earlier, Bogarde had managed perfectly well to give the impression of being able to play the piano in "The Alien Corn," one of the four stories of *Quartet* (dir. Harold French et al., 1948), where his vulnerability and highly strung persona was perhaps more appropriate for Somerset Maugham's tale of an aspiring pianist from an aristocratic family, who studies hard but fails to make the grade and consequently shoots himself, in a film to which we will be returning later.

Liszt has been played by other actors over the years. Two years before Paderewski turned film star, the Chilean concert pianist Claudio Arrau, who specialized in Liszt interpretations, actually acted out the role in the 1935 Mexican production *Dream of Love* (dir. José Bohr), the title of which refers to Liszt's most famous composition, the *Liebestraum No. 3*. The same year, Heinz Hille directed an Hungarian film with the same title (at least when translated from the original Hungarian of *Szerelmi álmok*), with Ferenc Táray as the long-haired prestidigitator. *Szerelmi álmok* is also the title of a Soviet-Hungarian production directed by Márton Keleti in 1970, in which Imre Sinkovits' Liszt sits at a great many impressive grands, wearing an equally impressive variety of outfits. The St. Petersburg locations also enhance the proceedings, especially when Liszt stops playing (interestingly on a white grand with gilded scrollwork) when the Tsar of Russia starts talking.

In 1944, toward the end of World War II, the Third Reich brought the world *Träumerei,* directed by Harald Braun. In this story of Robert and Clara Schumann, Emil Lohkamp provided a very good visual approximation of Liszt, while Mathias Wiemann's Schumann seemed to sum up what had happened to Germany by this time, being a Romantic who went mad. Meanwhile, in Hollywood, Henry Daniell bought hauteur to his Liszt impersonation in *Song of Love,* in which Robert and Clara are played by Paul Henreid and Katharine Hepburn. Together, they observe Liszt playing his virtuosic warhorse *Mephisto Waltz No. 1,* during which one of the men in the audience asks of his companion: "When does he pull out the rabbit? He always pulls out some kind of rabbit." Bugs Bunny is nowhere to be seen, but suddenly a string breaks instead. Liszt stops, shrugs his shoulders and strides over to another instrument, resuming where he left off and concluding the piece to rapturous applause. "There's your rabbit," says the companion in the audience. (Liszt was indeed a notorious string snapper, playing, as he often did in his early years, older pianos made before the 1830s, before technology caught up with his technique.) We also observe Hepburn convincingly miming to Artur Rubinstein on the

Brahms and the woman: Katharine Hepburn as Clara Schumann, Robert Walker (center) as Johannes Brahms and Henry Daniell as Liszt in *Song of Love*.

soundtrack. (She practiced perhaps as hard as Bogarde, and certainly with more success.)

Brilliant though Clara was, she was a very different pianist from Liszt, and *Song of Love* emphasizes this in a scene that also reflects the general feeling about Liszt's reputation in 1947. While listening to Liszt's virtuoso transcription of Schumann's song "Widmung" or "Dedication" (the opening number of the first of his Lieder collection *Myrthen*), Clara asks, "Dedication to love, or a dedication to pyrotechnics?" Later, at Liszt's request, she sits down at the piano and plays the piece without embellishments, observing as she plays:

> You're a brilliant artist, Franz. I envy you. I wish I had the power to translate the commonplace into such stupendous experience. Once in a while, though, a little moment comes along, which seems to defy such translation. Do you know what I mean, Franz? The littlest thing: the wonder and the magic, two hearts that speak perhaps one to another. The unimportant things: love, Franz, as it is. No illusions. No storms at sea. No gilt. No glitter. Not the rustle of silk and the diamond garter, Franz, just love, unadorned.

Far from feeling insulted by this critique, Liszt admits that Clara has "described" him, and concedes: "I seem always to be tampering with works by men greater than myself." While this was certainly how Liszt used to be regarded, attitudes have changed since 1947, and Liszt's importance as a composer in his own right has long since been reassessed. So too has Clara's reputation as a composer, which was far from being addressed in this film, as the following speech, intoned with all of Hepburn's sugar-coated MGM intensity, makes clear:

> I'm a performer, nothing else. I have a kind of fleeting popularity, which people are willing to pay for. What I do is here today and forgotten tomorrow, but you create, Robert. The things you do will last forever.

Hepburn's Clara is therefore very much a wife and mother first, a performer second, and a composer not at all. *Song of Love* is therefore as absurd as so many other composer biopics, though unusual in offering a disclaimer at the end of the main titles (superimposed, incidentally, over a long shot of Hepburn, as Rubinstein plays Liszt's First Piano Concerto). The caption reveals that "certain necessary liberties have been taken with incident and chronology," which is certainly true, while simultaneously suggesting a seriousness of approach, at least in intent, which it fails to deliver. What we have instead is yet another variation on that old movie favorite of the love triangle: Schumann marries Clara, and then Brahms (Robert Walker), who moves in with them as Robert's student, falls in love with Frau Schumann. Schumann goes mad for good measure, which is always a bonus, and "Uncle" Brahms also turns nursemaid for the Schumann's seven children, playing his famous Lullaby to send one of them to sleep before, absurdly, doing the dishes in a pinafore. In the film's silliest scene, Clara rushes through her recital when the housemaid arrives backstage, indicating that Clara's latest baby needs feeding. "Amazing!" whispers a lady in the audience. "I've never heard her play that fast before!"

Also in 1947, a French film directed by Christian Stengel, again called *Dreams of Love* (*Rêves d'amour*), cast Pierre Richard-Willm as Liszt, followed in 1952 by the appearance of the great Sviatoslav Richter, playing both the music and the man Liszt, in *Man of Music* aka *The Composer Glinka*, a Russian-made biopic of Glinka, directed by Grigoriy Aleksandrov. Richter, one of the greatest of all twentieth-century pianists, excels here in his personification of his great predecessor. With full flowing locks, Liszt presides at a richly carved black grand, raised on a dais and encircled by his aristocratic audience. With head held high, he signals all the gestures of the Romantic hero before deigning to take requests, which are delivered to him on a large platter. He selects the "completely new and original" piece by Glinka (Chernomor's March from *Ruslan and Lyudmila*). With a bunch of red roses beside him, he takes off his gloves and attacks the piano like a rider digging his spurs into the flanks of a fiery stallion. His hair falls in his face, the piano thunders, the audience is electrified. "I don't know who the author is," Liszt admits after the rousing conclusion, "but I assure you he is a genius!"—as which point Glinka (Boris Smirnov) arrives, just in time to be pelted with flowers and to shake hands with the man who has provided him with the best publicity stunt anyone could hope for.

In 1956, Carlos Thompson played Liszt in William Dieterle's Wagner biopic *Magic Fire*. It maintains all the absurdities of the genre while still managing to follow the main outlines of the historical facts. Famously, Erich Wolfgang Korngold (who made a cameo appearance as the conductor, Hans Richter) condensed the entire *Ring* cycle to about five minutes to accompany the enjoyable pastiche of that epic towards the end of the film. Earlier, we see Alan Badel's Wagner pleading his cause to Meyerbeer (Charles Regnier), who receives him while lying in bed, like Louis XV. During this *levée*, Liszt performs Wagner's overture to *The Flying Dutchman* on Meyerbeer's white piano (rather like the one Sinkovits' Liszt plays in Keleti's *Szerelmi álmok*). "Bravo, Franz Liszt!" Meyerbeer exclaims at Wagner's expense, when the final chord dies away. (Wagner always painted Meyerbeer as his enemy.) "Bravo, Richard Wagner!" counters one of Meyerbeer's *levée* guests.

After the condensed *Ring*, we move to Venice, where Wagner sits before a big, black gondola of a grand on which he demonstrates passages of his final music drama, *Parsifal*, to Liszt, who now wears the famous long white hair and Abbé's cassock. We do not see Badel's hands at the keyboard, but we hear Korngold on the soundtrack, as Wagner explains the music's dramatic significance:

WAGNER: *Parsifal*.... It was inspired by the "Amen" sung many years ago by the choir boys in the court chapel at Dresden [in fact the city's Frauenkirche]. ... The bells of Montsalvat, hailing the young Parisfal's approach to the Holy Communion.
LISZT: Heresy, Richard! Heresy!
WAGNER: I tried to take what is best in all religion to show their common path to salvation through suffering, compassion, service and renunciation.
LISZT: No, Richard, you shouldn't.
WAGNER: Hear the temptation scene in Klingsor's garden when Parsifal, like Tannhäuser in the Venus grotto, resists all manner of temptations.
LISZT [beginning to be won over]: Ah, but it's exquisite.
WAGNER: The final scene of Parsifal's redemption. The Holy Speer! I bring it back to you!
LISZT [joining him on the piano stool]: Magnificent!
WAGNER: Suffering, sacrifice, renunciation sums up what I've done with my life!

Wagner stops playing and the next shot shows a calendar page: February 13, 1883. Another shot of the empty piano stool and silent keyboard conveys that this was the day Wagner died. His wife Cosima (Rita Gann) adds the final symbolism of closing the lid of the piano before seeking retreat on a chaise lounge. The piano thus comes to symbolize music itself, with the unintentional irony that Wagner wrote so little for this particular instrument.

All these cinematic Liszts certainly have more in common visually with the maestro than Bogarde's performance, but perhaps one of the most convincing impressions of Liszt's personality is Ekkehard Schall's in Tony Palmer's *Wagner* (1983). Schall develops from the proud and confident young virtuoso to the more diffident, elderly Liszt, who unsuccessfully attempts to interest Richard Burton's Wagner in his compositions. Wagner, who played the piano only in a rudimentary manner, mostly as an aid to composition, was always jealous of Liszt's technique and brilliant fame, and usually walked out of the room whenever Liszt started to play his *Mephisto Waltz*. Toward the end of Palmer's film, Wagner ridicules Liszt's musical innovations as having been only "in fingering," failing to admit that he had appropriated many of Liszt's musical ideas for his own works. Earlier, he described Liszt as the darling of the salons: "They see his fingers on the keyboard and imagine them ... *up their skirts!*" We are treated to a recreation of exactly this environment on the occasion of one of Liszt's birthday celebrations. An immense tiered cake stands on the piano, surmounted by an elaborate, edible, iced "L," which Liberace would have much admired. (The shared initial helps reinforce the comparison.) This kind of thing actually happened in 1839, when Liszt was performing in Pest: "Even the pastry-cooks excelled themselves by producing a new type of biscuit, in the shape of a grand piano, inscribed with the name 'Liszt' in icing sugar."[14]

Liszt thunders meaningless chords on the instrument, seeming bored, as the candles flicker, surrounded by admirers. As in *Lisztomania*, Liberace's recreation of the Liszt legend makes itself felt even in this much more careful, intentionally "faithful" recreation of musical history. (Both films share the same costume designer.)

Though Wagner only wrote a handful of occasional pieces for the piano, mostly in his youth, and claimed never to find inspiration at the keyboard, the piano was an essential piece of equipment for him to try out ideas, and Palmer's film demonstrates this by showing Wagner's Érard grand ("the only decent thing to come out of Paris," he claims) constantly on the move, under wraps, as it follows the composer's itinerant lifestyle, over borders, across the Alps, and winched into a Venetian palazzo. For dramatic effect, Wagner is also shown hammering out themes at this instrument while composing *Siegfried*, often intercut with images of a Nibelung at his forge. The piano thus becomes a mighty anvil for Wagner's musical

Grand master: Trevor Howard (right) as Richard Wagner and Mark Burns as Hans von Bülow in *Ludwig*.

smithy. And while Liszt does not appear in Visconti's *Ludwig* (1973), Wagner and his piano do. Trevor Howard gives perhaps the most lifelike portrayal of Wagner to be found in any film, his grand piano forming an essential component of the opulent surroundings (mostly at his patron, King Ludwig's expense), without which the Master could not compose.

Five

Piano Lessons

Anthony Burgess includes an account of a child's first encounter with a piano keyboard in his novel *The Pianoplayers*, in which Ellen Henshaw is instructed by her father:

> The white note to the left of the first of the twin black notes, not the triplets, is always C. At the top or the bottom, it makes no difference, always C. The C in the middle of the Joanna is middle C, which stands to reason. Then all the rest follow—D E F G A B, down as well as up: BAG FED. You can play the scale of C eight times over, very fast, from the bottom of the keyboard to the top, just by using your thumbnail. ... Then he got me on to chords. C E G, F A C, G B D. Those, he said, are the most important ones. Easy, really. Triads, he said, meaning chords made of three notes, tri meaning three like in a tricycle. ... The black note to the right of C is called C sharp. The black note to the left of D is called D flat. But it's the same sound, Dad. "Ah, my girl," he said, "there's a great mystery there, isn't there? You have a choice between calling it C sharp and D flat, and let that be enough for the time being."[1]

Kings Row (dir. Sam Wood, 1942), the ultimate American movie soap opera, begins with a piano lesson. Clever young Parris Mitchell (Scotty Beckett) runs into a music room to be greeted by Maria Ouspenskaya's Madame von Eln. "I'm late with my practicing," he exclaims after embracing her. He sits at the keyboard; but before he can begin, he is handed an invitation to a birthday party, so we never hear what piece he is learning. Madame von Eln is a benevolent teacher, so Parris is lucky. He also seems to enjoy practice, unlike many children who are subjected to the ordeal. For such unfortunates, the whole experience can be a tyrannous nightmare, as the British composer John Ireland recalled in an interview in 1963:

> I have the most unpleasant memories attached to my first piano teachers. They used to use a round, black and quite hefty ruler which would descend on my fingers the moment they got into trouble. But the difficulties didn't disappear as a result of the ruler treatment; they only became worse, and I became more and more terrified. At the age of ten, I associated Beethoven with suffering and

punishment. The crowning catastrophe occurred after I had come to London to study. I was studying the piano then with Frederick Cliffe in a group lesson where each student would play the piano for twenty minutes and spend the remainder of the time listening, it was hoped, with profit. On the occasion I arrived for my lesson badly prepared and broke down completely. "Where do you live?" thundered Mr. Cliffe. "West Hampstead, sir," I replied. "Go home at once, practise that passage three hours and come straight back here to me!" And such was the discipline in those days that I didn't dream of disobeying him.[2]

Learning to play the piano used to be an ordeal experienced by far more middle-class women than men, whether they had any feeling for music or not, as being able to play was a badge of desirability in the marriage market. Minna von Kerich, in Romain Rolland's novel *Jean-Christophe*, has no love for music, and finds her lessons with the story's eponymous hero a crashing bore, but nonetheless persists:

Minna would arrive late, her eyes still puffy with sleep, sulky; she would hardly reach out her hand to Jean-Christophe, coldly bid him good-day, and, without a word, gravely and with dignity sit down at the piano. When she was alone, it pleased her to play interminable scales, for that allowed her agreeably to prolong her half-somnolent condition and the dreams which she was spinning for herself. But Jean-Christophe would compel her to fix her attention on difficult exercises, and so sometimes she would avenge herself by playing them as badly as she could. She was a fair musician, but she did not like music—like many German women, But, like them, she thought she ought to like it, and she took her lessons conscientiously enough, except for certain moments of diabolical malice indulged in to enrage her master....

Young Jean-Christophe, sitting by her side, was not very polite. He never paid her compliments—far from it. She resented that, and never let any remark pass without answering it. She would argue about everything that he said, and when she made a mistake she would insist that she was playing what was written. ... As a relief from boredom she would invent stupid little tricks, with no other object than to interrupt the lesson and to annoy Jean-Christophe....

But she did not fail to take her lesson, and all the subsequent lessons, because she knew very well that Jean-Christophe was a fine musician, and that she ought to learn to play the piano properly if she wished to be—what she wished to be—a well-bred young lady of finished education.

But how bored she was! How they bored each other![3]

George Eliot was also very well aware of this particularly female problem, describing the dilemma in *Daniel Deronda*. The heroine of this novel, Gwendoline Harleth, consults her piano teacher, Herr Klesmer, about her future, which is now uncertain, as her family has suddenly lost all its money. Gwendoline must "do" something, but what? Acting? Singing? Klesmer, a character based on Liszt (whom Eliot had known while residing in Weimar with George Henry Lewes), is quite certain that she should put the idea of a professional career in music out of her mind:

> "You are a beautiful young lady—you have been brought up in ease—you have done what you would—you have not said to yourself, 'I must know this exactly,' 'I must understand this exactly,' 'I must do this exactly'"—in uttering those three terrible *musts,* Klesmer lifted up three long fingers in succession. "In sum, you have not been called upon to be anything but a charming young lady, whom it is an impoliteness to find fault with."
>
> He paused an instant; then resting his fingers on his hips again, and thrusting out his powerful chin, he said—
>
> "Well, then, with that preparation, you wish to try the life of the artist; you wish to try a life of arduous, unceasing work, and—uncertain praise. Your praise would have to be earned, like your bread; and both would come slowly, scantily—what do I say? They might hardly come at all."
>
> The tone of discouragement, which Klesmer half-hoped might suffice without anything more unpleasant, roused some resistance in Gwendoline. With a slight turn of her head away from him, and an air of pique, she said—
>
> "I thought that you, being an artist, would consider the life one of the most honourable and delightful. And if I can do nothing better?—I suppose I can put up with the same risks as other people do."
>
> "No, my dear Miss Harleth, you could do nothing better—neither man nor woman could do anything better—if you could do what was best or good of its kind. I am not decrying the life of the true artist. I am exalting it. I say, it is out of the reach of any but choice organisations—natures framed to love perfection and to labour for it; ready, like all true lovers, to endure, to wait, to say, I am not yet worthy, but she—Art, my mistress—is worthy, and I will live to merit her."[4]

However, Klesmer's artistic ideals were usually far from the minds of Victorian parents who had marriageable daughters on their hands. To be able to play at all was an accomplishment that made one more valuable on the marriage market, for it signified respectability, providing such musical activity was confined to the drawing room. Bernard Shaw was fully aware of this, and complained of the increasing prevalence of music being sacrificed on the altar of "a female with no music in her whole composition, simply getting up an 'accomplishment' either to satisfy her own vanity or to obey the orders of her misguided mother."[5] Respectability required middle-class women to be removed from the profane world and turned into ministering domestic angels. Thus, in Gustave Flaubert's critique of such a state of affairs in *Madame Bovary,* the eponymous Emma sits at the piano, easily impressing her boring husband:

> As for the piano, the more quickly her fingers ran over it, the greater was his amazement. She struck the keys with assurance and could run over the keyboard from top to bottom without an interruption. Thus shaken up by her,

the old instrument, the chords of which were all out of order, could be heard to the end of the village if the window was open, and often the bailiff's clerk, passing along the highway bareheaded and in canvas shoes, would stop to listen to it, his sheet of paper in his hand.⁶

Consequently, when nineteenth-century novels were made into movies, the piano usually came along with them. Orson Welles' adaptation of Charlotte Brönte's *Jane Eyre* (1943) has a scene in which Rochester (Welles) instructs Jane (Joan Fontaine) to play the grand piano in his cold and gloomy mansion. "Sit down at the piano and play a tune!" he insists. She does so, lit by a candelabra, which, unlike Liberace's, is actually required for illumination, so dark is the chamber. She plays a few bars of Mendelssohn's first *Lieder ohne Worte*, but is interrupted by Rochester, who shouts: "Enough! You play a little, I see, like any other English schoolgirl; perhaps rather better than some. Not well. Good night, Miss Eyre."

In his social history of the instrument, Dieter Hildebrandt quotes Hans Salmen's description of a rather more typically middle-class parlor, an environment that replaced the more patrician salon, to which the term "salon music" aspired:

> "In sharp contrast to the meager workers' dwelling in grim ghetto districts, people here surrounded themselves with plush furniture, oil paintings, artificial flowers, bric-a-brac, heavy curtains and busts of Beethoven...." The enthusiastic décor was an unconscious bolster against any number of anxieties.
>
> Furthermore, for the many thousands of new enthusiasts who flock to the piano from the middle of the century, the term "salon music" held a promise to raise the front parlour to the level of a true salon.⁷

A rather more accomplished performer is found in Henry James' novel *The Portrait of a Lady*: Madame Merle provides a veritable checklist of feminine accomplishments. She is a mature lady, and not in the marriage market, but her talent is nonetheless presented as an "accomplishment" rather than a professional skill. She is too respectable to aspire to professionalism of any sort. Playing the piano for Madame Merle is just as much confined to the domestic arena as it was for younger, less respectable and less accomplished ladies. It ranks no higher for her or for the society in which she lives, than any of her other pastimes:

> That she was a brilliant musician we have already perceived, and it was evidence of the fact that when she seated herself at the piano, as she always did in the evening, her listeners resigned themselves without a murmur of losing the entertainment of her talk. Isabel, since she had known Madame Merle, felt ashamed of her own playing, which she now looked upon as meager and artless; and indeed, though she had been thought to play very well, the loss to society when, in taking her place upon the music-stool, she turned her back to the room, was usually deemed greater than the gain. When Madame Merle

was neither writing, nor painting, nor touching the piano, she was usually employed upon wonderful morsels of picturesque embroiders, cushions, curtains, decorations for the chimneypiece; a sort of work in which her bold, free invention was as remarkable as the agility of her needle. She was never idle, for when she was engaged in none of the ways I have mentioned, she was either reading (she appeared to Isabel to read everything important), or walking out, or playing patience with the cards, or talking with her fellow inmates.[8]

As Hildebrandt also reminds us, it was actually Robert Schumann who invented the phrase "salon music" (in 1838), merely to describe music intended for intimate, domestic consumption. Originally, the term had nothing disparaging about it. Hildebrandt also refers to Adolf Bernhard Marx's observation that music in the nineteenth century was considered "an imperative part of education; every family demanded it, wherever possible for every family member, with no particular regard for talent or inclination ... [E]ven among small traders and artisans, precious time and money was diverted to secure, at least for the daughters, piano sheet music, teachers and music education, in the hope of thus being counted among the 'educated.'"[9]

Hence, the importance of the piano in Louisa May Alcott's novel *Little Women*, in which the word "piano" appears 27 times, and is mostly associated with Beth's love of them. She "envies girls with nice pianos."[10]

Beth had her troubles as well as the others; and not being an angel, but a very human little girl, she often "wept a little weep," as Jo said, because she couldn't take music lessons and have a fine piano. She loved music so dearly, tried so hard to learn, and practiced away so patiently at the jingling old instrument, that it did seem as if someone ... ought to help her.[11]

Help comes from the March family's wealthy neighbor Mr. Laurence, who allows Beth to practice on his impressive grand. He doesn't play himself, but his son does, and before long, Beth is regularly visiting this temple of music, which she calls her "Palace Beautiful" and "Mansion of Bliss." Beth "yearns" for this piano with "trembling fingers."

Beth at last touched the great instrument, and straightaway forgot her fear, herself, and everything else but the unspeakable delight which the music gave her, for it was like the voice of a beloved friend.[12]

The piano becomes a symbol of all that Beth desires. She knits Mr. Laurence a pair of slippers by way of appreciation, and he thanks her by giving her a piano of her own, "a little cabinet piano, with a letter lying on the glossy lid." The glossiness is significant here, as it conveys the opulence Beth yearns for as well as music she craves. Indeed, the piano's form and decoration are described in sensual detail: "the cunning brackets to hold candles, and the nice green silk, puckered up, with a gold rose in the middle, and the pretty rack and stool, all complete." Mr. Laurence arrives, and as Beth plays, everyone else joins in. The piano thus forms the nucleus not only of society but also of civilization itself, as Ralph Waldo Emerson versified it at the beginning of his essay on that subject:

> From the log cabin Beethoven's notes
> On the piano, played with master's hand.
> "Well done!" he cries; "the bear is kept at bay,
> The lynx, the rattlesnake, the flood, the fire:
> All the fierce enemies, ague, hunger, cold,
> This thin spruce roof, this clayed log wall,
> This wild plantation will suffice to chase.
> Now speed the gay celerities of art,
> What in the desert was impossible
> Within four walls is possible again—
> Culture and libraries, mysteries of skill,
> Traditioned fame of masters, eager strife
> Of keen competing youths, joined or alone,
> To outdo each other and extort applause."

Of course, the March girls do not live in a log cabin, but the reverence Beth feels for her piano is fully in accord with Emerson's sentiments here, which Alcott would have known all about thanks to her father, Colonel Alcott, who was part of Emerson's "Transcendentalist" circle in Concord, Massachusetts. Beth pays for her musicality, however, with the cliché of physical weakness. Like Mimi in Puccini's *La Bohème*, she must die, having glimpsed esthetic perfection, much as Laurence's granddaughter, the previous owner of the piano, also died. In Mervyn LeRoy's 1948 film adaptation of the story, Beth's piano has red silk decoration rather than Alcott's green, thus emphasizing its sensuous nature. Gillian Armstrong's 1994 version presented a much plainer affair, still with the candlesticks but no silk. The close-up of Beth's fingers caressing the keys, before she begins to play, is, however, deliberately sensuous in its intent. As everyone joins in to sing "Deck the Halls," the piano is again shown to be the foundation stone and unifier of bourgeois security, which of course respectably contains and defuses all those much more bohemian emotions.

Respectability

To emphasize her own eminent respectability, Rose Hobart's Muriel Carew in Rouben Mamoulian's *Dr. Jekyll and Mr. Hyde* (1931) is shown at the piano, playing (rather slowly) one of Robert Schumann's *Fantasiestücke* ("Aufschwung" or "Soaring," to be precise). She has obviously received expensive tuition in her youth, in accord with her social standing, and her lessons have paid off in her considerable, though strictly non-professional accomplishment. Her grand piano, adorned with flowers and a pre–Liberacean candelabra, appears towards the end of the film, just before Jekyll arrives to bid her farewell. Their encounter, which encapsulates the story's basic theme of culture vs. barbarism, takes place almost entirely on the piano stool, the piano nearly always being in shot. Disturbed by his repressed emotions, Jekyll can no longer contain the Mr. Hyde within him. Left alone, Muriel collapses on the keyboard, the ensuing discord expressing her despair. (When Anthony Corlan's Paul Paxton slams the keyboard of the grand piano in Peter Sasdy's *Taste the Blood of Dracula* [1970], he similarly expresses his anger and frustration. Otherwise, it is purely an item of set dressing, indicative of the film's middle-class Victorian milieu.)

Hyde now appears and contemplates the prostrate pianist. He advances towards her, lifting her from the keyboard. She screams. Her father runs to her aid, and in the ensuing struggle, the keyboard cover crashes down with a clash of notes, silencing the world of culture that Hyde cannot endure. That Dr. Jekyll also plays the organ in his own establishment further bolsters the dichotomy. (The film itself begins with Bach's Toccata and Fugue in D minor, which was later to be associated with *The Phantom of the Opera* thanks mainly to its use of the diminished seventh chord, that cliché of musical terror. Horror films have often interpolated it for this reason.)

To be musical is to be civilized, or, more precisely, to admire the *right kind* of music is to be civilized. Mr. Hyde enjoys a good tune in the lowly music hall at which he first encounters the working class Ivy Pearson of Miriam Hopkins; but that kind of music is obviously not "respectable." (Mamoulian returned to this theme in *Golden Boy* [1939], in which young violinist Joe Bonapart [William Holden] earns money for his lessons from boxing, but eventually settles for the more respectable and civilizing effects of music.)

Hammer films learned Mamoulian's music lesson, when including music teacher Anton Hoffer (David Warbeck) in John Hough's 1971 *Twins of Evil*; Hoffer even composes a song. (The movie is set in Puritan times and the instrument on which he plays the accompaniment is a harpsichord, but the implication is the same.) Hoffer's musicality is thus in stark contrast to the brutality of the witch-hunters led by Peter Cushing's Gustav Weil, who are even more evil than the vampires they attempt to eradicate. Similarly, in Mario Bava's *Black Sunday* (1960), we are introduced to Barbara Steele's character, Katia Vajda, while she is playing somewhat anachronistic music on a square piano, complete with candelabra. (Liberace had by this time made that accessory almost essential.) Katia's civilized respectability is confirmed by her well-instructed musical ability. Later, she will be corrupted into the barbarous condition as the vampire, and thus lose this ability.

In the real world of nineteenth-century middle-class respectability, however, too much proficiency could prove socially disadvantageous. Early on in the century, virtuosity was already considered "professional" and therefore vulgar. Jane Austen makes this very clear in *Pride and Prejudice* (1813), when Lady Catherine explains that too much accomplishment is *infra dig*, as it suggests professionalism, which of course indicates a much lower social standing. In Joe Wright's 2005 film adaptation of the novel, Elizabeth Bennet (Keira Knightley) is forced to play before Dame Judi Dench's formidable Lady Catherine. Elizabeth begs to be excused, but Lady Catherine insists:

> Music is my delight. In fact, there are few people in England who have more true enjoyment of music than myself. Or better natural taste. If I had ever learnt I would have been a great proficient. [The fact that she didn't proves her social standing.] So would Ann, if her health would have allowed her.... No excellence can be acquired without constant practice. I have told Mrs. Collins this. Though you have no instrument of your own, you are very welcome to come to Rosings and play on the pianoforte in the housekeeper's room. You'll be in nobody's way in that part of the house.

As Dieter Hildebrandt explains, "A proper young lady, in other words, would be sure to practice diligently, though without disturbing the household, so as to have something to offer society—although of course the very fact that she could play would prove that she was not a lady in the truest sense."[13] But if one was not sufficiently accomplished, social embarrassment lay in another direction, as Mary Bennet discovers: After she sings to the assembly at the Netherfield Ball, her father prevents further renditions with the line: "That will do extremely well, child. You have delighted us long enough. Let the other young ladies have time to exhibit."[14] Hildebrandt also reminds us that in Thackeray's *Vanity Fair*, "the piano is no longer an entirely innocent pursuit: somehow, along with the excessive use of powder and paint, too many petticoats and extravagant hats, it has become a mark of coquettishness. Amelia Sedley, the positive heroine, can play, but only just. Becky Sharp on the other hand, with her green eyes and half–French artistic heritage, is an accomplished pianist; little wonder that she is destined to lose her virtue. Dexterity implies frivolity; skill in performance implies shamelessness. Anyone who can play the piano that well is surely not to be trusted."[15]

This is a lesson painfully learned by Laura Tweedle Ramsbottom (Susannah Fowle) while attending the finishing school for young women in Bruce Beresford's 1977 adaptation of Henry Handel Richardson's 1910 novel *The Getting of Wisdom*. When Laura plays rather magnificently, her disconcerted piano teacher Miss Hicks (Dorothy Bradley) asks, "You taught yourself that during the holidays?"

"There wasn't that much to do."

"Well, oh dear.... Well, another half hour's practice, Laura."

Laura begins to play again, something much more florid, and Miss Hicks leaves her to it. Laura's friend Tilly then enters the practice room, saying, "That sounded very like Thalberg to me."

"Oh, Tilly, I didn't know what I was playing. I wasn't thinking."

"You play like that when you're not thinking! No wonder Hicks is in a dither."

The music of Thalberg, Liszt's greatest rival, would not have been regarded as quite suitable for merely "accomplished" young ladies. It was too virtuosic, too "professional." Richardson points this out quite clearly in his novel, which the film faithfully recreates. When Laura plays Thalberg before the assembled tutors in the drawing room, "dead silence" greets her bold display:

> Laura learnt that she had been guilty of a gross impertinence, in profaning the ears of the Principal and Mrs. Strachey with Thalberg's music, and that all the pieces she had brought with her from home would now be taken from her. Secondly, Mr. Strachey had been so unpleasantly impressed by the boldness of her behaviour, that she would not be invited to the drawing-room again for some time to come.[16]

The dismay of Laura's repressed and small-minded tutors is made all the greater because her virtuosity is instinctive and she herself lacks any of their pretensions to culture (the title of the novel is deeply ironic). Young women were simply not required to display undue passion or to have real talent, which is also why Helena Bonham Carter's Lucy Honeychurch in *A Room with a View* (dir. James Ivory, 1985) causes such surprise (though this time encouraging and appreciative) from Simon Callow's Mr. Bede. Lucy plays Beethoven's extremely demanding and passionate "Waldstein" Sonata on a "Steinwal" upright in the parlor of her hotel in Florence (if only it had been a "Steinwald!"). The scene is reminiscent of what Anthony Trollope had to say about hotel pianos in his 1862 book *North America*:

> There is always a piano in an hotel drawing room, on which, of course, some one of the forlorn ladies is generally employed. I do not suppose that these pianos are in fact, as a rule, louder and harsher, more violent and less musical, than other instruments of the kind. They seem to be so, but that, I take it, arises from the exceptional mental depression of those who have to listen to them.[17]

Lucy later plays Schubert's A-minor Sonata in a drawing room setting back home in England, the contained passion of Schubert being far more appropriate for such an eligible young lady. It is also Schubert which Laura plays at the recital she gives at the end *The Getting of Wisdom*. Having been awarded a place to study music in Germany, she is congratulated in front of the whole school by Barry Humphries' Reverend Strachey, and she launches into Schubert's D-flat Impromptu, her ability now having been given the accolade of scholarly respectability, which, of course, reflects well on the status of the school.

Sin

But it wasn't just middle-class girls who played the piano. If over-accomplishment in young ladies was considered bad manners, any man who used music simply to seduce was obviously not to be trusted. Hildebrandt offers Count Fosco in Wilkie Collins' *The Woman in White* as a good example of this: He never plays Mozart, merely Italian opera overtures to hypnotize his victims like a musical snake. "There was something horrible—something fierce and devilish—in the outburst of his delight at his own singing and playing, and in the triumph with which he watched its effect upon me as I shrank nearer and nearer to the door."[18] This is bad enough in a foreigner, but for an Englishman to indulge in such seductions was, for most Victorians, quite beyond the pale. Such, however, is the situation in William Holman Hunt's famous 1853 painting "The Awakening Conscience," in which an immoral, materialistic "arriviste" is depicted entertaining his mistress (ironically modeled on Hunt's own mistress, Annie Miller). She is indeed very close to falling—and not just off the piano stool on which she and the seducer are perched. This is very obviously *not* the pose of a pupil and teacher. She sits on his lap, gazing out into the purity of the garden, symbolically far away, though in fact only a few paces from this over-stuffed interior, her conscience just having awoken to beckoning redemption. Responding to the confusion the painting caused among the general public at the time, art critic John Ruskin explained all in his helpful letter to *The Times* on May 25, 1854:

> The poor girl has been sitting singing with her seducer; some chance words of the song "Oft in the stilly night" have struck upon some numbed places of her heart; she has started up in agony; he, not seeing her face, goes on singing, striking the keys carelessly with his gloved hand.

Ruskin also refers to the "fatal newness" of the interior furnishings of this little love nest (probably situated in St John's Wood, London, where many similarly bewildered birds were kept in gilded cages). The piano is "carefully painted, even to the last vein of the rosewood"—and is thus brand new. The man is therefore identified as a ghastly member of the *nouveau riche*, and the piano's "terrible lustre" indicates that there is nothing of "the old thoughts of home upon it, or that it is ever to become part of a home."[19] By inverting the iconography of middle-class respectability—the piano, the woman, the domestic arena—Hunt demonstrates the immense power of the piano as an icon of domestic bliss, of feminine virtue and above all of social respectability. Even the painting's frame ironically echoes his point. It is embossed with bells, which are certainly not going to be ringing, as there is obviously to be no wedding. A similar situation awaited Emma Bovary in Flaubert's once scandalous novel about her. Emma is a very accomplished pianist ("She struck the keys with assurance, and could run over the key-board from top to bottom without an interruption"[20]); but marriage with M. Bovary proves to be so soul-destroying, Emma stops playing, for what would be the point? She has no hope of ever breaking free from her provincial monotony. She later decides to take up the instrument again and pleads for lessons from her well-meaning bore of a husband, who fails to realize that the piano lessons are in fact a subterfuge, which allows her to visit her new lover, Léon.

Another woman, whose conscience failed to awaken in time, plays another piano in Visconti's 1971 adaptation of *Death in Venice*. In fact, there are two pianos in the film (three if we count the scene in which Dirk Bogarde and Marc Burns discuss musical esthetics). The first is a concert grand in the Hotel des Bains, at which Björn Andresen's Tadzio, the seductive muse of Bogarde's Gustav von Aschenbach, picks out Beethoven's "Für Elise." This immediately reminds Aschenbach of his visit to a prostitute years before. The prostitute does not in fact feature in Thomas Mann's original story, having been drawn from another of Mann's works, *Doctor Faustus*, in which the composer Adrian Leverkühn visits a prostitute called Esmeralda, who will later infect him with syphilis and in so doing provide him with musical inspiration. (This is the Faustian pact implied by the novel's title.) The whole episode is in fact drawn from the biography of Friedrich Nietzsche, a resonance Mann was keen to exploit in this critique of German culture. In Visconti's vision, Aschenbach doesn't catch syphilis (it is Venice's cholera that eventually carries him off) but the scene is important in equating Tadzio (and the piano) with dangerous seduction. In a flashback scene, the prostitute peers around her out-of-tune upright as she continues the piece, which Tadzio began in the previous scene. (When Nietzsche visited his own prostitute, he apparently played certain "significant" bars from Weber's Romantic opera *Der Freischütz*, but Visconti realized that "Für Elise" would be much better known. Many years later, when Hermonia [Emma Watson] teaches Ron [Rupert Grint] to play the piano in *Harry Potter and the Deathly Hallows* [dir. David Yates, 2010], she plays the

Seductive strumming: Björn Andresen as Tadzio in *Death in Venice*.

same "romantic" piece.) Aschenbach's nervousness as he approaches this piano-playing siren suggests the apprehension of a piano pupil attending a lesson. The prostitute, like a piano teacher, will instruct him in her art; but Aschenbach, who has not been practicing, is understandably apprehensive.

In Franz Seitz's 1982 adaptation of Mann's *Doctor Faustus*, Leverkühn, played by Jon Finch, strikes the flat of his hand on a piano keyboard, much as Anthony Corlan does in *Taste the Blood of Dracula*. Leverkühn then strides out, unready, at this stage, to engage sexually with Esmeralda. The seduction occurs later, after he has tracked her down to Sarajevo (Mann's way of equating Leverkühn's pact with the downfall of European culture, which began in that city in 1914). Leverkühn's pact depends on his renunciation of love, so when he begins to show fatherly affection for the winsome infant, Nepomuk, towards the end of the story, Nepomuk eventually contracts meningitis and dies. Seitz compresses this episode into a conversation between Leverkühn and the boy, which takes place over an open grand piano, again suggesting a pupil-teacher relationship. This particular setting is not in the book, but by placing Leverkühn and Nepomuk at opposite ends of the instrument, Seitz is able to imply the corrupting power of Leverkühn's musical gift.

Six

Practice Makes Perfect

Piano Stool Blues

The prostitute in *Death in Venice* is hardly a virtuoso, but any kind of musical accomplishment must nonetheless be attained through practice, and an astonishing number of films have featured this essentially private and often grueling process. Musicians themselves like to keep their practice hours to themselves, though Saint-Saëns satirized scale drill in the "Pianists" section of his *Carnival of the Animals*, thereby suggesting that pianists are just another kind of curious animal, which, like the others, makes its own characteristic noise. Though Saint-Saëns could smile at the drudgery of scales, there *is* a kind of desolation about the sound of piano practice, suggestive of incarceration and oppression; and that is why the sound of it haunts the deserted Venetian piazzas in Nicolas Roeg's *Don't Look Now* (1973). This film's hero, John (Donald Sutherland), is trapped by his own destiny. Haunted by a premonition, his mounting realization of what it means becomes increasingly oppressive for both him and the audience. The sound of the piano in one scene thus subtly intensifies his state of mind. Similarly, in Seitz's adaptation of *Doctor Faustus*, Leverkühn visits a doctor about the syphilis he has contracted. He arrives to find the doctor dead, and hears a singer practicing scales accompanied by a piano. The sound provides an eerie counterpoint to an already uncanny scene.

Bland Playing

In the *Quartet* segment "The Alien Corn," George Bland (Dirk Bogarde), an aspiring pianist, hides himself away in a Paris garret to study. Having come to an agreement with his un-musical, upper-class family, he is to study for two years before subjecting himself to professional opinion. If this goes against him, he must give up all thought of the piano as a career.

His girlfriend Paula (Honor Blackman) visits and informs him that his parents had expected him to give up after a month:

"Good Lord, no!" George exclaims. "I love it!"

"Have you got a good teacher?"

"Yes ... he's a bit hard to please but he's good. Trouble is, I only get a couple of lessons a week, you see. The rest of it's all practice: ten hours a day."

"Are you satisfied?"

"Yes, I think so."

He then launches into a Chopin Waltz, a Peters Edition of pieces by Liszt lying on the piano lid, so we know that we are meant to think of the great Romantics, even though the story is set in 1948. Later, back in England, his judge Lea Makart (Françoise Rosay) arrives wearing a kind of Valkyrie bonnet to preside over the trial. (The bonnet was perhaps a reference to Rosay's other career as an opera singer.) George plays another Chopin Waltz, and the verdict is crushing. According to Makart, he will never be a pianist of the first rank, "not in a thousand years."

> Of course, I can see that you have worked very hard, and have acquired technique, brilliance, but you lack the magic, the quality that is a combination of soul and fire, without which no artist can reach the heights. I'm sorry, but your playing is ... square. If I thought you had in you the makings of an artist, I shouldn't hesitate to beseech you to give up everything for Art's sake. Art is the only thing that matters. ... I don't think that you can ever hope to be anything more than a very competent amateur.

George may not have Makart's talent but he certainly agrees with her belief that Art is all that matters, for soon after hearing her verdict, he shoots himself. Practice, therefore, does not always make perfect.

Dr. Terwilliker's House of Horrors

This rather disturbing perspective on practice was lavishly explored in the curious and surrealistic Dr. Seuss fantasy film *The 5,000 Fingers of Dr. T.* (dir. Roy Rowland, 1953). Tommy Rettig, who would soon become Lassie's TV partner, plays a boy named Bart Collins. He is condemned to piano practice by his widowed mother, who believes the discipline of practice will be good for him. The actual music is therefore a bi-product of her protestant work ethic. His teacher, Dr. Terwilliker (Hans Conried), is a martinet and might also very well be a pedophile. His name is suggestive of this (a conflation of "willy" and "wanker"), and in the conservative circles of 1950s America, any "artistic" figure was already a dubious commodity.

Dr. T. asks Bart, "Don't you realize, if you don't practice, you will never become a concert pianist?"

Dr. Terror: Hans Conried and Tommy Rettig in *The 5,000 Fingers of Dr. T.*

"I don't think the piano is my instrument," Bart complains. Dr. T., obviously a product of nineteenth-century esthetics, replies, "What other instruments are there, pray tell? Scratchy violins, screechy piccolos, nauseating trumpets, etc., etc. We'll make a Paderewski of you yet."

The ghost of Paderewski thus makes its presence felt at a time when his famous fan, Liberace, was taking American TV by storm, and it is illuminating to contextualize *The 5,000 Fingers of Dr. T.* alongside *The Liberace Show*: Bart's mother is a lower middle-class, presumably working mother. She has a TV set in her living room, only a few steps from Bart's upright piano, and is thus exactly Liberace's target audience: upwardly mobile, culturally aspirational, politically conservative (esthetically also), white and "wholesome." Bart loves his mother but fears that Dr. T. is hypnotizing her. Bart would much rather be playing baseball, but he is forced to waste his time practicing so that Dr. T. can collect his fee. Bart also misses his father and worries that Dr. T. is intent on marrying his mother. He would much prefer her to marry the friendly plumber, Mr. Zabaldowski (Peter Lind Hayes), which is indeed what happens in the end. "Dr. Terwilliker is the one enemy I've got," Bart complains, before falling asleep at the keyboard and dreaming the rest of the film.

The action now takes us to Dr. T.'s "Happy Fingers" Musical Academy: a Piranesi prison, indeed, redesigned by Dr. Seuss, filled with steps, holes in the floor and ladders that lead nowhere. Bart's dream soon becomes a totalitarian nightmare, fully in accord with Communist paranoia of the time in which the film was made. It also channels the Nazi terrors that came to an end eight years earlier. Dr. T. presides over his academy in a vast hall through which swirl two gigantic whiplash curves of piano keyboards. Regularly spaced before them stand stools, like ice cream parlor perches, which await 500 young male bottoms. The tyrannical Dr. T. looks forward to the arrival of his boys (it seems psychologically significant that they are all boys). Soon they will be practicing 24 hours a day, 365 days a year. The Academy is nothing short of a musical concentration camp. Indeed, the "Happy Fingers" slogan is not so far removed from the Nazi's "Kraft durch Freude" slogan: "Strength through joy." "Arbeit Macht Frei" ("Work Sets You Free") on the gates of Auschwitz is also echoed here. There is even electrified barbed wire to prevent escape, and threatening guards make sure that no one attempts it. When the children arrive, they carry suitcases like concentration camp victims, while Dr. T. becomes a parody of Hitler presiding over a Hitler Youth assembly, wearing an absurd military uniform. Bart's brainwashed mother introduces him as "your lovable leader," and the speech he gives before his assembled musical slaves, atop his Seussified Nuremberg or Kremlin podium, is suitably crazed: "This is my day! Five thousand little fingers, all playing together on my piano! Every finger obedient to the whim of me, the master!"

We then cut to a shot of one little boy crying, obviously in considerable distress, which is unquestionably upsetting: piano lessons, as John Ireland knew too well, can indeed be terrifying ordeals, but the political, not to mention psycho-sexual implications of this image are even more disturbing.

"Every infinitesimal microscopic piece of living tissue of these 5,000 little fingers, cringing and trembling and groveling before *me*!" Dr. T. continues, commanding the boys to raise their hands in what only marginally differs from a Nazi salute. Bart challenges Dr. T.'s musical tyranny with an "atomic" device, which causes havoc (though not destruction). Liberated from the tyrant, he conducts the 4,999 other boys in a rendition of Liberace's favorite musical classic: "Chopsticks."

Pianazimmo

The totalitarian terrors of *Dr. T.* definitely bear comparison with Daniel Mann's 1980 CBS-TV film *Playing for Time*. Vanessa Redgrave plays the incarcerated cabaret musician Fania Fénelon, who finds herself, as a Jew, playing in the Auschwitz orchestra to entertain the likes of Dr. Mengele. As Sophy Roberts describes in her book about the migration of pianos to Siberia, musicians in Stalin's Gulags were similarly detailed to such duties:

> If it weren't for the barbed wire, guards' towers and prison slang, the troupe's performances would be as good as anything heard in the capital, remarked one of the artists, who remembered the sound of waltzes floating across Arctic marshes under the glance of prison lights. If there is a dark irony in this remark, it's hard to determine the desperate depths given the complex nuances, censorship and fear of reprisal (the musicians also commented on the better living conditions they enjoyed, and clean sheets).[1]

Life for the musicians in Auschwitz was precarious, depending, as it did for Fénelon and her fellow players, on how well they played. "There is life or death," explains the orchestra's conductor, Alma Rosé (Jane Alexander). "There is no room for anything else whatever." Fénelon is auditioned (she sings, to her own accompaniment, "One Fine Day" from Puccini's *Madame Butterfly*), but before she begins, she kisses the grand piano, never thinking that she would ever see, let alone play one again. "Music is the holiest activity of mankind," Rosé insists (and she is well qualified to do so as her uncle was Gustav Mahler).

"I like to think I'm saving my life rather than pleasing the SS," Fénelon replies. Rosé counters with: "Do you think you can do one without the other?"

A piano in Auschwitz is a contradiction in terms, and to observe Nazis listening to a Jewish musician playing the piano is the ultimate cultural contradiction; and yet the Nazis made it happen. (The piano's symbolic power as an icon of civilization is also central to Roman Polanski's *The Pianist* [2002], in which the piano and its player are similarly placed in stark contrast to Nazi Germany as a whole.) In fact, the Nazis' pursuit of an esthetic ideal in racial terms helps explain their perverted interest in music. Being *the* German art form, music was central to the Nazi worldview. As Thomas Mann spent so long repeating, estheticism is "the herald of barbarism."[2] The ultimate example of this in terms of the piano is the scene in which Fénelon works at her orchestrations on the same grand at which she auditioned. The lights flicker and go out, and in semi-darkness she continues to work against the sounds of screaming, gunfire and howls in the dark.

After a concert some days later, one of the Nazi officers congratulates the players: "I was opposed to this idea of an orchestra, but I must say now with singing of your sort, it is a consolation that feeds the spirit. It strengthens us with this difficult work of ours."

A piano also features in Jochen Alexander Freydank's 2007 *Spielzeugland* (*Toyland*), which condenses into a mere 14 minutes all of Germany's guilt and a little of its heroism in the face of tyranny. A mother (Julia Jäger) tells her young son Heinrich (Cedric Eich) that their neighbors, the Silbersteins, will soon be leaving their flat. The Silbersteins are Jewish and their son David (Tamay Bulut Özvatan) enjoys playing piano duets with Heinrich. Unable to reveal the truth to him, Heinrich's mother tells him that the Silbersteins are going to visit Toyland, and Heinrich is angry that he can't go with them. We are then led to believe that Heinrich runs away from home to join David, ending up on the train to Auschwitz. We see Heinrich's mother desperately searching for him, but in fact she is enacting a rescue plan. By pretending to be looking for her son, who is actually quite safe, she manages to persuade the SS officers to believe that David is Heinrich and thus release him from the train. Reunited, the two boys sit down at the piano and play their duet, their hands now those of their later adult selves. Freydank thus uses a piano not only as a metaphor for friendship but also as an antidote to Nazi atrocity.

Jewish musicians suffered before the Third Reich, though not in quite the same way as they did in Auschwitz. Gustav Mahler was one of them. In Ken Russell's *Mahler* (1974), the young Gustav (Gary Rich) attends the grim Sladky Academy. Poor but talented, he plays a tune on Sladky's upright. (The tune will later feature in his Fourth Symphony.) Meanwhile, Otto Diamant's Sladky avariciously hoards coins in his cashbox which, with grim irony (Sladky is also Jewish), he keeps under a bust of Wagner.

"And what do you call that, may I ask?" Sladky enquires. Gustav explains that he wrote it himself: "'The Kitten's Serenade.'"

"More like the tune the cat died of. 'Eine Kleine Katmusik'! Where did that come from?"

"Out of my own head."

"And that's where it should have stayed. Even a monkey's more clever. He can pick out a tune on one finger, pick out his nose with another and eat a banana all at the same time, but to play the piano calls for genius!" Sladky insists, rapping a picture of Liszt on the wall with his violin bow. "And genius calls for scales! Scales! Scales!"

He prods Mahler, shouting, "Elbows in! Wrists out! Elbows! Wrists!"

Sladky is obviously not the most enlightened teacher, but many were like him. In Rolland's *Jean Christophe*, the young hero must endure "learning to run as fast as possible over the keys, by loosening the thumb, or exercising the fourth finger, which would cling awkwardly to the two next to it. It got on his nerves; there was nothing beautiful in it. There was an end of the magic sounds, and fascinating monsters, and the universe of dreams felt in one moment…. Nothing but scales and exercises—dry, monotonous, dull."

His father, who instructs him, "had a heavy ruler. At every false note, he struck the boy's fingers, and at the same time shouted in his ears, so that he was like to deafen him. Jean-Christophe's face twitched under the pain of it; he bit his lips to keep himself from crying, and stoically went on hitting the notes all wrong, bobbing his head down whenever he felt a blow coming."[3]

In the nineteenth century, piano-playing became an industry. Manuals, Methods and Studies mushroomed from piano stools across the world. The piano was as much a machine as any steam hammer. Piano manufacture rocketed, and the need for teachers grew alongside it. Things changed when jukeboxes began to replace pianos in pubs and records replaced, in living rooms, Burne-Jones' "altar of homes" and "second hearth."[4] It was therefore appropriate to have represented the piano teacher played by Shirley MacLaine in *Madame Sousatzka* (dir. John Schlesinger, 1988) as something of a throwback.

Bohemian Rhapsody

Madame Sousatzka, a failed concert pianist, makes her living as a strict and idealistic piano teacher. She lives in faded grandeur in an apartment filled with framed photos of great pianists from the past, alongside which the youth culture of the 1980s is shown to sit uncomfortably, and, for her, irrelevantly. The apartment block in London is, however, long overdue for renovation, and everyone else is moving out. The rising damp, the dirty fingerboards of the doors and the peeling wallpaper all conjure the bourgeois idea of bohemianism, which is enshrined in Puccini's opera *La Bohème*. The film is also nourished by the Romantic idea that concert pianists are somehow "different" and on a higher plane than ordinary mortals (though that kind of elitism is distinctly middle-class rather than aristocratic). Schlesinger presents "classical" music as a kind of religion for initiates only, which is a supremely Romantic idea, originally fostered by E.T.A. Hoffmann and Robert Schumann in the nineteenth century. There is consequently very little music by any but Romantic composers in the film. Gluck is the only notable exception. Like the echo of his Dance of the Blessed Spirits from *Orpheo ed Euridice* in the title music of *Theatre of Blood* (dir. Douglas Hickox, 1973), classical music becomes a symbol of an esthetic that is now out of date. (In Hickox's film, Vincent Price plays an actor-manager of the old school, out of sympathy with the 1970s, just as Madame Sousatzka finds herself alienated by the 1980s.) When piano prodigy Manek Sen (Navin Chowdhry) gives his first public concert, it is appropriately with a performance of Schumann's Romantic A-minor Piano Concerto.

This overall esthetic accounts for the choice of the piano as the film's featured instrument. A flute or even a violin would not support the Romantic message anywhere near as successfully. Music is to be worshipped, and the piano becomes a shrine, before which one invokes the muses. "Caress the phrases," Sousatzka urges her charge, in much the same way that Margaretta Scott's Danielle Ryman encourages her psychopathic son in *Crescendo* (1970), Alan Gibson's psychological thriller for Hammer ("That's right, my darling. That's right. Strong declamatory chords leading into the appassionata.")

Money is also deemed vulgar in this temple of music. When Manek performs at a commercial music festival, Madame Sousatzka is horrified, which is an absurdly Romantic reaction, as musicians have always needed to make money. To cap this naïvely middle-class perspective, Schlesinger employed the BBC arts presenter Humphrey Burton to play himself as a BBC Radio 3 presenter during the relay of Manek's big concert.

All the practice clichés are also here. Manek begins as a confident show-off, and is soon cut down to size by Madame. After working for hours on the same piece, he begins to attain beauty through suffering, which, according to Madame, is the only way. "Begin. I want you to forget everything you've ever learnt. Begin with the C major scale. You don't have to impress me with how clever you think you are. You move around far too much, Mr. Virtuoso." Madame Sousatzka believes that music comes not from the fingers ("ten poor little worms") but from the abdomen, "and it rises higher and higher from the depths of your very soul. Higher and higher from your deepest instincts to the height of reason." While expounding all this mumbo jumbo, which would perhaps be more appropriate for a singer, she fingers Manek in a manner that might cause politically correct parents of today some concern. Later, when he's studying the Chopin C minor Prelude, Sousatzka manically munches a biscuit and creeps around the piano muttering, "Pianissimo ... now, very, *very* soft" (which is what "pianissimo" means). "Remember the position of the shoulder! ... Just a vibration...." She advances vampire-like upon Manek, her hands like claws as she swallows her biscuit, purses her lips and stares at her pupil, before feeding him another biscuit like a well-trained dog.

The next scene shows Manek practicing one of Mendelssohn's *Songs Without Words*, with Madame shouting, "No! Allegro! Allegro! No! It's too heavy!" thus confusing tempo with intonation. Manek then receives more meaningless commands: "Don't collapse the fingers! You sound like an old man shuffling in his slippers!" None of this means very much, especially as the Song Without Words in question (Op. 67, No. 4) is actually marked "Presto," not "Allegro." But pedantry is not what this film is about. Rather we are in the territory of Svengali: music as a mystical process, and practice as a religious rite. Madame Sousatzka is another Svengali, which is perhaps why she talks about the abdomen to a pianist.

Phantoms

In George du Maurier's *Trilby*, Svengali teaches a singer. Like Dr. Terwilliker, Svengali practices hypnosis. He also lives in poverty, a prerequisite for the Romantic artists who scorn bourgeois comfort and mediocrity. According to du Maurier,

> He was not a nice man. He had but one virtue—his love of his art; or rather, his love of himself as a master of his art—*the* master; for he despised, or affected to despise, all other musicians, living or dead—even those whose work he interpreted so divinely. ... He had been the best pianist of his time at the Conservatory in Leipsic.[5]

Svengali's hypnotic mantra is: "And you shall see nothing, hear nothing, think of nothing but Svengali, Svengali, Svengali!"—to which John Barrymore brought an equally hypnotic stare when he performed the role in Archie Mayo's 1931 *Svengali*. Svengali also influenced Gaston Leroux's Erik, the infamous and tyrannical music teacher known as the Phantom of the Opera, who first appeared on the scene in 1910, 16 years after *Trilby*. Whereas Svengali is a Jew, Erik is one of Nature's freaks, a hideously deformed genius who presides over his lair below the Paris Opera House, playing on the organ his own "Don Juan Triumphant" when not instructing the unfortunate young singer who has fallen into his clutches. His cinematic offspring are many: the several adaptations of the novel, of course, but also Dr. Phibes, as played twice by Vincent Price, and the other tortured maestros we meet in films such as *Dangerous Moonlight, Crescendo, Hangover Square* (dir. John Brahm, 1945), *The Hands of Orlac* (dir. Robert Weine, 1924), *The Kiss of the Vampire* (dir. Don Sharp, 1963) and *The Mephisto Waltz*.

Though the Phantom plays the organ rather than the piano, the organ keyboard reminds us of the piano, and Erik also shares in common with so many cinematic pianists the desire to dominate, the ability to subdue others to his will, psychopathic tendencies that lead to murder, mad genius and, most of all, a profound alienation from society. Erik is the archetypal music teacher—a tyrant who lives solely to dominate both his muse and his interpreters. A demonic composer, his disfigurement symbolizes his genius. Both signify his aloof distance from mediocrity. He is insane—criminally so—and according to Romantic ideology, insanity is the ultimate badge of inspiration. In fact, few of the great nineteenth-century Romantic composers were clinically insane. Schumann and Hugo Wolf were indeed certified, thanks to syphilis, and Scriabin might have been if he had lived long enough, but the rest were eminently sane. (Tchaikovsky was a depressive but quite rational.) Mental instability does affect some performers (one thinks of the pianist John Ogden in the twentieth century) but this too is rare. A concert pianist must be that rare combination of sensitivity, physical resilience and mental strength. There is little room for Phantoms of the Opera or anywhere else in real life; but Erik is a particularly resonant personification of the myth. He epitomizes the Romantic ideal of divine afflatus being visited to the socially exceptional, the inspired individual who does not conform to the standards of bourgeois life.

To demonstrate his difference, Erik sleeps in a coffin, like Sarah Bernhardt; the notes of the *Dies Irae* are incorporated in the decoration of his underground lair; he keeps apart from others, composing his masterpiece *Don Juan Triumphant* in private. "I sometimes work at it for 14 days and nights together," he explains, "during which I live on music only, and then I rest for years at a time."[6] Erik is the ultimate Romantic anti-hero: a virtuoso without an audience. It is for others to perform his work before the gawping multitude. He remains behind his mask, an enigmatic recluse. Erik's function is to create and to instruct. Suffering is essential, and Erik is the epitome of suffering. Music itself makes one suffer. "You see, Christine," he explains to his protégé in Leroux's novel, "there is some music that is so terrible that it consumes all those who approach it."[7] Erik's *Don Juan* "burns." The organ expresses all that his disfigured features and withered body no longer can: his sexual passion.

Lon Chaney's Erik in the 1925 film is the closest any cinematic Phantom ever got to Leroux's conception. Chaney's torturous makeup brought Leroux's description to life: "Know that I am built up of death from head to foot and that it is a corpse that loves you and adores you and will never, never leave you."[8] The only major omission is that in the film, Erik plays only the organ. In the novel, he also has a piano at his disposal, and it is at the piano that he first instructs Christine. The piano was removed in the film in favor of the more Gothic connotations of the organ, and the omission remained with all the remakes. In these (most notably in 1943, starring Claude Rains, and in 1962, with Herbert Lom), the Phantom is a rather more ordinary fellow: a composer who has been hard done by, his music stolen, his face accidentally disfigured. Chaney's Erik is much more demonic. As in Leroux's novel, Erik is *born* this way. He is not the mere victim of accident. He has no rational motivation. Each of these films, however, retains the concept of suffering for one's art, and the tyranny of tuition.

The Phantom of the Opera, therefore, haunts most of the films that feature keyboard virtuosi. Notable among these is *The Seventh Veil*, in which

Chaney reaction: Lon Chaney as Erik in the silent *The Phantom of the Opera*.

James Mason plays Nicholas, a tyrannical misogynist who terrorizes and simultaneously indulges Ann Todd's uptight concert pianist, Francesca, who has a phobia about damaging her hands.

The whole thing starts in a psychiatric hospital, a venue also featured four years before in *Dangerous Moonlight*. Pianists in psychiatric hospitals are really only an update on Erik in his subterranean lair. In *The Seventh Veil*, Francesca wants to kill herself, having burned her hands in a car accident with a man she was thinking of marrying. Her hands are not beyond repair, but her phobia makes her think they are and she attempts suicide by hurling herself into a river. Fished out by a policeman, she is treated by Dr. Larsen, a psychiatrist played by Herbert Lom (yet to interpret the Phantom in the 1962 version). Referencing Salomé's Dance of the Seven Veils, Larsen intends to remove the veils of Francesca's mind to learn what is really troubling her, and under hypnosis he discovers that her relationship with Nicholas has been a complex one. Nicholas himself is lame, a naturalistic equivalent of Erik's disfigurement. He is similarly reclusive, and his instructional relationship with Francesca mirrors that of Erik and Christine.

At first, Geraldine is too frightened of Nicholas to be able to play for him, just as Christine is paralyzed with fright by the Phantom; but Nicholas tempts her innate love of music out by playing the piano himself. He strums through a Chopin Prelude, and before long she is joining in with Mozart's "Facile" C major sonata. Francesca herself explains what happened next:

Mind control: Ann Todd and James Mason in *The Seventh Veil*.

Nicholas made me practice four or five hours a day. He was always beside me now, listening to everything I did. It was terribly hard work but Nicholas saw to it that I didn't shirk one minute of it. He was a slave driver, but he was a wonderful teacher too. He knew instinctively how to get the best out of me, and he knew more about the spirit of music than any man I have ever met.

Though theirs is not a sexual relationship, it is, psychologically speaking, sadomasochistic. Geraldine both loves and hates Nicholas: "I'm grateful for some of the things you've done for me," she confesses to him, "but I'll never forgive you for some of the others." When she fell in love with a fellow student at the Royal College of Music, Nicholas slapped her face and locked her in her room, putting all possibility of marriage out of the question by taking her on a long European tour. Principal among Nicholas' other misdemeanors was his jealous rage over the second boyfriend in her life. This inspired him to smash his walking stick over Geraldine's hands while she was playing the slow movement of Beethoven's "Pathètique" Sonata:

> Francesca, I've always treated you as though you were my own daughter. All the love and sympathy I have had, I've given to you. My life hasn't been a happy one. I've not told you about it and I'm not going to tell you now, but you are the one beautiful thing that's been in my life and I can't live without you, you must know that. I can't give you up. I won't give you up. You're a

great artist. Great artists don't just happen, they have to be made and I've made you. I've spent ten years training you, molding you, you've been my life's work and now you're going to throw it all away on a man who doesn't even want to marry you. Francesca, listen to me! You can't stand up against me. You haven't got the strength. You'll do as I say. I demand that you give up this man! I demand that you send him away! ... You belong to me. We must always be together. You know that, don't you! Promise you'll stay with me always. Promise!

However, when the seventh veil is removed and Geraldine is finally cured of her dilemma, it is to Nicholas that she runs. Their relationship is astonishingly like that of Christine and Erik in Leroux's novel. The other man who loves Christine, Raoul, shouts: "Why, you love him! Your fear, your terror, all of that is just love, and love of the most exquisite kind, the kind which people do not admit even to themselves. ... The kind that gives you a thrill, when you think of it."[9] The Christine of the Chaney film is less in love with Erik than he is with her, it is true, especially after she has unmasked him, but Erik is just as possessive of Christine as Nicholas is of Geraldine. The Phantom rants:

[R]emember, you are mine—mine—and you shall not see your lover again. If you do it is death to you both!

Erik has "created" Christine just as Nicholas creates Geraldine: "To you I have imparted the full measure of my art," Erik insists. "You will triumph—all Paris will worship you! But I warn you, you must forget all worldly things and think only of your career—and your Master! Soon, Christine, this spirit will take form and command your love!"

Erik is not only a master of his art but also a master in the sense of being a control freak with a desire to possess. He watches Christine from his opera box with the eyes of a stalker, just as Nicholas watches Geraldine perform Rachmaninoff's Second Piano Concerto from backstage like a puppet master. Geraldine is frightened of Nicholas because he knows what she's thinking and what she's going to do: "He has some extraordinary power over me."

The controlling impulse behind these teacher-pupil relationships is reflected by the obsessive nature of piano practice itself, to the point of excluding everything else. Erik's command that Christine must forget all worldly things is echoed in *The Seventh Veil* by a montage sequence that symbolically compresses the seven-year European tour on which Nicholas takes Geraldine. Her fingers moving up and down the keyboard are virtually masticated by the black-and-white teeth of the voracious musical beast that is a grand piano. Pages of musical scores are relentlessly turned as the practice persists. For Geraldine, playing becomes an ordeal rather than a pleasure. During her performance of Grieg's Piano Concerto, she frowns and frets, worried about her fingers, ultimately collapsing from shock after the final chords. Performing music is shown here as a sacrificial rite, not unlike the virgin who dances herself to death at the end of Stravinsky's ballet *The Rite of Spring*.

Such antics help us to understand what is really going on in the obsession of so many predominantly middle-class parents, who are so keen for their offspring to develop their musical talents. Musical hoops are set up and the children are encouraged to leap through them. They are subjected to graded examinations like the steps of the staircase leading nowhere in *The 5,000 Fingers of Dr. T.*; but the music is perhaps the least significant part of the process, as so much of the emotional motivation of pedagogy is about the will to power. The pursuit of "classical" music differs from the performance of pop. Pop looks after itself, but classical music must be "nurtured." Its social status is consequently immensely appealing to the socially ambitious. Nicholas is dismissive of popular music in *The Seventh Veil*. He disdainfully calls Geraldine's first boyfriend Peter "the apostle of a new religion: it's called 'swing.'" Of course, the true religion for Nicholas is the classical canon. For him, Peter is a false prophet with none of the social power and psychological hold Nicholas has over Geraldine. (Interestingly, it was in the cinema that the crossover between pop and classical, which we now take so much for granted, was first explored. Nowhere else in 1940s Britain would they have been found side by side as they are here, thanks to Geraldine's jazz-band flame.)

Prodigies

Subsequent films on the subject follow a similar path, even though their outward style might differ. In 1987, Lee Mishkin directed an animated cartoon version of the once astonishingly popular 1948 Capitol Records vinyl disc which told the story of *Sparky's Magic Piano*. Sparky, the reluctant piano pupil, discovers that his piano can play the classical piano repertoire for him, thus not only releasing him from the drudgery of practicing but also turning him into a idolized infant. The film version, which resembles the style of both the original Hanna-Barbera TV series of *Scooby Doo Where Are You!* (1969–1970) and the CBS series *The Archie Show* (1968), has the advantage of star names on the soundtrack, such as Vincent Price (playing Sparky's father Henry), Price's real-life wife Corale Browne and even Tony Curtis, along with ubiquitous Warner Brothers voice artist Mel Blanc. It also reprises the all-important vocoder timbre of the piano itself, which had caused such an impact when first used on the Capitol disc.

Trashy though it is, *Sparky's Magic Piano* says much about popular ideas of pianos, classical music and infant prodigies. On one level, the story is a pretext for introducing the standard piano classics to a young audience. The list of pieces is much as one might expect, but fulsome for all that, including Chopin's "Revolutionary" Etude, *Fantasie-Impromptu*, C-sharp minor Waltz, the Op. 10, No. 4 Étude (described by one of Sparky's elderly female fans as "a terribly difficult piece") and, inevitably, the "Minute" Waltz, which Sparky announces he will play in half a minute (in fact it takes him 50 seconds). Along with all this inevitable Chopin, we have Rimsky-Korsakoff's "Flight of the Bumblebee," Mozart's Sonata in C-major, Beethoven's "Pathétique" and "Moonlight" Sonatas, Rachmaninoff's infamous C-sharp minor Prelude and, when Sparky becomes really famous, Rachmaninoff's *Rhapsody on a Theme of Paganini*, Brahms' A-flat Waltz, Schumann's "Aufschwung," Gottschalk's "The Banjo" and, for Sparky's Hollywood Bowl appearance, the Grieg Piano Concerto.

Alas, Sparky's success goes to his head, and the piano, which always plays appallingly out of tune, grows resentful, eventually refusing to play for the arrogant, ungrateful boy. The hoax is exposed, Sparky's reputation is demolished. But in the end, all is revealed to have been a daydream anyway.

Sparky's original frustration with practice, along with his hated lessons, which are presided over by a sharp-featured female teacher, are fully in accord with Bart's predicament in *The 5,000 Fingers of Dr. T.*, but the story's most vital aspect is the attitude first of his parents and then of his adoring fans. Infant prodigies, particularly of the piano, reveal much about the will to power and our latent utopian yearnings to become perfect—even godlike. John Gray has identified Leon Trotsky as a particularly good example of this ultimately very dangerous way of thinking, which Trotsky believed Communism would bring about:

> Man will become immeasurably stronger, wiser and subtler; his body will become more harmonized, his movements more rhythmic, his voice more musical. The forms of life will become dynamically dramatic. The average human type will rise to the heights of an Aristotle, a Goethe, or a Marx. And above this ridge, new peaks will rise.[10]

Such utopian thinking, which underlies all the yearnings of religion, explains much about the worship of musical prodigies. Mothers with a Madonna complex suddenly discover that they have given birth to a musical Christ, while fathers realize that their income might increase beyond their wildest dreams. (Mozart's father Leopold fell into the latter category, which had negative emotional consequences for them both.) Sparky's story, however, marks him out as a false Messiah—a musical anti–Christ, if you will—who promotes his own counterfeit kingdom in the furtherance of his own will to power.

Sparky's costume changes are also significant. During his first flush of fame, he wears sunshades, a big blue bow tie and a shirt decorated with love hearts, obviously in homage to Elton John (even though his repertoire is strictly "classical"). His greater fame requires more formal evening dress, though exaggerated along Liberace lines.

The ghost of Sparky hovers in a short segment from *Fantasia 2000* (dir. James Algar *et al.*, 1999), in which an infant pianist is shown tackling a virtuoso passage from Gershwin's *Rhapsody in Blue* on an upright piano, while his stern mother or teacher stands, hands folded together, beside him. As the music grows more demanding, the piano stool slides away from the instrument, and the child clings desperately to the keyboard, still playing. The camera then swoops to the floor of the apartment above to reveal a cartoon Gershwin in shirtsleeves continuing the piece on his own piano. That is all we see of the prodigy, but we might not have even had that without the memory of Sparky.

In *Shine* (dir. Scott Hicks, 1996), Geoffrey Rush and Noah Taylor play the real-life Australian virtuoso David Helfgott, who has a far more exploitative father than Sparky. Helfgott's father Peter (Armin Mueller-Stahl) is positively abusive, leading to severe mental problems for his son. Like Leopold Mozart, Peter projects his own violence and sense of failure onto his prodigal son with the aim of redeeming himself. The world of classical music is often exploitative. One of the *Midsommer Murders* TV episodes, "Master Class" (dir. Renny Rye, 2010), concerns just such an environment, which in this case leads to the murders we expect. I also know of a mother who interrupted a pupil's harp lesson at a private school simply to unnerve the student to the extent of making him fail his exam and thus pave the way for her own son's success. When a young person attains a transcendental technique in the already arcane and (some might say) elitist realm of "classical" art music, a great deal of reflected God-like glory becomes available to be enjoyed by those who nurture and promote them. Those who fail to make the grade are, of course, disposable; in the case of "Master Class," they are simply murdered by James Fox's Sir Michael Fielding, who runs his own musical hothouse, and who would no doubt have felt at home in Nazi Germany, where esthetics so often triumphed over morality. (While I was teaching a course on Romantic piano music for Cambridge University, an adult student announced quite shamelessly during a coffee break, "Hitler had the right idea: Keep the people down and the art going.")

When a student at the Royal College of Music, the young Helfgott decides to perform Rachmaninoff's Third Piano Concerto for his graduation piece. His avuncular professor (John Gielgud) attempts to dissuade him: "No one has ever been mad enough ever to attempt the Rach. 3." But young David has madness on his side. "Am I mad enough, professor?" he asks. "Am I?" A montage of manic practice ensues, with all the meaningless metaphors of struggle and triumph. "Think of it as two separate melodies jousting for supremacy," the professor suggests, as the camera swirls around the piano in a whirlwind of afflatus, whisking Helfgott into musical heaven. In the spirit of Wilhelm Busch, Gielgud's professor continues: "Hands are giants! Ten fingers each!" This is not so much the preparation of a concert as musical bungee-jumping. "Performing's a risk, you know. No safety net. Make no mistake, David. It's dangerous. People get hurt." It's also a kind of stunt. As the camera rotates over the mystical musical hieroglyphs that are such a mystery to those who can't read them, the professor adds: "You have to learn to be able to play it blindfolded." This was something Mozart was forced to do as a boy, so when we later see Helfgott actually playing with a blindfold, he is anointed by the spirit of another genius. Gielgud is then reduced to shouting anything to give the impression that he is Helfgott's Erik: "The page, for God's sake. The notes! Would it be asking too much to learn them first?"

"And then forget them," Helfgott adds.

"Precisely," the professor agrees, which fully accords with the audience's need to "feel the feeling" rather than understand the process.

When the professor says, "Just give me the fingering," we cut to a shot of Helfgott rapping his fingers over a tabletop, much as Liszt apparently did with a dummy keyboard on his long travels between venues in his youth. The impression is spiderish, reminiscent of the crawling hand in that other piano classic *The Beast with Five Fingers* (dir. Robert Florey, 1946). *The Seventh Veil* is also fascinated by fingers. But not all piano films are: So many of the actors cast as pianists can't actually play, and so their keyboard maneuverings are hidden from view or replaced by stand-ins. Ann Todd *could* play, and watching her fingers, her hands, her exposed arms, her swaying body and finally her anguished features has an undeniable sexual charge. The subtext in these *Seventh Veil* scenes is that Geraldine is being raped by Nicholas. As we have seen, piano playing is certainly erotic in a way that playing a wind instrument could never be. A trombone can suggest an erection (and detumesence, as it does in Shostakovitch's opera *Lady Macbeth of Mtsenk*) but it is not *sensual* in the way that fingers are when caressing the keyboard. This was fully understood by Gabrielle D'Annunzio, who includes a piano recital in his novel *Il piacere* (*The Child of Pleasure*). The hero, Andrea Sperelli, cannot take his eyes off the pianist's gloves (suggesting a kind of fetishism to which Max Klinger devoted an entire series of etchings in his portfolio *The Glove*):

From time to time, his eyes wandering from the fingers of the pianist to the long gloves hanging from the music stand, which still retained the form of those hands, still preserved an inexpressible charm in the small opening at the wrist where, but a short time ago, a tiny morsel of her soft flesh had been visible.

Maria rose amidst a round of applause. She left the piano, but she did not take away her gloves. Andrea was tempted to steal them.—Had she not perhaps left them for him?—But he only wanted one. As a connoisseur in amatory matters has said, a pair of gloves is a totally different thing from a single one.[11]

The Helfgott fingers are not sensual, however. Obsession is the main thing here. So obsessed with fingering does he become that he burns his toast, and his flat becomes increasingly chaotic. (As the Phantom of the Opera says, "You must forget all worldly things.") The professor now adds that key element already identified by Madame Sousatzka: "You must let it come from here." He pounds his chest. "From the heart." This is what audiences want to hear: not the technical aspects of music or harmonic progressions, not the complexities of cadences and counterpoint, nor aspects of orchestration, not even fingering proper, but that music must come "from the heart."

The professor then casts all discretion to the winds and shouts, "Don't you just love those big fat chords?" which one can hardly imagine Rachmaninoff, who played them so often, ever saying. Rachmaninoff was a model of restraint when it came to the performance of his own and others' music, as is made clear in a *Times* review of a concert he gave in London on May 26, 1908, under Sergey Kusevitsky:

> The direct expression of the work, the extraordinary precision and exactitude of his playing, and even the strict economy of movement of arms and hands which [Rachmaninoff] exercises, all contributed to the impression of completeness of performance. The slow movement was played by soloist and orchestra with deep feeling, and the brilliant effect of the finale could scarcely have been surpassed, and yet the freedom from extravagance of any kind was the most remarkable feature. We wished that all the amateur and other pianists, who delight in producing sensational effects with his prelude in C sharp minor, could have heard the composer playing it as his second encore. His crisp, almost rigid, treatment of it would be a revelation to many.[12]

A greater contrast with *Shine*'s sweat-drenched, disheveled performance could hardly be found. Contemporary audiences, equally drenched in the imagery of rock concerts, want to *see* passion as well as hear it, and they would probably be disappointed by Rachmaninoff's formidable control, if his performances had been captured on film. *Shine* also caters to our love affair with conflict, struggle and victory. Rachmaninoff's methodical approach to practice ("You have to peer into every corner, take every screw apart, so that you can then easily put the whole thing together again"[13]) is in marked contrast to Gielgud's line in *Shine*: "You have to tame the piano, David.... It's a monster. You have to tame it or it will swallow you whole." This is a piano lesson from the perspective of *The Lord of the Rings*. Finally, in another tribute to Liszt, one of Helfgott's piano strings breaks. This rarely happens on a modern iron-framed concert grand, but, as we observed in *Song of Love*, it did happen quite often on the old wooden-framed pianos on which Liszt often performed. We have thus checked all the boxes: the ghosts of the classical tradition, the master of the Romantic one, conflict, "from the heart," otherworldliness, madness and obsession.

The Japanese teen-drama, *Your Lie in April* (*Shigatsu wa Kimi no Uso* [四月は君の嘘], dir. Takehiko Shinjō, 2015), a live-action version of a popular Manga TV series, echoes the clichés of *Love Story*, but is packaged for millennials: A boy suffers a nervous breakdown during an audition, but is redeemed by the influence of an inspirational girl violinist who, we later learn, "has always loved him" from the age of five and who took up the violin because she was so impressed by his piano-playing. Alas, she becomes terminally ill and eventually dies, leading to the final moral about music inspiring love, which, as we know, conquers all.

Hothouse Horrors

There is always room for these Romantic ideas to be reworked, as they are perennial human concerns in the quest for meaning. To make sense of chaos, we use passion to justify struggle, even if we fail, which Helfgott ultimately did (notwithstanding the fact that he had a film made about him). Michael Haenke's *The Piano Teacher* (2001) is another child of *The Phantom of the Opera*. It is set in Vienna with a severely contemporary style rather than the Gothic melodrama of Lon Chaney's film; we nonetheless encounter a tyrannical music teacher who uses music as a way of finding sexual gratification, which her disability has so far denied her. Whereas Erik is disfigured, the intriguingly named piano teacher of Haenke's film, Erika (Isabelle Huppert), is emotionally scarred. Whereas Erik's face was a screaming skull, Erika's is a blank death mask. She rarely smiles (neither did Ann Todd's Geraldine), her whole life, like Erik's, is wrapped up in music to compensate for a loveless life spent living with her domineering mother. Her sexual repression manifests itself in sadomasochism and self-harm. She controls her latest pupil Walter Klemmer (Benoît Magimel) in much the same way that Erik controls Christine and Nicholas controls Geraldine. The sex scenes here convey the activities of porn: handjobs, fellatio, humiliation, sex in toilets—all those things that Chaney kept below

Masterclass: Isabelle Huppert and Benoît Magimel in *The Piano Teacher*.

the surface in favor of facial horror, and which Geraldine confined to the keyboard. The dynamic is exactly the same, however. Erika also indulges in sabotage, again like Erik. Erik lets loose the chandelier of the Paris Opera House, while Erika contents herself with putting broken glass in the coat pocket of another student, Anna (Anna Sigalvitch), whom Walter has had the audacity to court. Anna's fingers are sufficiently lacerated to prevent her from performing at a concert.

Overly ambitious parents are also exposed in *The Piano Teacher*. Anna's mother, like Erika's, uses music to promote her own social mobility. Because classical music, particularly in Vienna, is the pinnacle of cultural aspiration, to attain it, even at second hand, is to have "arrived." Again, it is power (social, sexual and psychological), not music, that this film is really all about. *The Piano Teacher* is consequently quite rightly a rather unpleasant film, bleak rather than baroque, mean rather than melodramatic, but in essence no different from the ultimate meaning of *The Phantom of the Opera*.

Similarly, Sophy Laloy's 2009 film *You Will Be Mine* (the original title is more cannibalistic: *Je te mangerais*, "I will eat you") concerns a psychotic lesbian relationship between music student Marie (Judith Davis) and medical student Emma (Isild Bordeu). Not only does this story suggest that homosexual women are unstable and even dangerous but, perhaps even more tellingly, that classical pianists are deranged too—a trope we can again trace back to the Phantom via *Hangover Square* (see below). There are no murders here, but the combination of neurotic gay sex with pianos is just another layer on top of the already well-established idea of the alienation of the artist from bourgeois norms in general, and the "strangeness" of classical music in particular. Lesbians also feature in Denis Dercourt's *The Page Turner* (2006), in which Mélanie (Déborah François), a failed pianist, works at a law firm where she encounters the husband of the pianist, Ariane (Catherine Frot), who examined her some years before. Midway through her audition for Ariane, an admirer appears and asks for Ariane's autograph. This is highly unlikely, but it generates the plot. The interruption distracts Mélanie, who promptly gives up her hopes of the concert platform; but she never forgets her resentment for the famous pianist. When she becomes a friend with her new employer's family, she uses her ability to turn pages so well to ingratiate herself with Ariane, who grows to depend on her emotionally; and this is all part of Mélanie's plot to seduce and then abandon Ariane in revenge for her humiliation at that years-ago audition. There are elements of Henri-Georges Clouzot's *Les diaboliques* (1955) and Roman Polanski's *Repulsion* (1965), but more significantly, it is the central image of the piano that generates the sense of unease: Those who play it are unstable, not to be trusted, easily led astray and dangerous. Mélanie is Erik's great granddaughter.

The trauma of breaking down during a piano audition also generates the plot of Phil Dorling and Ron Nyswaner's 2012 comedy *Why Stop Now?* Other films have pursued the parent-prodigy syndrome. *Vitus* (dir. Fredi M. Murer, 2006) concerns Vitus (played by Fabrizio Borsani and Teo Gheorghiu at the ages of 6 and 12 respectively), who dislikes being a prodigy and wants merely to be ordinary. His parents think otherwise, as parents have so often thought in the past when presented with a gifted child. Vitus would much rather be a pilot, which good fortune later brings about, but the scenes featuring Vitus playing the piano are what the film is really about: the wonder others feels for a musical ability, which the owner of it takes for granted. In one scene, Vitus plays his black grand wearing a jacket and tie, signaling the social conservatism of classical music, and it is this connotation that drives some filmmakers to go against the grain and place musical talent in under-privileged circumstances.

Jenny von Loeben (Hannah Herzsprung), the imprisoned pianist in Chris Kraus' *Vier Minuten* (2006), has been convicted of murder, but unlike George Harvey Bone in *Hangover Square*, is actually innocent. (The real criminal is Jenny's boyfriend, for whom she has been covering.) However, the union of crime and art explored in *Hangover Square* is a particularly resonant one for a German film director to explore, given the Nazis' interest in the arts as tools of propaganda. (Flashbacks to Nazi times, accompanied by a Schubert piano Impromptu, occur in the film relating to the past of Jenny's prison piano teacher, Traude Krüger [Monica Bleibtreu].) Thomas Mann also made many references to the relationship between art and crime. In "Tonio Kröger," he tells of a banker who was imprisoned and "it was actually first *in prison* that he became conscious of his gift" as a writer:

> And his experiences as a convict are the main theme of all his works. One might be rash enough to conclude that a man has to be at home in some kind of jail in order to become a poet. But can you escape the suspicion that the source and essence of his being an artist had less to do with his life in prison than they had with the reasons that *brought him there*? A banker who writes—that is a rarity, isn't it? But a banker who isn't a criminal, who is irreproachably respectable, and yet writes—he doesn't exist.[14]

The Jenny of *Vier Minuten* is also the victim of her overly ambitious father, who raped her as a child when she resisted his attempts to enroll her in musical competitions; and the relationship she has with Krüger is again comparable with *Phantom of the Opera*, being authoritarian and possessive. Kraus is keen to show us genuine blood on the keyboard, along with graphic prison violence, including the burning of Jenny's hands by fellow prisoners jealous of her "prodigy" privileges. Fingers are also crushed by a slammed piano lid, reminding us of Louis Gottschalk's terrible ordeal, not to mention Tom the cat's at the hands of Jerry the mouse. Krüger demands complete obedience from her pupil, referring to her experimental way of using the piano as "Negro music," which she forbids. But this strumming of the strings with her fingers, drumming on the wood casing of the piano, and playing violent note clusters with the flat of her hand (all reminiscent of Henry Cowell's experiments in the 1920s) triumph in the end, when she is given the opportunity to perform at a concert. A prison guard assists in her escape, but with the police in pursuit, she has only four minutes to play before they arrest her again—hence the title of the film. Beginning with the opening of Schumann's Piano Concerto (the planned repertoire for the event), she then launches into a virtuosic demonstration of her "Negro music" to a standing ovation; but her triumph comes after so much suffering—and it was all set in motion by an overly ambitious, abusive parent. The film's portrayals of psychological torment and body horror again suggest *Phantom of the Opera* as a distant progenitor.

The body horror of the Phantom, along with his pedagogical meaning, was magnified in *The Perfection* (dir. Richard Shepard, 2019). Here, the pursuit of musical perfection through suffering reaches its logical if horrific conclusion in an elite musical academy where students are gang-raped if they make any mistakes during their performances. To save her cellist friend Lizzie (Logan Browning) from this fate, Charlotte (Alison Williams) arranges a complex plot involving hallucinogenic drugs, which ends in Lizzie chopping off her own hand. Thus mutilated, she will not be able to perform and thus will escape the rape.

Keyboard Killers

Graphic violence is often exploited for its comic potential, comedy being largely about the misfortunes of others. The creators of Warner Brothers' cartoons were well aware of the curious affinity pianos have with violence. The joke was simple, but always effective: an explosive device is triggered by the depression of a particular key. MGM's *The Cat Concerto* had used a similar idea with the mousetrap Jerry places on Tom's keyboard, but the idea goes back a couple of years to a U.S. Army animated training film, made for the Army by Warners and featuring Private Snafu. In *Booby Traps* (dir. Robert Clampett, 1944), Snafu leaps onto a piano stool and plays "Believe Me If All Those Endearing Young Charms," but he keeps missing the booby-trapped note by a semitone. An automaton of Hitler then plays the correct tune to him on a triangle and Snafu rushes back to the piano only to blow himself up. Now an angel on a cloud playing a harp, he consoles himself: "Well, at least up here I don't have to worry about no booby-traps." He plucks the same tune on his harp and blows himself up again.

What started life as a warning against very real wartime dangers soon became a running Looney Tunes gag. In *Ballot-Box Bunny* (dir. Friz Freleng, 1951), Yosemite Sam tries it out on Bugs, with the expected but always hilarious consequences. *Show-Biz Bugs* (Friz Freleng, 1957) replaced the piano with a xylophone. "When he strikes this note, instead of a xylophone he'll be playing a harp," Daffy explains, while connecting the TNT. Wile E. Coyote hopes the same trap will kill the Road Runner in *Rushing Roulette* (dir. Robert McKimson, 1965). "Learn to play the piano FREE here," reads a sign in the middle of the desert. Road Runner takes up the offer but keeps playing the wrong note, which prompts Coyote, like an infuriated piano teacher, to demonstrate how it should be done. After the explosion, his mouth is filled with rotating piano keys.

A variation on this theme propels the plot of Eugenio Mira's *Grand Piano* (2013). Absurd though this plot is, it does have some serious things to say about stage fright and the pressure of attaining perfection. Pianist Tom Selznick (Elijah Wood) is in danger of assassination while performing a virtuoso piece by a deceased composer. A message on his sheet music informs him that if he makes a mistake during this performance, he will be killed; a red laser dot demonstrates that a sniper is watching him. Within the piano, a locked compartment holds the key to the deposit box wherein the composer's fortune is secured; only a flawless performance will open the compartment. The composer's assistant, who helped him create the complex mechanism, now wants the money, but as he cannot play the piece himself, it is up to Tom to play it for him.

All this is what Hitchcock referred to as a MacGuffin. The real purpose of the film is to explore the nature of performance itself: the desire for perfection, the stress of attaining it and the need to slay the audience before it slays you. I have often played a similar game when practicing a piece: What if a wrong note were actually to kill me? It is quite an incentive to get things right. Tom's would-be assassin is a personification of the audience as well as another kind of Phantom. Needless to add, the way in which this film's grand piano is photographed emphasizes the coffin-black of the modern grand, along with the almost dental nature of the keyboard which threatens to devour him.

Being a MacGuffin-based thriller, the film inevitably owes much to Hitchcock's example, in particular the scene in *The Man Who Knew Too Much* (1956) in which Doris Day performs, for the second time in the film, "Que Sera Sera," accompanying herself on another shiny black grand piano. This instrument is situated in an embassy building, and Day's character, Jo Conway, uses the performance to let her kidnapped son Hank know she is in the building. Hank has been abducted to prevent his parents from revealing what they know about a plot to assassinate a V.I.P., and Jo's anxiety as she performs the song foreshadows Tom Selznick's distress on seeing the red lazar dot on his musical score. Indeed, music in general is strongly associated with assassination in Hitchcock's film, as the attempt to kill the Moroccan prime minister occurs during a performance of Arthur Benjamin's "Storm Clouds Cantata" at the Royal Albert Hall in London, conducted by the film's composer, Bernard Herrmann.

The same general idea informed David Miller's lesser-known espionage thriller *Hammerhead* (1968). This involves an imposter who has been employed to steal military information in the possession of the British ambassador, Sir Richard (Michael Bates). Sir Richard and his wife (Kathleen Byron) arrive at the concert hall where their son, young Brian (Earl Younger), is to perform David Whitaker's sub–Rachmaninoff–style concertante piece. Before that is due to start, the ambassador just has time to attend a secret security meeting to discuss his missile defense plans. Having settled his wife in her seat and assured Brian that he will be back in plenty of time to hear his performance, he sets off for the meeting, unaware that Kit (Diana Dors), who has a microphone concealed in her lipstick, is watching his every move. She coughs into her device to communicate with her boss Hammerhead (Peter Vaughan), the mastermind behind all this skullduggery. Sir Richard is chloroformed, the imposter puts on the ambassador's clothes, attends the meeting in his place, reads the information into a concealed tape recorder and then proceeds to the concert hall, by which time Brian has begun to play his Bechstein grand.

Whitaker also included a concertante piano in the final cue of his score for *Dr. Jekyll and Sister Hyde* (dir. Roy Ward Baker, 1971). A piano is not involved in the plot, but Whitaker felt that a piano was the obvious choice to accompany what he described as "the dramatic moment."[15] Fritz Lang would no doubt have agreed with him, as he used a grand piano to bring his 1928 spy drama *Spione* to a climax. Being a silent picture, we have to imagine the sound of the instrument (unless a live pianist provides it for us, of course), but Lang suggests the sound visually by having the front section of the lid removed, allowing large cut-outs of musical notes to protrude from the sound board and fan out over the keyboard at which Rudolf Klein-Rogge, as the espionage mastermind Haghi, performs a mock recital disguised as a vaudeville clown. Police enter the auditorium and surround him. Realizing there is no escape, he shoots himself in the head, bringing the film to an equally abrupt end.

Rehearsing and Composing

Henrik Ibsen's play *A Doll's House,* which has been filmed several times since its premiere in 1879, contains an important rehearsal scene featuring a piano. Nora, the wife of Torvald Helmer, has a guilty secret. To raise money for a trip to improve her ailing husband's health, she took an illegal loan from the unscrupulous Krogstad. Nora had to forge her own father's signature as surety (married women at this time not being permitted to engage in such transactions). Krogstad uses this fact to blackmail Nora. He will expose her unless she manages to persuade her husband to promote him to a higher position in the bank where they both work. When Nora fails in this, Krogstad writes a letter to Torvald explaining the situation. The letter lands in the locked letterbox behind the front door of their home and waits there like the sword of Damocles. Torvald, meanwhile, wishes to rehearse Nora's moves in the Tarantella she is to perform at a social gathering that evening, and Nora, beside herself with anxiety, dances with increasing enthusiasm, in a desperate attempt to distract her husband from collecting his letters. Nora ultimately realizes that her entire life with Torvald has been a sham, that she never loved him, and that to find out who she really is and what she really wants from life, she must leave everyone— including her children—behind. The door slams behind her, echoing, as it did, across Europe.

The rehearsal scene encapsulates the whole of her dilemma, not least the obedient way in which she has submitted to instruction from Torvald all through their marriage. She is now quite literally dancing to his tune. Ibsen's stage directions require the piano to play an important role in this scene. As the "altar of the home" and a symbol of bourgeois respectability, its symbolism is particularly powerful here. As first, Torvald plays (again, Ibsen takes it for granted that an educated middle-class man would be able to), but Dr. Rank soon takes over, to give Torvald more opportunities to watch his wife's moves:

> [RANK sits down at the piano and plays. NORA dances more and more wildly. HELMER has taken up a position beside the stove, and during her dance gives her frequent instructions. She does not seem to hear him; her hair comes down and falls over her shoulders; she pays no attention to it, but goes on dancing.]

"My dear darling Nora," says Torvald, "you are dancing as if your life depended on it," as indeed it does—at least her former life.

This is one of the piano's most famous rehearsal scenes, but one in which the pianists are not women, as one might expect in such a domestic setting. In 1973, *A Doll's House* was filmed twice. In Patrick Garland's version, Claire Bloom and Anthony Hopkins take the leading roles; Joseph Losey's version stars Jane Fonda and David Warner. Hopkins (playing Torvald) had the advantage of being able to play the piano. After only a few bars Rank (Ralph Richardson) takes over, at which point Torvald says that in not playing the piano, "it'll make it much easier for me to control her." It is one of Ibsen's most telling lines.

Rehearsals are a form of control, the director and music director exerting their will over the performers, who may creatively retaliate. Ideally, the process should be collaborative. An enjoyable example of a piano rehearsal can be found in Tony Palmer's *Wagner*, in which Richard Burton's Wagner puts Gwyneth Jones' Malvina von Carolsfeld and Peter Hoffmann's Schnorr von Carolsfeld through their paces as the first-ever Tristan and Isolde. Singing to piano accompaniment, they explore the famous love duet, which Wagner continually interrupts. "No, no, no. Look, if you look after the little notes, the big ones will look after themselves. So try it again now. No, no, no. 'Bist du mein?' Do you realize what it means? 'Art thou mine?' It's a confession of love! Let's have some passion in it! Now, try it again." Malvina looks doubtfully at her husband and Wagner, who continues:

> Just remember the words. Remember what the words mean. Forget the music for a second. Just look at the words. You must remember that the words are equally as important as the music. It is, after all, meant to be poetry. I hope it is poetry, so let us think of the words and the meaning will then be perfectly obvious to the audience. We mustn't just get mellifluous like those funny Italian operas. Let's try again.

The piano resumes. Later: "I don't know whether your voices are tired, but you're shouting now, you're not singing, you're shouting."

"But it's so high, Meister. We're almost forced to," Malvina complains.

"If you can't sing the top C, we'll find someone who can sing the top C, shall we?" Wagner threatens.

"Well, I think you'll find it rather difficult!" Malvina protests.

"Well, let's not lose our tempers," Wagner insists, on the verge of losing his own. "Let's try again!"

In fact, Wagner found the process of rehearsing this particular music-drama very rewarding, as with just piano accompaniment he could indeed hear all the words. (The huge orchestra he calls for in the full score often obliterates them.) With just a piano accompaniment, everything was clear.

Pianos also regularly feature in the "backstage" scenes of Hollywood musicals, which are so often about the mounting of a production rather than the production itself. A notable comparison with Ibsen's earlier rehearsal scene, also set in a parlor, occurs in *Easter Parade,* in which Fred Astair's Don Hewes auditions Judy Garland's Hannah Brown while operating a pianola, which plays the accompaniment to Irving Berlin's "I Love a Piano." At first Don is unimpressed by Hannah's talents, but he changes his mind when he watches her dance. They then dance together, and a change of key transports them to the stage on which they interact with a diminutive white upright: Hannah sits on top of it while Don pushes it off stage. The comparisons with Ibsen end here, however, as they eventually get happily married.

Astaire was no mean pianist himself, and often played pianos in his film musicals. He demonstrated what he liked to call "dirty" stride piano in *Roberta* (dir. William A. Seiter, 1935), introducing his dance routine with a performance of Jerome Kern's melody on white grand piano amid the expected art deco splendor. In *Follow the Fleet* (dir. Mark Sandrich, 1936), he wears a sailor's uniform, smokes a cigarette and tunes an upright, with all the hammers exposed, before he sits down on a barrel to strum out "I'm Putting All My Eggs in One Basket" in another "backstage" number. In Norman Taurog's *Broadway Melody of 1940*, Astaire sits at another upright to accompany himself in a rendition of Cole Porter's "I've Got My Eyes on You," incorporating the instrument into his tap routines by hitting the side of the piano with his feet. Again the scene is played "backstage," Astaire performing to himself, so to speak, though he is secretly being watched by Eleanor Powell.

Astaire's partnership with the piano reached its peak in 1950 when, in *Let's Dance* (dir. Norman Z. McLeod), his choreographic interaction with it makes any need for a human partner redundant. Again in a rehearsal environment, with a black grand piano being played by someone else, Astaire executes his routine, hanging from the open lid, swinging himself under the instrument, climbing inside, draping himself over the lid, dancing onto of it, and sliding down the slope of the lid before moving over to an upright, which he plays himself (hammers again exposed). His fingers now take over from his legs, dancing, as they do quite literally, over the keys before he once more dances on top of the piano, using the lid as punctuating percussion, and hitting the side of the instrument with his foot. He then moves back to the grand, executing glissandi with his feet while standing atop it. Surreally, a group of cats emerge screeching from the piano before he finally slams the lid as the piece comes to an end.

The piano also makes its seemingly inevitable appearance in Ken Russell's much more British perspective on the musical in *The Boy Friend* (1972). In a tribute to Astaire, one of the dancers (Antonia Ellis as Masie) leaps onto this battered old upright at the end of "Won't You Charleston with Me," though with considerably less grace than the American star; and Russell also references the style of his beloved Busby Berkeley in the many dance routines, one of which features a chorus line of girls wearing skirts decorated with piano key patterns. More importantly, the action takes place on three levels: the backstage drama of the performers, the onstage performance of the musical of *The Boy Friend*, which takes place in a provincial theater on a wet afternoon, glamorous fantasy sequences, which bring to life the dreams of the characters with idealized versions of their dance numbers. To emphasize the contrast between these fantasy scenes and the somewhat seedy reality of theatrical life, Russell deliberately makes the stage production feel more like a rehearsal: Not only is the matinée audience very thin, but the score is also performed by piano and percussion, and a somewhat out-of-tune upright piano at that. Played by a simpering pianist (Peter Greenwell) who clenches a cigarette holder between his teeth, the piano accompaniment echoes the long-standing practice of the rehearsal répétiteur, which we see realized in Herbert Ross's 1980 *Nijinsky*.

Pianos are usually present in cinematic rehearsal scenes. In *The Tender Trap* (dir. Charles Walters, 1955), Frank Sinatra sits at a battered upright in a rehearsal room to demonstrate how to sing the title song, after Debbie Reynolds has sung it with what Sinatra calls "surface schmaltz." Sinatra takes it much slower: "You see what I mean? You just have to let it settle a little." Instruction over, they go off for lunch, Sinatra ending the scene with a glissando. Unlike Astaire, Sinatra isn't actually playing the piano here, but he does pick out the notes we see at the end of *Pal Joey*, at the beginning of the final number, "What Do I Care for a Dame?" The camera then rushes over the keys to cover an orchestral glissando, leading us into the routine. The process is reversed at the end, after which Sinatra's Joey slams the lid shut.

In *Deception*, Claude Rains' arrogant composer, Alexander Hollenius, rehearses his new cello concerto, playing the orchestral part on the piano

Appassionata: Bette Davis plays Beethoven in *Deception*.

in his opulently appointed home as Paul Henreid's cellist, Karel Novak, plays the solo part. Pianos play an important role in this film in general, as Bette Davis' Christine Radcliffe performs the opening of Beethoven's "Appassionata Sonata" during the party that celebrates her marriage to Novak. (Davis went to the considerable trouble of learning it especially for the film.) The occasion is all too "appassionata" for Hollenius, who has fallen possessively in love with Christine. Listening to her playing Beethoven on such an occasion causes him to crush his champagne glass and cut his hand. Erich Wolfgang Korngold, who wrote both *Deception*'s underscore and Hollenius' potted cello concerto (later expanded into Korngold's Op. 37 C-major Cello Concerto), also includes a concert grand as part of the orchestration. We see it in the orchestral rehearsal scene reduced to a mere member of the orchestra, as pianos were by so many other twentieth-century composers.

We don't observe Hollenius actually composing, though Christine does burst into his music room just as he is playing the furious final bars of his composition on the piano, wrapped in a dressing gown, his hair ruffled with Wagnerian intensity. Neither do we watch Marius Goring's composer Julius Crasner composing his score of *The Red Shoes* in Powell and Pressburger's 1948 film of that name, but we do see him playing it to Anton Walbrook's impresario Boris Lermontov (loosely based on the great Diaghilev). Lermontov's office in the rooves of the Paris Opera has its own grand piano, of course. While sugaring his breakfast melon, he listens to Crasner's ideas, but Crasner, noting Lermontov's apparent lack in interest, stops playing. "Have you finished already?" Lermontov asks, reminding one of Stravinsky, who played through his score of *The Rite of Spring* on a piano in much the same circumstances to Diaghilev. Stravinsky went on to explain in a well-known film interview that Diaghilev, surprised by 59 repetitions of a particularly disorient chord, "didn't want to offend me; he asked me only one thing, which was very offending. He asked me, 'Will it last a very long time?' I said, 'To the end, my dear! And he was silent.'"

We also see a group meeting between the set designer, choreographer and others, discussing the ballet's production, with Crasner at another grand. Later, a cigarette between his lips, he plays the score to Moira Shearer's Victoria Page during her lunches in Lermontov's office. There are also some rehearsal scenes featuring an upright on stage, with arguments about tempo, along with a ballet class in which a grand piano is even more out of tune than Sparky's famously out-of-tune instrument.

Other films show us the process of composition, which usually takes place at the piano. In 1943's *The Constant Nymph* for example. Joan Fontaine's Tessa is in love with Charles Boyer's Lewis Dodd, who suffers from lack of inspiration. Tessa plays the theme of Lewis' latest piece on the piano, which inspires him to sit down at the keyboard to complete it, the implication being that Love is the key, rather than hard work.

Not all composers have approved of composing at the piano. Berlioz couldn't play the instrument at all, which is one reason why his orchestral music sounds so different from composers who could. He was, in fact, grateful for this apparent handicap:

> My father would not let me take up the piano; otherwise I should no doubt have turned into a formidable pianist in company with forty thousand others. He had no intention of making me an artist, and he probably feared that the piano would take too strong a hold of me and that I would become more deeply involved in music than he wished. I have often felt the lack of this ability. On many occasions I would have found it useful. But when I think of the appalling quantity of platitudes for which the piano is daily responsible—flagrant platitudes which in most cases would never be written if their authors had only pen and paper to rely on and could not resort to their magic box—I can only offer up my gratitude to chance which taught me perforce to compose freely and in silence and thus saved me from the tyranny of keyboard habits, so dangerous to thought, and from the lure of conventional sonorities, to which all composers are to a greater or lesser extent prone.[16]

Schoenberg was appalled when he was once discovered composing at piano, but Ravel actively encouraged Gershwin to use a piano, which he thought the only way to discover new harmonies. Stravinsky also regularly composed at the keyboard and admitted his dependence upon the piano as a compositional tool:

> Whether or not I am a pianist ... the instrument itself is the center of my life and the fulcrum of all my musical discoveries. Each note that I write is tried on it, and every relationship of notes is taken apart and heard on it again and again. The process is like slow motion, or those greatly reduced-in-speed recordings of bird calls.[17]

Film footage exists of Stravinsky seated at the piano strumming one of the famous chords from *The Rite of Spring*: "I like very much this chord. It was rather a new chord, you know: an eight notes chord. The accents were even more new, and the accents were really the foundation of the whole thing."

Whether composers use the piano or not, when it comes to demonstrating such a mysterious and largely abstract process for cinema audiences, directors require some kind of visual symbolism beyond the wielding of a pen, which is why films like to show their composers conceiving their masterpieces at pianos. Not all films do this: Ken Russell's *Mahler* is a case in point. Mahler composed in a hut on Lake Attersee and had recourse to a piano there. Consequently, Russell shows Robert Powell's Mahler writing music at a desk, while simultaneously suggesting that the sounds of nature all around him are "dictating" the score to him.

When Russell turned his attention to Delius in TV's *Song of Summer* (1968), the piano is shown as merely an aid to composition. Blind and paralyzed as Delius became, it was up to his amanuensis Eric Fenby to transcribe his instructions, using the piano as a guide. Russell and his actors (Max Adrian as Delius and Christopher Gable as Fenby) recreate the process vividly. Fenby sits at the grand, while Delius is brought into the room and laid on a chaise lounge opposite. "Now I want you tell me exactly what you think of it," Delius asks. "Now play." Fenby does so.

"It starts off with clarinets and bassoons. Frankly, I don't like that second chord. I don't like the way that fifth is doubled there."

"Well, well, well, go on, then. Yes?"

"I'll play that again for you."

"Well go on—straight on."

"I don't care for the way it's repeated. The music seems to sag there."

"Sag?"

Fenby continues to play and comment on the orchestration. A while later, he confesses, "I feel this is very weak here. It's lacking in taste."

The criticism proves too much for Delius, who asks to be carried away; but the following day, they try again, Fenby at the piano, Delius sitting next to him:

"Now then, Fenby, where were we from yesterday? Cellos and basses."

"Yes, I think it should be an A—cellos and basses."

"Good. Now inner parts! Get your violins a C-sharp. Yes, yes, yes. Play it! Yes, and yes, violas—what have you got in the violas?"

"Well, I've nothing there."

"Well, better get a B-flat there."

Fenby plays.

"Yes, yes!" Delius enthuses. "Play it like that! Yes, yes, a little excitement!"

"Now I'll try and play it all." He plays.

"Yes! Now take your C-sharp to E, second violins. Yes, that's it! Against F-sharp and A, next bar, first violins."

Fenby writes, drops his pencil on the lid of the piano and plays.

"Put a G there."

"Where does the G go?"

"Divide your cellos! G in the first part. Low A in the second. Yes. Add a bassoon there. Write that down!"

"Shouldn't the bass move a little there, Delius?"

"No, no, no, no! Put a pizzicato on the first—no, better on the third beat. Yes, now move your inner parts down a semitone. Bring the oboe in—top A! Triplet on the first beat. Yes, now play it all! No, no! You forgot the pizzicato in the basses." Fenby tries again. "*That's it, Eric.* Very good!"

Rarely has the process of composition and the excitement of creation been so vividly captured on film. All this could, of course, have been done at a desk, but the demonstrations at the piano make the process much more dramatic and easier to comprehend. Again, the piano indeed becomes a kind of altar at which the spirit of music is not only being worshipped but also invoked.

In *Lisztomania*, Russell has Liszt working at an upright in a Chaplinesque pastiche of silent film style. The naïve idiom cleverly suggests the happy days of Liszt's romance with Countess Marie d'Agoult, who persuaded him to retreat from the concert hall and devote his time to composition during their elopement in Switzerland. The idyll did not last, but it encouraged Liszt to take composition seriously—and Liszt always conceived his music at the piano.

His son-in-law, Richard Wagner, as played by Richard Burton, is also shown composing at the piano in Tony Palmer's *Wagner*. We have already encountered Palmer's metaphor of the piano as a kind of musical forge. Later, in Venice, Wagner works on the third act of *Tristan und Isolde* in a lavishly decorated palazzo on the Grand Canal. He sits at the piano, writing his ideas down with a quill pen. Wagner liked to boast that he didn't compose at the piano, but the instrument was nevertheless an essential piece of equipment. In his *Autobiographic Sketch* he confessed, with regard to the composition of his opera *The Flying Dutchman*:

> In order to set about its composition, I required to hire a pianoforte; for, after nine months' interruption of all musical production, I had to try to surround myself with the needful preliminary of a musical atmosphere. As soon as the piano arrived, my heart beat fast for very fear; I dreaded to discover that I had ceased to be a musician. I began first with the "Sailors' Chorus" and the "spinning-song"; everything sped along within me as though on wings, and I shouted for joy as I felt within me that I still was a musician.[18]

Without a piano, he might not have done. Wagner may not have been a very good pianist, but without one he was lost: hence the regular shots of Wagner's Érard Grand being hauled around Europe on a cart in Palmer's epic.

When Palmer turned his attention to Shostakovitch in *Testimony* (1988), he contradicted his own screenplay by showing Ben Kingsley's Shostakovitch composing his Seventh Symphony at an upright piano.

"Where does the music come from?" his daughter asks.

"From my head," he replies.

"From where in your head, Dad?"

"My head is a big round world. Little demons in it open little doors and poke their faces out. Here's a particularly naughty little demon. [*He plays the famous theme from the Seventh Symphony.*] Nobody takes any notice. We think he's friendly, but he gets bigger. Bigger! And *bigger*! Before you know, he's trampling everybody down!"

An earlier scene, however, has Shostakovitch arguing with Robert Stevens' Vsevolod Meyerhold: "With respect, you're wrong, Comrade Meyerhold, I don't orchestrate. I hear. Prokofiev orchestrates from a piano score. I write *for* the orchestra."

Another important appearance of the piano and its role in composing occurs during the discussion on esthetics and musical meaning in Visconti's *Death in Venice*. Mark Burns plays Alfred, the friend of Dirk Bogarde's Gustav von Aschenbach, and Alfred's role is to play devil's advocate. He argues that music has no meaning and consequently no virtue.

> ALFRED: Beauty belongs to the senses—only to the senses.
> ASCHENBACH: You cannot reach the spirit through the senses. You cannot. It's only by complete domination of the senses that you can ever achieve wisdom, truth and human dignity.
> ALFRED: Wisdom? Human dignity? What use are they? Genius is a divine gift—no! no! divine *affliction*! A sinful, morbid flash-fire of natural gifts.
> ASCHENBACH: I reject—I reject the demonic virtues of art!
> ALFRED: And you are wrong! Evil is a necessity. It is the food of genius

Alfred goes over to the grand piano, takes off his jacket and plays a chord.

> ALFRED: Listen to this chord—or this one. You can interpret them in any way you like. You have before you an entire series of mathematical combination [*he plays a glissando*]—unforeseen and inexhaustible: a paradise of double meanings, in which you more than anyone romp and roam about like a calf in clover.

Alfred then starts to play a motif from Mahler's Fourth Symphony, which stands in for one of Aschenbach's own compositions.

Mr. Holland's Opus (dir. Stephen Herek, 1995) begins with piano music on the soundtrack before we see Richard Dreyfuss in the title role composing the eponymous opus on his grand piano. Taking a job as a college professor, he soon learns that his students do not share his passion for the classics. Consequently, after five wasted months, he demonstrates to them that the Toys' hit "Lover's Concerto" is actually based on a minuet by J.S. Bach, and thus does rock'n'roll open the gateway to the masters. He insists: "Playing music is supposed to be fun. It's about heart. It's about feelings and moving people and something beautiful and being alive and it's not about notes on a page."

Most people don't want to know about notes on a page. The technicalities of music are complex, but its effects are immediate and instinctive, and cinema has always been about the immediate and instinctive. As a result, pianos, being the most immediate and recognizable symbol of music, have always been the cinema's primary musical icon.

Seven

Surrogate Pianos

Organs

The organ is a very different instrument from the piano, but because the sound is summoned from a keyboard, it is often regarded as a necromantic piano. The Gothic resonance of the organ in *The Phantom of the Opera* was knowingly echoed in Billy Wilder's *Sunset Blvd.* (1950) in which Gloria Swanson's Norma Desmond is entertained by Erich von Stroheim's butler Max with a performance of the Bach D-minor Toccata and Fugue (again) on the instrument in her Hollywood-Gothic mansion. (When Max is not playing, the wind whistles eerily down the organ pipes instead.) The "abnormal" Gothic resonance of Desmond's organ is emphasized when contrasted with the "normal" upright piano at Artie Green's New Year Party, which William Holden's Joe Gillis joins after life with Norma becomes too much for him.

Sunset Blvd. is a kind of crime story, its narrator (Gillis) is killed at the end, thus making the narration technically "impossible." Crazed by jealousy, Norma Desmond shoots Gillis when she finds out that there is another woman in his life, and leaves his body floating in her swimming pool. *The Phantom of the Opera* is also a great crime story, and Erik's most immediate post-modern descendent in this respect is Dr. Anton Phibes, played in two films by Vincent Price. Phibes is the victim of a car crash which disfigured him just as hideously (if less artfully) as Chaney's screaming skull. Whereas Erik wears a mask (and later, a Death's Head at the Opèra Ball), Phibes reconstructs his face prosthetically. Price's face—"pallid and wan," as Poe would have described it—thus become Phibes' mask: a living face turned into a death mask and able to speak only through a mechanical device attached to a hole in his neck (through which he also takes nourishment).

With Erik as his ancestor, Phibes could never have been a pianist. His instrument has to be the organ; but Phibes is flamboyant (and not a little

Bad phibrations: Vincent Price in the title role of *The Abominable Dr. Phibes*.

camp), and so specializes in organ lollipops. Not for him the over-used Toccata and Fugue in D minor of Bach. *The Abominable Dr. Phibes* (dir. Robert Fuest, 1971) opens with a transcription of "The War March of the Priests" from Mendelssohn's oratorio *Athalie*. Phibes is cloaked in black, his arms aloft like the tentacles of a sea anemone or the billowing lianas of a poisonous vine, as the passage work alternates from one hand to the other. He performs on an organ tricked out with art-deco adornments (the film is set in the 1920s), which rises from the floor of his London mansion, much as many a Wurlizer rose from the basements of London cinemas—and not just London, of course. (We see just such a phenomenon occur in the provincial setting of *Brief Encounter*.)

The organ is appropriate for Phibes because he is meant to be dead. Pianos are for the living—often the psychotic or murderous living, but the living nonetheless. As if to demonstrate the contrast, a grand piano features in Brian Eatwell's designs for the art deco living room of Joseph Cotten's Dr. Vesalius. Vesalius, who was the chief surgeon of the team that attempted (but failed) to save Phibes' wife Victoria, has a son called Lem (Sean Bury). We learn that Lem is a pianist, but we never hear him play. His musical interests are merely part of the plot, and the main purpose of the piano here is to help identify the opposing domains of the living and the dead. It also aids the film's visual sophistication (one of Fuest's main preoccupations).

Phibes performs on his organ alone, much like Erik, though in rather more lavish surroundings. His muse, Vulnavia, does not sing like Erik's Christine, but she does dance with her disfigured sugar daddy, who certainly seems to have no shortage of funds. No expense is spared in his grotesque revenge on the surgeons who failed to save his wife's life (Phibes' car crash occurred as he rushed to her hospital bed).

Of course, the whole thing is a gloriously knowing satire on Leroux's creation, and perfectly suited to Price's equally knowing yet simultaneously disturbing performance. Death has never been such fun as it is when in Dr. Phibes' company, and perhaps only a musician could make it so. The virtuosity of the various deaths he arranges echoes his own virtuosity at the organ manuals. All his plans go like clockwork, which is precisely the mechanism that animates his musical automata (one of which is a piano player). These perform the music Phibes cannot play himself when dancing with Vulnavia. (Phibes is no musical snob and is never averse to syncopation.) The name Vulnavia, with its suggestion of "Vulva," along with the preserved body of Victoria, only emphasizes his connection with Erik, the obsessive necrophile.

As organs are instruments of death, they are most at home in churches, which, being portals of paradise, are also temples of death. The ghostly billowing of air down all those pipes in *Sunset Blvd.* is a deathly sound as well—not so far removed from the disembodied bleat once demonstrated to me at school when a biology master blew down a sheep's larynx; and in the context of a school, particularly a British "public" school of the kind we encounter in Lindsay Anderson's satire of such institutions in *If....* (1968), the organ is positively oppressive in its connotation. Accompanying the boys and masters in their rendition of the hymn "To Be a Pilgrim" in the school chapel, the organ connotes the flattening authority of such an institution, its dominating sonority brooking no opposition to the loyalty and conformity to one's social class, which such schools aim to inculcate and perpetuate.

Harps

If the organ is an instrument of death and fundamentally pessimistic, the harp is nearly always angelic and optimistic, and therefore of less semiotic value to the cinema, despite several honorable exceptions. I bring in harps at this point because the piano is, as Leigh Hunt once described it, "a harp in a box." The iron frames of grand pianos, which tension the strings, do indeed strongly resemble harps, and this similarity, despite the fact that harps have no keyboard, requires us to consider the harp as another surrogate piano. In the Marx Brothers' *A Day at the Races* (dir. Sam Wood,

1937), Harpo Marx gives a graphic demonstration of what I mean. Taking over from his brother Chico at a grand piano, Harpo begins to wreck Rachmaninoff's infamous C-sharp minor Prelude, a joke with real-life inspiration behind it, as he recounted in his book *Harpo Speaks!* Having hired a practice place, Harpo suddenly found he had a noisy neighbor:

> The new guest, whose playing was driving me nuts, was Sergei Rachmaninoff. They were not about to ask him to move.
>
> I was flattered to have such a distinguished neighbor, but I still had to practice. So I got rid of him my own way.
>
> I opened the door and all the windows in my place and began to play the first four bars of Rachmaninoff's Prelude in C-sharp Minor, over and over, *fortissimo*. Two hours later my fingers were getting numb. But I didn't let up, not until I heard a thunderous crash of notes from across the way, like the keyboard had been attacked with a pair of sledge hammers. Then there was silence.
>
> This time it was Rachmaninoff who went to complain. He asked to be moved to another bungalow immediately, the farthest possible from that dreadful harpist.[1]

In *A Day at the Races,* Harpo also wrecks the piano itself, anticipating the nihilistic antics of rock groups like The Who with their penchant for smashing instruments on stage as part of their act. Finally, with the piano in pieces, Harpo removes the iron frame, props it on its side, and begins to play it exactly like a harp.

The way in which music for the harp is notated in orchestral scores is also much the same as it is for pianos. Their parts similarly occupy two staves, usually treble and bass. Harps have also lent the term "arpeggio" to pianos, which use this rippling broken chord effect just as often. Pianos can also execute glissandi, but not quite as elaborately as the harp. On the piano, only two glissandi are possible: a white-note glissando, performing, in effect, a rapid C-major scale, and the potentially flesh-tearing black-note glissando, which is inevitably pentatonic. Harps, however, thanks to the pedal mechanism invented by Sébastien Érard in the early nineteenth century, can create very many more glissandi combinations, permitting all the major, minor and chromatic scales. Once the composer has indicated which pedals should be selected to tighten the relevant strings up a semitone, all he has to do is indicate the glissando execution by means of a diagonal line through the stave, indicating the note on which the glissando is to start and end. The prevalence of glissandi in harp-writing might suggest that the harp is played with a rake rather than the fingers, but the effect is always exhilarating, adding much to the glamor of many an orchestral climax.

The most celebrated appearances of the harp in film are those moments in the Marx Brothers' films when Harpo entertains the audience with his virtuoso impromptus. During these delightful intermissions, the clown usually disappeared and complete concentration and musicianship took over. In *A Night at the Opera* (dir. Sam Wood, 1935), after having hammered a piano for laughs (pretending to slam the piano lid on his fingers, for example—another joke Tom and Jerry would remember), he silences the noisy crowd with a magical harp solo, aided by his own whistling skills. Everyone watches with rapt attention, as they should. In *The Big Store* (dir. Charles Reisner, 1941), he wears eighteenth-century costume and plays his harp before three mirrors. His reflections later take on lives of their own, playing independently, before transferring their allegiances to violin and cello and finally adding some contemporary syncopation to what had started out as Mozart's "Facile" Sonata. In the Marx Brothers' Western comedy *Go West*, Harpo plays a "primitive" harp, while an Indian attempts to join in with his equally "primitive" flute; but Harpo's introductions just keep coming, much to the chief's frustration. Again, syncopation triumphs in the end. In *A Night in Casablanca*, Harpo, like his brother Chico, cannot resist the circus-stunt possibilities of Liszt's Second Hungarian Rhapsody, which he plays straight until again jazzing things up during the "Friska" section. In *Love Happy* (dir. David Miller, 1950), he gives a moving rendition of Stephen Foster's "Swanee River."

All this should not give a false impression: While lending its magic to many an orchestral film score, the harp makes relatively few appearances on screen, and when it does, it is usually in its angelic context. (Harpo's apparent innocence does indeed qualify him for this role.) In *The Bishop's Wife* (dir. Henry Koster, 1947), Cary Grant plays Dudley, a suave angel come to Earth. His mission is to help David Niven's bishop restore relations with his own family, which have been woefully neglected due to his determination to raise money for the restoration of his cathedral. Dudley demonstrates his angelic musical accomplishments in a scene set in the music room of the wealthy Mrs. Hamilton (Gladys Cooper), whose money Dudley intends to direct towards alleviating the pressing needs of the poor. A piano is part of the furnishings here, but it is inevitably the harp toward which Dudley is attracted, and on which he performs a glissandi-laden rendition of a piece called "Lost April." His virtuosity, which is given the full Liberace charm (Cary Grant style), works like all the other magic Dudley organizes throughout the film: Mrs. Hamilton's heart is warmed and the funds pour from it.

Niven was not involved in this scene, but he encountered the harp in a much later film, which he apparently enjoyed filming much less: *Eye of the Devil* (dir. J. Lee Thompson, 1967). Here, another male harpist entertains the guests of Niven's Philippe de Montfaucon, during which

Montfaucon learns that he is expected to sacrifice himself along the lines of Sir James Frazer's *The Golden Bough,* to ensure a successful grape harvest for the family's wine business. The (uncredited) harpist plays the main theme of Gary McFarland's underscore, which lends it a mysterious mood of expectancy and elegance, along with an equally appropriate implication of other-worldliness. The harp is, after all, the quintessential instrument of Heaven. As St. John in "Revelations," 14:2, somewhat tautologically puts it: "I heard the voice of harpers harping with their harps." The fact that we are really about to enter a more demonic arena in the sinister chateau does not disqualify the harp here, as ambiguity is everything in a film of this kind, and this one in particular could perhaps have done with rather more of it.

Another reason that the harp is appropriate for this film is that the origin of the instrument may well go back to the huntsman's bow, the twanging string of which, after the propulsion of the arrow, gave rise to the idea of making music with it. Later in the film, it is the bow and arrow of David Hemmings' hunter, Christian de Caray, which dispatches Montfaucon through the heart. Could the harp recital at the beginning therefore be something of a premonition?

Disney's *Fantasia* also dwells upon the more conventionally feminine connotations of the harps seen in the opening reel amid the predominantly male orchestral players. Two elegant ladies appear (one of whom disposes of her handbag) and take their places at their angelic instruments, between which the compere later appears to introduce the film. During the Toccata and Fugue section, they perform appropriate arpeggios bathed in the blue light of Disney's synesthetic scheme.

By way of balancing the male and female examples we have been discussing, two more examples will complete this brief survey of harp semiotics. The aforementioned *The Angel Who Pawned Her Harp* stars Diane Cilento as an angel sent back to Earth to help various characters who live in the Angel, Islington, district of London. She has no money so pawns her harp and thus enters the lives of those she has been sent to assist. When she plays to the pawnbroker Joshua Webman (Felix Aylmer) and his Irish friend Ned Sullivan (Joe Linnane), Ned says, "What an opportunity, Josh—a real angel playing celestial music, not to mention the stupendous novelty of hearing it while we're still alive." The harp is believed to be by a (fictional) maker called Delmanda, "the only mortal who made harps for angels." The angel's duty done, and everyone living happily ever after, she reclaims her harp and returns to Heaven.

Hansjörg Thurn's 1999 film *The Harpist* begins in the slightly pretentious magical realist style we find in David Rudkin's celebrated BBC-TV dramas *Penda's Fen* (dir. Alan Clarke, 1974) and *Artemis 81*, and ends in rather more like one of Hammer's Grand Guignol psychodramas such as *Paranoiac* (dir. Freddie Francis, 1963). Christien Anholt's aspiring young novelist Ferdinand Rupitsch encounters Irish harpist Rebecca Kennedy (Geraldine O'Rawe). He first sees her on a Lohengrin-like boat, plucking Bach's C-major Prelude like a figure from Tennyson, but she is in fact engaged on a promotional photo-shoot for her latest tour, and this is no more than a publicity stunt. It is, however, love at first sight for Ferdinand, who follows her to Hamburg with the help of a seemingly magical stranger, Henry (Stephen McGann). ButHenry is Rebecca's distinctly incestuous brother, who has escaped from psychiatric hospital and is intent on revenge. This revelation is, however, kept back until much later, Thurn allowing us first to believe in Henry's potentially magical nature. "It hurts to discover that one's angel is merely flesh and blood," Henry remarks to Ferdinand, for that is really what Ferdinand at first believes, the heavenly connotations of the harp greatly enhancing Rebecca's mystery and fascination.

Harpsichords

It is fitting that when Roger Daltrey's Liszt ascends to Heaven at the end of *Lisztomania*, he does not strum a piano, but rather the inevitable harp. Paradise is not the place for passion, the predominant emotion of the piano. The harp is angelic and ethereal but hardly passionate; and it is even more difficult to ascribe passion to the harpsichord, an instrument that more closely resembles the piano, while relying on the harp's plucking of strings. Sir Thomas Beecham's comparison of the harpsichord's timbre to "two skeletons copulating on a corrugated iron roof" lends it a certain necrophilia connotation, but in terms of red-blooded sexual passion, it is nowhere beside the piano. Charles Rosen has expressed this well:

> The importance of the piano was not ... simply its greater sonority, or even its ability to realize dynamic nuances. It was, I think, above all the fact that it was the only instrument that could both realize an entire musical score on its own and at the same time call into play all the muscular effort of the body of the performer. A loud note on the organ requires no extra effort on the part of the performer, and only a minimal increase on the harpsichord is necessary (coupling the manuals to gain more sonority makes the action slightly more resistant). ... With the piano, every increase of sound is felt by the whole body of the pianist, bringing into play back and shoulder muscles. The performer has to cooperate directly in every crescendo and decrescendo: playing the piano is closer to the origin of music in dance than performing on the earlier keyboards that it superseded. The danger of the piano, and its glory, is that the pianist can feel the music with his whole body without having to listen to it.[2]

It is perhaps unfair to compare the harpsichord with the piano, as they are very different instruments. D'Annunzio, for one, was not impervious to the harpsichord's charms. In his short story "Leda Without Swan," written in the 1880s, the narrator attends a harpsichord recital of Scarlatti sonatas, the virtuosity of which inspires a surreal sequence of responsive pseudo–Baroque imagery. The effect is positively cinematic:

> From the shorn grass, from among the symmetrical shrubs, the trimmed box-hedges, from the Naiads' breasts, the Tritons' shells, the dolphins' backs, the cheeks of the bronze frogs squatting beside the benches or at the grottoes' thresholds, from the mouldings of the balustrades along with terraces and ramps, from the domes of the small rotundas and the arches of the covered walks, from every side the jets spurt, leap, whip out, pursue, smite, formidable as swords, as rapiers, as pikes in ambush.
> Ladies and courtiers shriek, laugh, run, shy away, recoil....
> And lo! Suddenly the first pearl necklace snaps, the grains come spilling off the string, flow tumbling down along the smooth roseate steps which the water descends in minuscule cascades.
> There snaps the second necklace—of seven strands?—then the third—of twenty-one?—and another, and another yet, of strands beyond number.
> The pearls multiply, imitate a mild hail, scatter in all directions, resplend, resound, rebound, mingle with the rivulets—now they look like precious bubbles of the water, now like drops scattered by drenched, pouring beauty.[3]

Even more remarkably, the heroine of George Moore's 1898 novel *Evelyn Innes* goes into raptures over the music of Wagner's *Tristan* with as much intensity as the lovers in Mann's "Tristan" story, but she does so while listening to her own lover play it on the harpsichord:

> Evelyn lay back in a wicker chair thinking. He had said that life without love was a desert, and many times the conversation trembled on the edge of a personal avowal, and now he was playing love music out of *Tristan* on the harpsichord. The gnawing creeping sensuality of the phrase brought little shudders into her flesh; all life dissolved into a dim tremor and rustling of blood; vague colour floated into her eyes, and there were moments when she could hardly restrain herself from jumping to her feet and begging of him to stop.[4]

Curiously, harpsichords regained a little of their popularity in the mid-twentieth century when they were associated with the glamorous world of espionage drama. Edwin Astley used them in his scores for British television shows in this genre such as *Danger Man* and *Department S*, combining this "old" sound with driving ostinati and jazz elements. Just as orange became the defining color of the 1970s, the harpsichord acquired a new signification in terms of timbre. The harder, less emotional sound of the harpsichord suited these urbane and often ruthless dramas, but the harpsichord failed to make a comeback outside this particular eccentricity.

It is not just its hammers, general glossiness and sonic power that make the piano the pre-eminent erotic instrument, but also, as Rosen points out, the engagement of the pianist's entire musculature while performing upon it. This is why no harpsichordist could ever aspire to the erotic appeal of a pianist, particularly so in their cinematic incarnations.

Eight

Sex and Violence

Fetishissimo

Ken Russell's presentation of Liszt as the ultimate musical Lothario in *Lisztomania* is made clear by his juxtaposition of giant phalluses with piano motifs throughout his satirical extravaganza. Liszt himself was quite aware of his erotic appeal and played up to it. The mother of his three children, Countess Marie d'Agoult, had given up everything for the maestro. She soon came to regret her infatuation with a man who could not resist the attentions of other women. She wrote him at the end of their relationship, "What have I to do with a charming good-for-nothing, an upstart Don Juan, half mountebank, half juggler, who makes ideas and sentiments disappear up his sleeve, and look complacently at the bewildered public that applauds him? Ten years of illusion! Is that not the very sublime of extravagance? Adieu; my heart is bursting with bitterness."

Marie confessed that she had "no objection to being your mistress, but I will not be one of your mistresses." Liszt eventually settled for Countess Carolyn Sayn-Wittgenstein, who worshipped him as a god:

> I kiss your hands and kneel before you, prostrating my forehead to your feet, laying, like the Orientals, my finger on my brow, my lips, and my heart, to assure you that my whole mind, all the breath of my spirit, all my heart exist only to bless you, to glorify you, to love you unto death and beyond—beyond even death, for love is stronger than death.[1]

But even Carolyn's devotion did not prevent further dalliances, the most sensational being Liszt's affair with Olga Janina, the "Cossack Countess" who had horse-whipped her own husband before abandoning him and eventually making her way to Rome where she encountered Liszt in 1869. They were infatuated with each other. He gave her private piano lessons during which she confessed her love for him. "Never speak to me of love," Liszt replied, but this didn't stop him from embracing her. "I ought not to love you; but I do love and cannot conceal it," he admitted later, before fleeing. Olga followed him, dressed as a peasant boy. When he realized who she was, he collapsed at her feet, unable to deny himself further. Olga then thought of killing him and doing away with herself with the same dagger, as a way of ensuring that no one else would ever love him. It was the kind of fanaticism that foreshadowed John Lennon's murder over a hundred years later. Olga changed her mind at the last moment, but continued to stalk him. After bankruptcy, a laudanum overdose and a recovery, Olga then tried to poison herself again before spinning out of Liszt's orbit and settling in Paris.

Such was the nineteenth-century Romantic background to so much piano imagery in twentieth-century cinema. Liberace had sex appeal, though this was muted as "romance" in *Sincerely Yours*. There is no overt sex on display in that film, though there is a disturbing hint of necrophilia in Liberace's performance in *The Loved One*. Far more to the point is Jane Campion's *The Piano* (1993), which adds a twist to Ralph Waldo Emerson's observation, "'Tis wonderful how soon a piano gets into a log-hut on the frontier."[2]

The piano here is not only the "voice" of its mute, significantly female heroine (something she shares with Dr. Phibes), but also the means by which an adulterous affair is arranged. This heroine, Ada McGrath (Holly Hunter), finds herself transplanted from her native mid-nineteenth-century Scotland to the muddy terrain of New Zealand when married off to Sam Neill's ex-patriot frontiersman, Alisdair Stewart, whom Ada finds it impossible to love. She takes with her her brown wood, square piano, which survives a stormy voyage only to be left on the beach at its termination, being far too bulky to transport through the inhospitable terrain to Stewart's home; but this piano is essential to Ada, as she cannot speak. The piano, like Phibes' trumpet, speaks for her. Despite its long sea voyage, the piano is in remarkably good tune, as Ada pries off one of the planks of its packing case and, along with her daughter Flora (Anna Paquin), plays some of Michael Nyman's specially written though anachronistically minimalist music on the revealed keyboard. But this impromptu performance on the beach is to be her last contact with the instrument for some time. At Stewart's home, she has to make do with the dummy keyboard she draws on a tabletop. Stewart later exchanges her abandoned piano for some land owned by his compatriot, George Baines (Harvey Keitel).

Baines has an ulterior motive in wanting the instrument. It is impregnated not only with sea salt but also with Ada's scent, and Baines can smell it. He dusts the instrument in the nude, suggestively rubbing his genitals against the wooden case and the piano's legs.

Rarely has a piano been made so explicitly erotic. Under the pretense that Ada will give him piano lessons, Baines invites her to his home, and a bargain is struck: If Ada grants him sexual favors, Baines will eventually

On the beach: Holly Hunter (left) and Anna Paquin in *The Piano*.

allow her to buy back her beloved "voice," one black key at a time. Baines asks her to lift her skirts, and as she plays he looks at her legs from under the piano, in a scene that echoes the famous story of George Sand sitting under Chopin's piano so as to be immersed in the musical vibrations. But Baines has a different kind of vibration in mind. He touches her as she touches the keys and they embark on a kind of musical strip poker. Each time she takes off an item of clothing, she advances one key further to repossessing her beloved piano. This is the ultimate devotion to music as a form of spiritual salvation. Without her piano, Ada has hardly an identity, let alone a voice. It is her principal mode of communication.

Baines holds her bare arms as she plays, and we are reminded of the erotic appeal experienced by so many Victorian lovers when playing duets together. Even accompanying a singer permitted this, as we see in Joseph Losey's *The Go-Between* (1971) in a scene wherein Alan Bates' farmer, Ted Burgess, sings Gilbert and Sullivan's genteelly erotic song "Take a Pair of Sparkling Eyes" at the cricket match supper. Bates needs an accompanist, and Julie Christie's aristocratic Marian Maudsley eventually obliges. Her parents (Margaret Leighton and Michael Gough) already suspect that these two have been having an affair, and the duet they perform is almost a public declaration of it, by virtue of their studied attempt to appear as unattached as possible. Gilbert's lyrics say it all, with their references to "rosy lips" "a figure trimly planned/Such as admiration whets" and the counsel to "act upon it." Marian's mother stares balefully during the performance, while her father lights his pipe, his furrowed brow conveying his suspicions. The boy hero of the story, Leo (Dominic Guard), later gets up to sing, also to Marian's accompaniment. His own half-formed erotic connection with her is made even more explicit in L.P. Hartley's novel on which Harold Pinter's screenplay was based: "I could see Marian's fingers at work, catch the gleam of her white arms and whiter neck, and imagine not one, but a whole series of deaths which I should die for her."[3]

Duets

Far more intimate than accompanying is the process of playing four-handed arrangements, as this requires much closer proximity between the participants. Arms, thighs, shoulders and legs often touch one another during the process, especially when hands cross over. This largely accounts for the immense popularity of piano duets in the middle-class drawing rooms of the nineteenth century. In Willi Forst's Schubert biopic *Leise Flehen meine Lieder* (1933), also known as *Lover Divine,* the camera gives us the point-of-view of Hans Jaray's Schubert, who instructs Màrtha Eggerth's Countess Ezsterhazy at the piano. They play scales together, and at one point, Schubert's hands brush those of the countess. There was perhaps no other way for a commoner to touch aristocratic flesh in Schubert's time, and it was the honor of the piano to be the only piece of furniture that broke social distancing between classes.

In his short story "Lady Barbarina," Henry James demonstrates how the piano was often regarded as a kind of chaperone, which allowed two lovers to be alone together under the pretext of a musical interlude:

> She had seated herself at the piano and had played perpetually, in a soft incoherent manner, while he leaned over the instrument, very close to her, and said everything that came into his head. She was braver and handsomer than ever and looked at him as if she liked him out and out.[4]

A grand piano in particular lends itself to this by the way it spacially configures the participants. One may lean over the lady who is playing in order to turn pages, for example, or the lady may nestle in the curve of the piano while the gentleman is playing, to say nothing of draping herself over the lid, as Michelle Pfeiffer demonstrated in *The Fabulous Baker Boys* (dir. Steve Kloves, 1989). There is no other instrument that permits this kind of assignation. Can one imagine a solo trombone providing the opportunity? A bassoon? Even more significantly, it is the solidity of the piano as an object of furniture and a symbol of respectability, and, most important of all, the way it permits the player to leave his or her head disengaged physically, which make the difference: Social intercourse during performance is thus made possible, which is out of the question where blowing and scraping are concerned. This long tradition was satirized in Tim Burton's 2012 *Dark Shadows,* in which a piano stands in the great hall of Collinsport Mansion. It is there merely to permit Eva Green's witch, Angelique, to sit on the keyboard, play a glissando with her buttocks and remind Johnny Depp's Barnabas Collins of the erotic fun they once had together side by side on the piano stool.

When, in *The Piano,* Ada allows Baines to caress and kiss her for the "price" of five black keys, it inevitably leads to full sexual intercourse and the realization that Baines' love for her is reciprocated. "Her playing is strange and like a mood that passes into you," says Kerry Walker's Aunt Morag. Indeed, the piano *is* Ada. It is a part of her. Alas, when Stewart learns about the affair with Baines, he chops off one of Ada's fingers as a punishment for cuckolding him; but this catastrophe is later overcome by the application of a prosthetic finger. Ada begins a new life with Baines as a piano teacher and her voice gradually returns to her.

The story of *The Piano* can be reduced to another simple love triangle, but it is the central role of the piano that makes it interesting. In the sexually repressed environment of nineteenth-century respectability, the piano became a cherished vehicle for female self-expression, and for the experience of all those fascinating Italian musical terms: "Appassionata," "Abandonandosi," "con amore," "tempestuoso," "con fuoco," etc. None of these emotions would have been encouraged—even in marriage—away from the piano stool, but, within certain confines and restraints of taste, they were accessible to young ladies of musical accomplishment.

Seduction

Visconti included a piano at the beginning of his adaptation of D'Annunzio's erotic novel of sexual jealousy, *L'Innocente*. Here, the pianist herself is not erotic. She is a formidable, middle-aged performer dressed in black, who plays Mozart's "Rondo à la Turka," Liszt's "Les Jeux d'eaux à la Villa d'Este" and Chopin's A-flat Waltz, Op. 69, No.1. What *is* erotic is the audience, comprised of elegantly silk-clad young women, whose bare arms and décolletage contrast powerfully with the formal evening dress of the good-looking men who sit amongst them on chairs upholstered in yellow silk brocade. They have all gathered, however, to experience the piano's erotic power, and it is this that inflames the sexual jealousy of the story, in which the unfaithful Tullio Hermini (Giancarlo Gianni) punishes his wife Giuliana (Laura Antonelli) when she gives birth to another man's baby. Tullio leaves the bastard child out in the snow until it catches cold and dies. Giuliana immediately realizes that her husband has murdered her baby and leaves him. When Tullio's former mistress tells him that she too no longer loves him, he shoots himself. That such a story begins with a piano recital says much.

In his 1889 novella *The Kreutzer Sonata*, Leo Tolstoy made very clear how music—and piano music in particular—can seduce and lead to immorality. The story concerns Pozdnischeff, whose wife has an affair with Troukhatchevsky, a violinist. Unlike Emma Bovary, who meets her lover in a hotel away from prying eyes, Pozdnischeff's wife performs her love affair in the drawing room. Together, they perform Beethoven's Violin Sonata of that name, which inflames Pozdnischeff's jealousy:

> Two persons are cultivating the noblest art—music—together, this requires a certain proximity, in which there is nothing unseemly, and no one but a stupid, jealous husband, forsooth, could find anything reprehensible therein. And yet, every one knows full well that it is, thanks to these very occupations, especially musical studies, prosecuted together, that by far the greatest proportion of wickedness takes place in our society.[5]

Infuriated by the music which symbolizes his wife's infidelity, Pozdnischeff stabs her to death with a dagger, and ultimately blames music itself for his crime:

> Music, they say, acts upon one by elevating the soul. That is absurd. It acts upon us, it is true, acts with terrible effect—at least I am speaking for myself—but far from elevating the soul. It neither elevates nor depresses the soul, but irritates it. How shall I make my meaning clear? Music forces me to forget myself and my true state; it transports me to some other state which is not mine. Under its influence I fancy I experience what I really do not feel, that I understand what I do not comprehend, that I am able to do what is completely beyond my power. ... Music instantaneously throws me into that state of feeling in which the composer of it found himself when he wrote it. My soul blends with his, and together with him I am transported from one frame of mind to another. But why I am so ravished out of myself I know not.[6]

The basic scenario of *The Kreutzer Sonata* was satirized in *The Witches of Eastwick* (dir. George Miller, 1987). Susan Sarandon's Jane Spofford is magically given musical powers by Jack Nicholson's devilish Daryl Van Horne. Instead of a violin, Jane plays a cello, accompanied with strident chords on the piano by Van Horne. At first Jane doubts she will be able to play at all, but Van Horne encourages her: "Let it go. What are you afraid of? You have great passion in you. Let it out!" As the music of Elgar's Cello Concerto rises to its emotional climax, the over-heated instrument starts smoking before Jane throws it down and hurls herself into Van Horne's arms. Van Horne crashes against the keyboard with a symbolic discord, and music sheets fall in flames over the burning cello.

This idea of musical ravishment was transferred to Gothic fantasy by

Eric, Count Stenbock, in his "The True Story of a Vampire," which appeared in 1894, three years before Bram Stoker's *Dracula*. Like Stoker's novel, it was inspired by J. Sheridan LeFanu's short story "Carmilla." Set in Styria, like LeFanu's tale, "The True Story of a Vampire" transfers the lesbian subtext of "Carmilla" to a homoerotic one, in which a vampire, Count Vardalek, seduces the narrator's brother, Gabriel. The curious anticipation of Doctor Who's most infamous nemesis in Vardalek's name is surely coincidental, but he is no less villainous. He is also musical:

> After dinner my father asked him if he played the piano. He said, "Yes, I can do a little," and he sat down at the piano. Then he played a Hungarian *czardas*—wild, rhapsodic, wonderful.
> That is music which makes men mad. He went on in the same strain.
> Gabriel stood stock still by the piano, his eyes dilated and fixed, his form quivering. At last he said very slowly, at one particular motive—for want of a better word you may call it the *relâche* of a *czardas* by which I mean that point where the original quasi-slow movement begins again—"Yes, I think I could play that."
> Then he quickly fetched his fiddle and self-made xylophone, and did actually, alternating the instruments, render the same very well indeed.
> Vardalek looked at him and said in a very sad voice, "Poor child! You have the soul of music within you."

Later, Vardalek continues to play the piano that has been moved into his bedroom:

> He was playing on a piano, which had been specially put there for him, one of Chopin's nocturnes, very beautifully; I stopped, leaning on the bannisters to listen.
> Something white appeared on the dark staircase. We believed in ghosts in our part. I was transfixed with terror, and clung to the bannisters. What was my astonishment to see Gabriel walking slowly down the staircase, his eyes fixed as though in a trance! This terrified me even more than a ghost would. Could I believe my senses? Could that be Gabriel?
> I simply could not move. Gabriel, clad in his long white nightshirt, came downstairs and opened the door. He left it open. Vardalek still continued playing, but talked as he played.
> He said—this time speaking Polish—*Nie umiem wyrazic jak ciehie kocham*,—"My darling, I fain would spare thee; but thy life is my life, and I must live, I who would rather die. Will God not have *any* mercy on me? Oh! Oh life; oh, the torture of life!" Here he struck one agonized and strange chord, then continued playing softly. "Oh, Gabriel, my beloved! My life, yes *life*—oh, what life? I am sure this is but a little of what I demand of thee. Surely thy superabundance of life can spare a little to one who is already dead."[7]

Intriguingly, much the same thing happens in Don Sharp's Hammer thriller *The Kiss of the Vampire* (1963). For this, composer James Bernard

Eight. Sex and Violence

was required to compose a piano piece, which one of the vampires in question plays with the intention of hypnotizing his victim, Marianne Harcourt (Jennifer Daniel). The piano is not coffin black, as one might expect, but a rather more homely rosewood in rococo style with ormolu decorations, which complements the Solomonic columns, gilded furniture and eau-de-nil décor of the room in which we find it. The pianist is Carl Ravna (Barry Warren), the suave and sinister vampire son of the film's villain, the equally vampiric Dr. Ravna, played with extreme menace by Noel Willman. ("I intend to play this part without changing my expression once," he told co-star Edward de Souza.[8]) Warren, like Dirk Bogarde before him, though with considerable less anguish, took piano lessons for the role, and the film's musical director John Hollingsworth was so impressed that he suggested that Warren take up the piano professionally.[9] The miming is thus convincing, though we actually hear Douglas Gamley's performance on the soundtrack.

Before that Rhapsody is unveiled, however, Carl is discovered playing Chopin's Nocturne in D-flat (op. 27 no. 2). Charles Rosen's thoughts on this piece offer a possible, if somewhat esoteric reason for its appearance in this context. He points out that the melody is implicit in its accompaniment ("The Italianate melody ... is already hidden in the opening bar of accompaniment"[10])—just as Marianne Harcourt is soon to become part of and hidden in the Ravnas' vampire cult. More simply, this seemingly tranquil night piece also contains subtly disturbing chromatic elements, which echo the ambivalence of the Ravnas' seemingly civilized surroundings.

"Something you've composed yourself? How exciting!" Jacquie Wallis and Barry Warren in *The Kiss of the Vampire*.

Returning from dinner, Dr. Ravna emphasizes the contrast between appearance and reality in his discussion of the food he and his guests have just consumed (these vampires, it appears, do not refuse normal nourishment): "It often happens in life that the most beautiful things are made from the most unpromising of materials, don't you find? That wine you enjoyed at dinner ... made from grapes trampled by the feet of a peasant. Dirty feet as like as not...."

"Father, *please!*" protests Ravna's daughter, Sabena (Jacquie Wallis), but the point has been made.

And then, the "Vampire Rhapsody" begins.

"Something of your own, perhaps, Carl?" Dr. Ravna inquires with a meaningful stare. Carl happily obliges, knowing full well what is intended. He stretches his fingers over the keyboard in predatory manner and commences his performance of Bernard's Liszt-inspired cue. The harmonies echo Liszt's *Mephisto Waltz* and *Première Valse oubliée,* with their augmented fourths—also known as "the devil in music," which in turn influenced Scriabin's mature style. Echoes of Scriabin are also present in Bernard's piece, particularly from Scriabin's so-called "Black Mass" piano sonata; Chopin also, in the arpeggio figurations that extend over the entire range of the keyboard, which echo the final bars of Chopin's D-minor Prelude (Op. 28, No. 24).

That is the Prelude that Hurd Hadfield's Dorian Gray plays to Angela Lansbury's Sibyl Vane in *The Picture of Dorian Gray* (dir. Albert Lewin, 1945). Bernard also indulges in the unusual time signature of 7/4, which metrical asymmetry adds to the general sense of threat. While Carl bends over the keyboard, and generally reveals his descent from Erik of the Opera, Marianne sits beside him, clutching a glass of luridly green crème de menthe, while Sabena stands on the other side, her hands resting on the piano lid, her head bowed in contemplation. Marianne's husband Gerald (Edward de Souza) stands apart. The seduction is not aimed at him.

The scene is not dissimilar to many images of Liszt or Chopin performing in salons. The audiences of both musicians were often as hypnotized by their demonic music as Marianne is with Carl's, and Carl later becomes so engrossed in the spirit of his inspiration that he seems to fall under his own spell as he turns to face Marianne with wildly staring eyes. Some might find the gesture overdone and unintentionally comic, but Warren seems to be referencing the expressionist anguish of Conrad Veidt in *The Hands of Orlac.*

As the spell increases in its intensity, Bernard brings in an orchestral accompaniment of dissonant strings and disorientating vibraphone, before the proceedings are interrupted by Gerald, who is concerned that

Marianne might be about to faint. "Please don't stop!" Marianne insists, her eyes clinging to Carl's with erotic intensity. It is surely one of Hammer's most magnificent moments, but such a thing had, in fact, already happened in in *House of Dracula* (dir. Erle C. Kenton, 1945), where the roles were reversed. John Carradine plays Dracula but it is not he who plays the piano. He leaves that to his victim, who is discovered innocently amusing herself with Beethoven's "Moonlight" Sonata.

"You like it?" she asks. Carradine stares back:

"It breathes the spirit of the night."

Then the film's composer Edgar Fairchild injects the influence of Debussy into the piece. The victim has obviously not played Debussy before.

"I've never heard this music before, yet I'm playing it."

"You're creating it. For me," explains the count. Stylistically we now move from Debussy to Scriabin. "It is the music of the world from which I come," the count explains, even though that is presumably Transylvania rather than Russia or France.

Carradine had played the "Moonlight" Sonata on the piano himself in the previous year's *Return of the Ape Man* (dir. Phil Rosen), but his character there, Prof. John Gilmore, limits his comments about it to the feeling that "it's so sad." Because of that, he at first demurs when asked to play, and speeds things up towards the end, not that anyone seems to notice. The "Moonlight" is suitable for horror films and the kind of Gothic sci-fi in which Monogram and Universal specialized because it is an obvious icon of "classical" music, which brings with it the status that horror films of this period were so eager to grasp, like Frankenstein's Monster reaching up to the sun. The "Moonlight" sobriquet, which was not Beethoven's, is obviously suggestive, but Beethoven's description of it was "quasi fantasia"—"almost a fantasy," and that fits well with fantasy films. Its fame has also made it ripe for satire (if its appearance in *House of Dracula* was not already tending in that direction). E.F. Benson certainly thought so in his Mapp and Lucia novels, having the pretentious Lucia play the first movement to her friends, but only the first, as the finale is much more difficult to bring off:

> Lucia turned off all the lights in the room except one on the piano, so that they saw her profile against a black background, like the head on a postage stamp, and first she played the slow movement out of the Moonlight Sonata. She stopped once, just after she had begun, because Diva coughed, and when she had finished there was a long silence. Lucia sighed and Georgie sighed, and everyone said "Thank you" simultaneously. Major Benjy said he was devoted to Chopin and Lucia playfully told him that she would take his musical education in hand.[11]

Lacking Hands

If Barry Warren's model for the *Kiss of the Vampire* piano scene was Conrad Veidt's anguished performance as a concert pianist in *The Hands of Orlac*, it was an appropriate choice: The eroticism that underlies director Robert Weine's film is made clear from the very first frame, wherein we observe Orlac's fiancée reclining in bed and reading a letter from her beloved, promising that soon he will embrace her: "My hands will glide over your hair ... and I will feel your body beneath my hands." This is pianist's talk. He wants to "play" his fiancée's body with his hands, just as Carl Ravna wants to ravish Marianne with his rhapsodic digits.

We cut to a shot of Orlac at the piano to emphasize the point. We watch his hands gliding over the keys, swaying back and forth as he performs what will be his last concert, for immediately after it he is involved in a train accident, in a scene that once more combines locomotives with pianos. Orlac survives but his hands are crushed beyond repair. Drastic action is necessary. Conveniently, a convict is to be executed that night, and the surgeon decides to graft the murderer's hands onto what are now merely the Stumps of Orlac. In another scene derived from one of Max Klinger's famous "Glove" etchings, in which an enormous glove hovers over a sleeping man (the glove symbolizing the sleeper's lust for the girl who dropped it), the enlarged fist of the executed murder descends in superimposition over Orlac's bed. Orlac's fate is sealed. "These hands must never be allowed to touch another person," he decrees. Unable to express love, they soon revert to type.

Before that happens, however, Orlac is reunited with his piano. In Maurice Renard's 1920 novel, on which the film is based, the piano is described as a "silent coffin that contained latently within itself the whole potentiality of music." Orlac "stroked it, as if he might the pelt of a thoroughbred bay stallion."[12] In the film, Orlac caresses it much as Baines will do in *The Piano*, though Orlac remains fully clothed. He glides his hands over the piano lid, bending over it as though in an embrace, and suggesting that the instrument is more erotically charged for him than his fiancée. He sits down on the stool, and as he carefully opens the lid, the fiancée appears through a door in the background, which juxtaposition eloquently demonstrates that for Orlac, opening the lid of his piano is like lifting the skirts of his beloved—only more thrilling. The fiancée watches, perturbed, but when Orlac attempts to play, he discovers he is suffering from the musical equivalent of impotence. (Renard describes Orlac shutting the piano lid "as he might a coffin lid on a dearly loved corpse."[13]) This is the cue for the fiancée to advance and reclaim her man—a man who can now no longer touch her for fear of murdering her.

In a café, Orlac reads about the crimes of his murderous donor, and back in his music room, he curses his new hands while standing next to his piano. His expression is not dissimilar to that of Carl Ravna in *The Kiss of the Vampire*. It is now murder rather than music to which his hands are dedicated. But a happy ending is provided: The original owner of the hands was not, in fact, guilty of the crimes he was meant to have committed. Another man was responsible, and Orlac need not worry any more. But this happy resolution does not interfere with the film's complex expression of the piano's erotic appeal.

Two much less satisfactory film adaptations followed. The first, *Mad Love* (dir. Karl Freund, 1935) shifted the emphasis from Orlac to Dr. Gogol (Peter Lorre), the surgeon who performs the transplant. (Lorre fully lives up to the name of his character with his famously goggle eyes, later to be encased in actual goggles in one of the film's most disturbing images.) A theatrical Grand Guignol background also informs the story (which would later be revived in Sam Gallu's *Theatre of Death*, 1967), along with the Pygmalion myth later exploited in Andre de Toth's 1953 *House of Wax* (Gogol worships a wax statue of the leading lady, Frances Drake).

Orlac's piano does make several appearances. We hear Colin Clive as Orlac playing part of a Chopin Sonata and the G-minor *Ballade*, along with a piece composed by Orlac himself (the work of the film's composer, Dimitri Tiomkin, in somewhat Scriabinesque style). The screen's Henry Frankenstein, Clive now finds himself in the position of being operated upon. This is traumatic for both him and his wife, and his subsequent nightmare is exquisitely summed up by Freund in a sequence in which the keys of a self-playing piano transform into the sleepers and track of the train, all accompanied by Chopin's suitably up-tempo "Black Keys" Étude (Op. 10, No. 5): Pianos and trains again.

After the operation, a few bars of Wagner's *Siegfried Idyll* restore a mood of calm, but not for long, as Orlac's hands now refuse to obey his musical will. Like many of us, he finds he cannot play Chopin's demanding *Fantasie-Impromptu*. The rest of the story really concerns Dr. Gogol's activities. Conflating *The Phantom of the Opera* with Michael Curtiz's *Mystery of the Wax Museum* (1933), Gogol also plays an organ in his gloomy retreat, contemplating, as he does so, his waxwork figure of Madame Orlac. The title of the film is apposite, as Gogol's infatuation with Madame Orlac is the main focus of this reworking of Renard's novel.

In 1960, the story returned to its native France in a version directed by Edmond T. Gréville. This starred Mel Ferrer as Orlac and a particularly sadistic Christopher Lee, speaking eloquent French, as a stage magician who exploits Orlac's predicament for cash. Whereas Clive's Orlac seems to specialize in Chopin, Ferrer's Orlac is a Liszt player. We begin with a performance of Liszt's *Hungarian Fantasy* for Piano and Orchestra; its final bars provide a background for the ensuing main titles. Later, after his operation, he plays one of Liszt's piano *Consolations* while his fiancée, Louise (Lucile Saint-Simon) looks on. "With you, everything is possible," Orlac insists. "You are a miracle."

But this proves not to be the case, as the hands revert to type, or so Orlac thinks. He attempts to strangle Louise in a sado-erotic moment again initiated by the piano. Another of Liszt's *Consolations* then initiates another love scene, while their formal engagement is accompanied by Chopin's E-flat Nocturne. After Orlac has been sent the gloves of the murderer by Lee's magician, Nero, he breaks down during a performance of the almost inevitable "Moonlight" Sonata. But after the denouement, he brings the story to an end with another performance of the *Hungarian Fantasy*.

A variation on Renard's theme occurred two years later in Newt Arnold's *Hands of a Stranger* in which pianist Vernon Paris (James Stapleton) undergoes the same operation, after which his new hands simply refuse to play anything. Expressing his despair, he strikes the keyboard and produces a series of discordant note clusters that unintentionally resemble the effects Henry Cowell asks for in the second movement of his Piano Concerto of 1928. The most visually interesting aspect of this otherwise standard fare is the moment when Paris gives piano lessons to the boy whose father caused the accident in the first place. Once again, the keyboard is photographed resting along the bottom edge of the screen.

Boned Up

In 1938, Eric Ambler juxtaposed crime with piano music in his novel *Epitaph for a Spy*, in which Frau Vogel plays a Chopin Ballade.

> Frau Vogel, it was clear, had once had a talent. There was about her playing a curious, faded brilliance, like that of a paste buckle in a hamper of old ball dresses. And then I forgot Frau Vogel and listened to the music.
> When she had finished there was a moment of dead silence in the room, and then a burst of clapping. She half turned in the chair, flushed and blinked nervously....

She then begins a Bach encore, which is interrupted by the arrival of the police. They are searching for Josef Vadassy, who has unknowingly been caught up in the world of espionage:

> When the interruption came I did not at first notice it. There was a murmur of voices from the hall, someone hissed a request for silence, a chair grated on the floor. I opened my eyes in time to see Köche disappearing hurriedly

through the door which he closed softly behind him. A few moments later I heard it open again noisily.

It all seemed to happen in the fraction of a second, but the first intimation I had that anything was wrong was that Frau Vogel stopped suddenly in the middle of a bar. Instinctively I looked across at her first. She was sitting, her hands poised over the keys, staring fixedly over the top of the piano, as though she were looking at a ghost. Then her hands dropped slowly on to the keyboard, sounding a soft discord. My gaze traveled to the door. There, standing on the threshold were two uniformed *agents de police*.[14]

A piano recital is such a symbol of civilized decorum, it makes the perfect foil for the rude intrusion of the police. Similar territory was visited in John Brahm's adaptation of Patrick Hamilton's 1941 novel *Hangover Square*. The 20th Century–Fox film was made as a follow-up to Brahm's *The Lodger* (1944) to capitalize on the success of Laird Cregar in the title role. In *Hangover Square*, Cregar plays George Harvey Bone, a pianist and composer who commits murders during blackouts. (Bone is a curious name for so burly a figure, unless it refers to the euphemism for an erection, but this is as unlikely as the title of a musical entertainment mentioned in the film—"Gay Love"—having a homosexual implication.)

The erotic element is, however, strong if decorous. Bone is loved by Faye Marlowe's Barbara, the respectable daughter of a well-known conductor; but Bone himself loves Linda Darnell's music-hall singer Netta, who has much looser morals. The piano provides a platform for both relationships to develop. Barbara's love in genuine (she also admires Bone's concerto, which was composed for the film by Bernard Herrmann in his most flamboyantly macabre manner), but Netta only pretends to love the pianist. All she really wants are the songs she persuades him to write for her. On discovering that Netta is already engaged to another man, Bone strangles her with a curtain cord before collapsing during the premiere of the concerto. By this time, of course, the police have worked out what was made clear to the audience from the beginning, but Bone refuses to be arrested until he has played the end of his masterpiece. He hurls an oil lamp at the police and provides the film with a fiery climax, during which he plays the final bars amid the flames of his self-created Hell.

In many ways, the whole affair is yet another reworking of *The Phantom of the Opera*. Like Erik, Bone not only lives for music, he also kills for it. Erik's demise is watery rather than fiery but the trajectories of both stories follow similar contours of solitude, yearning, revenge, triumph and death. Central to this confluence of sex and violence is Bone's piano, his more modest square piano symbolizing his introversion rather more eloquently than the black grand that takes over for the final concert. Significantly, the square piano is also adorned with a candelabra. (Chopin's candelabra in *A*

Bone of contention: Laird Cregar as George Harvey Bone in *Hangover Square*.

Song to Remember, which would so impress Liberace, had been seen earlier the same year.)

There are other parallels between Erik and Bone: Erik sends a chandelier crashing into the stalls of the Opéra to remove a singer he dislikes, whereas Bone climbs a massive Guy Fawkes bonfire, on top of which he deposits Netta's body. During his psychotic episodes, Cregar's wildly staring eyes are suitably illuminated with two pencil spotlights, providing a fleshy equivalent of Erik's skeletal death mask. Music and madness are again linked in a manner that suggests the coupling is inevitable. It's another example of how Hollywood endlessly recapitulates the myth that classical musicians are peculiar people. Music hall singers are less problematic, though, in Netta's case, no better than they ought to be. These differences are synthesized in Herrmann's score, which combines both the post–Romantic idiom of Bone's concerto with the somewhat anachronistic idiom of the popular songs he composes for Netta. (The film is set in the Edwardian era, but the songs are firmly in 1940s style.) Like Carl Ravna's "Rhapsody," Bone's composition is an expression of his inner corruption: It too emphasizes the evil tritone.

As Joseph LaShelle's camera swoops over the orchestral players in the climax, one shot in particular emphasizes the "difference" of the pianist from the others. The camera zooms towards Cregar, and we stare directly down over the keyboard as his fingers scamper over the keys like spiders, implying (erroneously, of course) that the devotion demanded by virtuosity and inspiration has social and psychotic consequences.

Piano Gangsters

The connection between keyboards and crime was recapitulated in rather different ways in later films. *Shoot the Piano Player*, directed by François Truffaut in 1960, stars Charles Aznavour as a pianist caught up in Paris' gangster underworld. It was based on David Goodis' novel *Down There*; Truffaut adopted the novel's French title *Tirez sur le pianiste* for his film adaptation.

Aznavour's Charlie Kohler is a dance hall and café pianist whose brother Chico re-enters his life along with two gangsters who are pursuing him. In fact, Charlie's real name is Edouard Saroyan; he was a concert pianist whose wife Thérésa tried to help further his career by becoming the mistress of an impresario. When Saroyan learned of this, he left Thérésa, who subsequently killed herself by defenestration. Back in the present, the gangsters in pursuit of Chico are now hiding at the Saroyan family home, whither Charlie, his brother and Charlie's prostitute girlfriend Léna dash. It is there that a rogue bullet hits Léna, who dies in Charlie's arms.

A landmark in French New Wave" cinema, *Shoot the Piano Player* is filmed in such a way as to be what Truffaut's biographers Antoine de Baecque and Serge Toubiana called a "musical film," not just because it features a piano player but also because of the way in which Truffaut edited it with "constant rhythm changes."[15] The main titles also feature the hammers and mechanism of the upright piano on which Charlie plays, suggesting something of the demonic nature of the instrument already discussed—the hammers of destiny, perhaps, the ruthless nature of which summon the discordant melody of Charlie's life.

Another "musical film" featuring jazz and attempted murder followed in 1962: Basil Dearden's *All Night Long*, in which the plot of Shakespeare's *Othello* was updated to the 1960s jazz scene in Patrick McGoohan plays the Iago figure, Johnny Cousin, opposite Paul Harris' Othello of a jazz pianist, Aurelius Rex. The only way Johnny will be able to finance his new band is to persuade Rex's new wife Delia (Marti Stevens) to sing for him; but Delia has retired at the possessive Rex's request. The film throws interesting insight onto the psychological motivation of Shakespeare's Iago, which Coleridge claimed was mere "motiveless malignity."[16] Johnny certainly has a motive here, but more than his professional need for Delia, he is also consumed

Jazz white: Dave Brubeck (left) and Charles Mingus in *All Night Long*.

with self-loathing. At the end, he snarls to his doormat of a wife (Betsy Blair) that he doesn't love her and loathes himself as well. He doesn't love anyone. Delia's Desdemona figure survives Rex's attack, and they are reconciled at the end, but it is a close run thing: Rex begins to strangle Delia with the same fingers we have seen him playing the piano with on several occasions. Only the intervention of Richard Attenborough's club manager, Rod Hamilton, and Keith Michell's Cass (the Cassio figure) prevents Shakespeare's tragic ending, but murder and music very nearly found themselves once more in unison. The theme of sexual jealousy is enhanced by the film's jazz milieu, especially when Cass explains that the attraction of music "is pure libido symbolism," and that jazz music in particular appeals to "Negroes, adolescents and intellectuals."

The piano plays a central role in the proceedings. Dave Brubeck even puts in a guest appearance. Jazz-white rather than classical-black, it is adorned with a glass ashtray and a glass of champagne rather than a candelabra, and two saxophones are draped over it as well.

Which brings me to Michelle Pfeiffer who, as singer Suzy Diamond, similarly drapes herself over the lids of the pianos in Steve Kloves' *The Fabulous Baker Boys*. The Baker Boys (Jeff Bridges and Beau Bridges) don't play jazz so much as tunes from the Great American Songbook—the kind of repertoire with which Liberace began his career when playing Manhattan supper clubs. Feeling the need to reinvigorate their tired, small-time act, they hire the sultry Suzy to sing along with their renditions. The sexual temperature rises accordingly, especially when Suzy sings "Makin' Whoopie" in a blood-red dress and exposes her extremely long legs, as she cavorts on top of the piano. The audience is transfixed, much as they were when Liberace wowed them in an earlier era.

The sibling rivalry of the Baker brothers never boils over into the violence of *All Night Long*, and it is also a long way from *Fingers* (dir. James Toback, 1978), in which we meet another musical psychopath, Jimmy (Harvey Keitel). "Jimmy is a man on the edge," the narrator of the film's trailer informs us. "If you've ever felt like fighting back, if you've ever felt madness surging inside you, you'll know this man: A man who hurts. If you've ever felt everything closing in, if you've ever felt ripped apart by passion, you'll know this man. Jimmy. A man who loves like he hates. A man who hurts." Jimmy also hurts other people, roughing up his gangster father's debtors when they fail to pay up, and it's fair to say that Jimmy's bite is much worse than his Bach. He's a talented classical pianist, desperate to play Carnegie Hall, but trapped in a violent underworld, not to mention a violent personality.

Similar territory was visited by Jacques Audiard's 2005 *De battre mon cœur s'est arrêté* (*The Beat That My Heart Skipped*). Thomas Seyre (Romain Duris), a eviction broker involved in the criminal underworld, decides to follow in his concert pianist mother's footsteps, and takes lessons from a Vietnamese woman who can only speak Chinese. But having spent the night before his conservatoire audition working with his somewhat untrustworthy business partners, he is unable to perform and leaves the stage. The film combines various themes we have already explored: practice (at one stage, he plays the Bach Toccata bare-chested to emphasize his obsessional approach; and as Audiard obviously wants as gritty and bohemian a style as possible, he makes sure that the music score from which Tom plays is very creased and heavily marked. "This is not an esthete at work," he seems to be signaling, "but a passionate artiste"). Two years after this failure, Tom encounters the Russian gangster Minskov, who once defrauded him of 300,000 Euros. A gun is pulled, which Tom wrestles from Minskov, but fails in the end to use. The final shot shows him sitting in the audience of his wife's concert; she turns out to be his Vietnamese teacher.

As in the previous films discussed, the aim here seems to be to strip the piano of its bourgeois accretions. The same can be said of Jeff Preiss's *Low Down* (2014), which is not so much about crime as it is about drug addiction in a jazz piano context. This biopic of pianist Joe Albany (John Hawkes) is as far removed from *I've Always Loved You* as it is possible to imagine, apart from the shared instrument and the fact that even in this wholly grimier context, a pianist is shown as being dysfunctional. Goronoff in *I've Always Loved You* may not be a drug addict but he is addicted to his own ego, and just as difficult to deal with.

Little Chopin Horrors

Pianos and pianists appear quite often in horror films, usually as signifiers of unease. In *The Walking Dead* (dir. Michael Curtiz, 1936), Boris Karloff virtually reprised his role as Frankenstein's Monster, not with the heavy makeup but instead a cadaverous expression and a shock of white hair in his toupee, his character, John Ellman having been electrocuted for a murder he did not commit. Restored to life by Edmund Gwenn's scientist Dr. Beaumont, Ellman becomes a divine messenger of retribution, seeking out the men who framed him, while at the same time returning to his former life as a concert pianist. During the film's central concert scene, Ellman plays Bernhard Kaun's specially composed pastiche of Chopin's improvisatory style, while staring out at his enemies in the audience. Again, like Erik, Ellman is dead but alive and it is music that sustains him.

In *The Monster Maker* (dir. Sam Newfield, 1944), the pianist in question, Ralph Morgan's Anthony Lawrence, is a victim, not a perpetrator of wickedness, and is in fact presented as a robust, all–American type. The opposite of a European "sensitive," he looks forward to the end of his concert tour so he can "relax, wear old clothes and let my beard grow," adding, "Most people don't realize it but giving a piano recital requires the stamina of a marathon runner." His professional attitude is made clear when his daughter Patricia (Wanda McKay) complains that she often feels she been sired by a grand piano: "Ahhh, don't bite the piano that feeds you, my darling," Lawrence replies. Throughout the film, we are treated to four extracts of Chopin, beginning with the "Revolutionary" Étude, during which we are introduced to the villain of the piece, J. Carrol Naish's Dr. Igor Markoff, who is attending the concert while making eyes at Patricia.

Lawrence's playing begins to deteriorate after Markoff injects him with a serum that causes acromegaly, the disease from which the actor Rondo Hatton also suffered. (Composer biopics also focus on the physical sufferings of Chopin [tuberculosis], Beethoven [deafness], Schubert [syphilis], Schumann [madness], not forgetting, of course, the reliable standby of poverty.) In the end, Markoff is killed and the pianist cured of his affliction, allowing him to end the film with a performance of a Chopin Polonaise. The piano thus helps form a narrative continuity, topping and tailing the film, providing musical interludes, emphasizing the tragedy of Lawrence's physical predicament and contributing cultural status to the proceedings.

It is not really surprising that Chopin should so often feature in such films whenever "classical" piano music is required. Chopin was, after all, the pre-eminent poet of the piano, and the inherent morbidity of this harmonic language made his music so appropriate for the Romanticism of Gothic fantasy. "He was dying all his life," Berlioz once remarked of the composer. One of his most flamboyantly morbid Preludes occurs at the very end of the Op. 28 set. No. 24 in D minor opens with a brooding but agitated ostinato in the left hand, over which a melody with querulous dotted rhythms appears. Unsettling trills also emerge, which eventually burgeon into fountain-like scalic passages, reaching right up to the highest F on the keyboard. As the Prelude reaches its peak, cascades of minor thirds in the right hand avalanche down from those heights, the ostinato continuing unabated throughout until the very end plunges us down to the darkest, most remote region of the keys, a sonorous and eldritch D-natural, which is repeated three times, like a hammer striking down on a coffin lid, or even Death itself knocking at the door. Chopin disliked such poetic allusions, but it is certainly the case that nothing more is possible after these three notes have been intoned, which is why the piece is placed at the end of the collection.

Contemplating Chopin: Hurd Hatfield and Angela Lansbury in *The Picture of Dorian Gray*.

It was this D minor Prelude that Albert Lewin chose for Hurd Hatfield to play in his adaptation of Oscar Wilde's novel *The Picture of Dorian Gray*, released in 1945, soon after *The Monster Maker*. Hatfield's Dorian plays it on an upright (but that is because we are backstage at a music hall), and he plays it specifically to seduce Angela Lansbury's innocent singer Sybil Vane. At first, she is intrigued but also troubled by this macabre music, which comes from a place of decadence far from her own horizons, and is thoroughly disliked by her brother, who appears in time to overhear Dorian's little recital. The choice of Chopin is doubly appropriate here, as Wilde himself has Gilbert, one of the characters in his essay "The Critic as Artist" confess:

> After playing Chopin, I feel as if I had been weeping over sins that I had never committed and mourning over tragedies that were not my own. Music always seems to me to produce that effect. It creates for one a past of which one has been ignorant, and fills one with a sense of sorrows that have been hidden from one's tears. I can fancy a man who had led a perfectly commonplace life, hearing by chance some curious piece of music, and suddenly discovering that his soul, without his being conscious of it, had passed through terrible experiences, and known fearful joys, or wild romantic loves, or great renunciations.[17]

"It's wonderful," Sybil says, after those three sepulchral Ds. She asks if Dorian wrote it, and Dorian explains that Frédéric Chopin wrote it "for a woman he loved." (The Preludes were indeed composed in Majorca where Chopin had somewhat crazily agreed to go on holiday with George Sand.) Dorian asks Sybil what the music meant to her.

"I don't know," she replies. "It is full of emotion, but it's not happy."

"No, it's not happy," Dorian agrees.

"Why was he unhappy?" Sybil asks.

Dorian plays the three notes of the melody again:

"Perhaps because he felt his youth slipping away from him."

"What an odd thing for you to say," Sybil remarks.

"Why?"

"You're so young."

Sibyl asks what the music is called: "Has it a name?" to which Dorian marvelously replies, "A kind of name. It is called 'Prelude,'" which explanation leads to their first kiss. Thus, what originated as a tribute to the Preludes and Fugues of Bach (the composer Chopin honored above all others) has now been thoroughly Romanticized as a prelude to seduction, and Dorian's performance of Chopin has transformed the backstage upright from its humble connotation to one of decadence and ultimately death. Upright pianos, being of the lower orders, rarely achieve this kind of transformation in films. Before Dorian's Chopinization of it, this piano would have been no different from the upright in front of the stage, which accompanies Sybil's performance of the wholly virtuous song "Goodbye, Little Yellow Bird." The lyrics of this indicate, with deep irony, her ultimate fate, for she, unlike the bird she is singing about, also succumbs to temptation:

> Goodbye, Little Yellow Bird,
> I'd rather brave the cold
> On a leafless tree
> Than a prisoner be
> In a cage of gold.

As an instrument of vengeance, the piano has never been presented more graphically than in the "Mr. Steinway" segment of Freddie Francis' portmanteau horror film *Torture Garden* (1967). It concerns a pianist (John Standing) whose piano is jealous of his new girlfriend (Barbara Ewing). The piano is called "Euterpe" after the Greek muse of music, but there is also an Oedipal element at work here. Rather like the portrait of Alejandra that hangs above Magno's piano in Raphael Baledón's 1959 *The Man and the Monster* (see below), a portrait of the pianist's mother hangs over "Euterpe." Indeed, the piano was a gift to him from his mother before she died, and her spirit now inhabits—and animates—the instrument. Playing Chopin's Marche Funèbre, the coffin-black, ivory-and-ebony toothed musical monster wheels itself across the shiny black floor of the music room and promptly defenestrates the unfortunate girlfriend.

Francis' direction here is masterful; he photographs the piano in disorientating oblique angles, echoing Seth Holt's monumentalization and alienation of the piano in Hammer's *Taste of Fear* (1961)—another piano that also apparently plays itself. Significantly, the piece in Holt's film is Chopin's E minor Prelude (Op. 28, No. 4), which accompanies of the moment in which Susan Strasburg's endangered and seemingly disabled heroine wheels herself down the corridor of her father's villa, drawn by the mysterious music. Chopin's harmonic scheme moves by semitones, successive chords, over a repeated semi-tonal melody, being chromatically altered in such a way that the piece does indeed appear to be moving through space as well as time. The melancholy desolation of Chopin's inspiration aptly matches the mood of the scene in which Strasberg believes her absent (in fact murdered) father to have returned and to be playing the piano. She is, however, being deliberately misled by those who are trying to drive her insane. Only her father plays this piano, so if he is not there, who has been playing? The idea of a heroine hearing mysterious music is a Gothic cliché reaching back to Ann Radcliffe's famous novel *The Mysteries of Udolpho*, but Holt imbues it with fresh resonance. First we hear the music. Then we see light under the threshold of the music room door. The music stops and we cut to the interior of the room itself. There stands the piano, its lid closed, its stool unoccupied. The camera moves forward towards Strasberg, who throws open the double doors, gliding past the locked lid of the instrument. She looks down at the piano, which we then see from her point of view, the angle not only approximating her eyeline but also disorientating ours. In some ways, this piano, in its enigmatic stillness, is more threatening than the much more predatory "Euterpe."

Chopin's music also appeared in Welles' *Jane Eyre* (Jane accompanies Adele's little dance with the A minor Waltz). The composer returned in the very different context of *Five Easy Pieces* (dir. Bob Rafelson, 1971), in which Jack Nicholson plays Robert Dupea, a middle-class refusenik who rejects his family and the promise of a career as a concert pianist to live a more "authentic" working-class life as an oil rigger, listening to Dolly Parton country western music rather than the Chopin he once practiced. He does, however, play two pieces of Chopin in the course of the film. The first (Chopin's Fantasy in F minor, Op. 49) is rattled out on a clapped-out upright, which he finds on the back of a removal truck on the freeway, though it is hard to recognize the piece as such, so noisy are the revving engines and car horns, and so out of tune the instrument. As the truck drives away with him still playing, one is reminded of the Dudley Moore sketch which I mentioned at the beginning of our pianistic odyssey. The second piece is the famous E minor Prelude, which Robert plays for his sister-in-law (with whom he later has sex). He plays it without feeling anything, despite his sister-in-law's admission of having been "very moved" by it. He explains, "I picked the easiest piece I could think of, and I first played it when I was eight years old, and I played it better then." He insists that he had no inner feeling while playing: "None." Middle-class culture in general, and Romantic culture in particular, is thus presented as shallow, artificial, remote and most of all inauthentic. Whether one agrees with that or not, there's no denying that Chopin is the ideal composer to represent the culture and values that the film so strongly attacks.

The same E minor Prelude turned up again in Stephen Frears' *Florence Foster Jenkins* (2016). Jenkins (Meryl Streep), infamous as the world's worst opera singer, trained as a pianist in her youth, but had to give it up due to an accident. She hires a pianist with the unlikely name Cosmé McMoon (Simon Helberg) to accompany the recitals her husband encourages her to put on, and the Chopin piece appears by way of nostalgia. She strums the melody while McMoon, dressed only in a singlet, adds the drifting chromatic accompaniment of the left hand. The shot of their hands playing together echoes the touching nature of their association: Originally horrified to find himself accompanying such a terrible singer, McMoon now begins to realize that Florence's love of music and love of life in general are perhaps more important than being able to hit the right notes. It is, in effect, yet another duet, with all that this implies. Chopin's Prelude in all its wistful sadness and simplicity is the perfect piece for such a moment.

Bach and Bights

Although Bach wrote copious music for keyboard instruments, he worked at a time before the invention of the piano; but Robert Florey's *The Beast with Five Fingers* made eloquent use of a transcription. Peter Lorre stars as Hilary Cummins, the crazed private secretary of Victor Francen's Francis Ingram, a wheelchair-bound, one-handed concert pianist with Lisztian locks. After Ingram's death, Hilary murders the other claimants of Ingram's will, making it appear as if it is Ingram's severed hand, come back to life, that is responsible. He eventually begins to believe his own fiction and, in a masterful dream sequence, imagines the hand is throttling *him*. The five-fingered beast is also seen strumming Bach's Chaconne in D minor at Ingram's coffin-black grand, which stands in magisterial isolation in the hall of his Gothic mansion. The film's composer, Max Steiner, also ensures that the Chaconne features throughout the underscore. One particularly evocative use of the piano occurs in Ingram's mausoleum: A light mysteriously shines through the window of his final resting place and, as though sounding from beyond the grave, a reverberant and otherworldly piano intones a few bars of Bach to suggest that a supernatural solution might indeed be the only one to this murder mystery. The motifs of disability, pianos that seemingly play themselves, and the piano itself as a sinister unsettling presence of power and even malignancy were all re-worked in the later films *Taste of Fear* and *Torture Garden*. Tim Burton no doubt had this film in mind when the Corpse Bride (in his 2005 animated film of that name) played a piano duet with Victor Van Dort, during which her hand detaches itself from her arm but keeps playing regardless. The scene is also yet another example of the social function of piano duets in bringing young lovers together.

El Hombre y el Monstro (*The Man and the Monster*) provided one of the most absurd, though simultaneously intriguing re-workings of motifs from *The Phantom of the Opera*. Baledón's film conflates various horrors around the central image of the piano: a pact with the Devil, werewolves, the Oedipus complex, necrophilia and the inherent unease with which popular culture seems always to feel in the presence of classical music. In this case, whenever the hero Samuel Magno (Enrique Rambal) hears Tchaikovsky's Second Piano Concerto, he turns into a werewolf. The Tchaikovsky piece, performed on the soundtrack by the great Mexican virtuoso Maria Theresa

Rodriguez (1923–2013), in fact masquerades as a "secret" concerto, written on black paper with white notes, which is presented as the work of the Devil.

Again like Erik, Magno gives lessons to Laura (Martha Roth), a beautiful student, in his remote retreat. As if this isn't suspect enough, he also lives with his mother (a sure sign in popular culture that something is amiss, and perhaps also an echo of Liberace's mother fixation, well-known to the world by this time). But again, "classical" music brings with it its own connotations of the weird. As is so often the case in horror films, musicians are presented as "different" and "alien," "not like us, the audience" and consequently not to be trusted.

Magno only plays the piano at night, having given up his public career because his hands have trembled ever since making a pact with the Devil to become the world's greatest pianist. Erik would have happily shaken hands with him, notwithstanding, for Magno, like him, is disabled, a genius, a recluse and in league with the Devil. The price for the Devil's assistance is murder: Magno must kill the pianist he most admires, Alejandra (also played by Roth), and then keep her dead body in his closet (anticipating Hitchcock's *Psycho*). Her portrait hangs above his piano. Magno's student Laura is a dead ringer, hence his interest in her.

"I'm the best pianist in the world, didn't you know?" he explains to camera. "It's true. And my fingers are moved by a superior power. Invulnerable. You know well what that great power is."

When Laura learns Magno's secret, he tries to kill her too. Jealousy also plays its part, as only *he* can be the greatest pianist in the world.

Faustian Pacts

The plot of *The Man and the Monster* is less interesting (not to mention coherent) than its imagery. The theme of artistic ambition causing emotional havoc is more rigorously echoed in a film one would normally place in a very different category. Ingmar Bergman's *Autumn Sonata* (1978) is, however, comparable. In it, Ingrid Bergman plays Charlotte Andergast, a genial but inherently selfish concert pianist. (Bergman was in fact an accomplished pianist, though her performances of Grieg's Piano Concerto and Sinding's *Rustle of Spring* in *Intermezzo* were dubbed by someone else.) The mother of two daughters, Charlotte has sacrificed familial bliss to her virtuoso career. In a sense she too has sold her soul to the Devil, though the context of this film is wholly naturalistic. During a visit to her married daughter Eva (Liv Ullmann), who is caring for her disabled sister Helena (Lena Nyman), the truth of Charlotte's neglect during her daughters' childhood is gradually revealed. The piano plays its part here, for one scene has Charlotte explain the meaning of Chopin's A-minor Prelude (Op. 28, No. 2). This unintentionally humiliates Eva, who has previously played the piece to her mother. "Let's just talk about the conception," Charlotte begins.

> Chopin was emotional but not sentimental. Feeling is very far from sentimentality. The prelude tells of pain, not reverie. You have to be calm, clear and harsh. Take the first bars, now. It hurts, but he doesn't show it; then, a short relief. But it evaporates immediately and the pain is the same: Total restraint the whole time. Chopin was proud, passionate, tormented and very manly. He wasn't a sentimental old woman. This prelude must sound almost ugly. It is never ingratiating. It should sound wrong. You have to battle your way through it and emerge triumphant.

This is all very well in art, but in life, Charlotte has been nothing but sentimental and unaware of the hurt, pain and torment of her daughter's own life. She has been so wrapped up in her career, none of the emotion she put into her music ever reached her own children. At the end of the film, as she sits on a train, unable to come to terms with the catastrophe she has left behind, Charlotte attempts to justify herself: "The critics always say that I am a generous musician. No one plays Schumann's concerto with a warmer tone, nor the big Brahms sonata. I'm not stingy with myself, or am I?"

The film has already answered that question for her. As Charlotte plays the Chopin prelude to her daughter, we see Eva gazing intently at her. Charlotte understands Chopin far better than she understands her own daughter, and Eva's gaze is both accusing and curious. It is also an uncanny echo of the equally devastating look Bergman gave in *Casablanca* (dir. Michael Curtiz, 1942), when listening to Dooley Wilson's Sam playing (on a suitably upright piano) "As Time Goes By." Time, for Charlotte, has certainly flown, and with it all hopes of a truly loving relationship with her daughters, one of whom has been physically struck down with a debilitating illness caused in part by her neglect. "Why can't she die?" Charlotte asks. "Do you think it's cruel of me to talk like that?" This is Bergman's entirely naturalistic equivalent to the dead body in Magno's closet.

Magno's pact with the Devil also had a psychedelic '70s make-over in Paul Wendkos' adaptation of Fred Mustard Stewart's novel *The Mephisto Waltz*. Another virtuoso in league with the Devil, the terminally ill Duncan Ely (Curt Jurgens) plans to transplant his soul into the much more vigorous body of music journalist Miles Clarkson (Alan Alda). (Alan's father Robert played Gershwin in *Rhapsody in Blue*.) Ely's party piece is Liszt's appropriately demonic warhorse, which not only gives the film its name but also inspired composer Jerry Goldsmith to re-work Liszt's diabolic nineteenth-century Romanticism in much more avant-garde, twentieth-century terms. The effect is electrifying. So too is the original Liszt piece, which is in fact Liszt's own piano transcription of what was originally an orchestral work. So idiomatic was Goldsmith's reworking, it sounds the other way round, and has become one of the archetypal cornerstones of the Romantic piano repertoire. It was an immense influence on Alexander Scriabin (would later write his own "White Mass" and so-called "Black Mass" Sonatas). Liszt's decadent tritone harmonies and languorous syncopations over the already erotic connotations of a waltz, make this piece the ideal signature of Ely's demonic quest for immortality. Novelist Stewart describes Liszt's piece in some detail, eloquently anatomizing its demonic effect. His adjectives include "eldritch," "sepulchral hollow," "biting," "maniacal" and "whispering." The music "swirled, smoked, shrieked and thundered."[18]

Shortly after Goldsmith's reimagining of the work in the main title, which dwells particularly on the disturbing open fifths at the start of the piece, and blends them with the medieval Dies Irae chant, we first hear the solo piano version when Miles arrives at Ely's mansion. Ely is practicing, so Miles must wait until he has finished, giving him an opportunity to admire Ely's breathtaking technique. We have already been shown Jakob Gimpel's hands, standing in for Jurgens, executing the flamboyant arpeggios that create cascades of Mephisthelean magic towards the end of the piece.

The music room is suitably furnished with chandeliers, a certain decadent extravagance and two Steinway grand pianos standing side by side.

"Did you recognize the piece I just played?" Ely asks.

"Late Romantic," Miles replies. "Liszt, I think."

"Not a bad guess: *Mephisto Waltz*. The Devil dancing with his paramours."

It is only when Ely notices Miles' hands that he becomes much more interested in him. They are "Rachmaninoff hands," he exclaims, and as such, an ideal replacement for his own.

"I happen to be the greatest pianist alive," Ely explains, with no false modesty, "and I tell you this, Mr. Miles Clarkson, hands like yours are one in a hundred thousand."

Thus begins the seduction of Miles by Ely's daughter Roxane, and the ultimate substitution of Ely's soul in Miles' body, much to the distress of his wife (Jacqueline Bisset). The failed Juilliard music student now finds himself playing duets with the greatest pianist in the world at soirees held at his mansion, and before long, a Satanic ritual effects the personality transfer.

Liszt's piece did as much to demonize the piano as his own reputation as "Mephistopheles disguised as priest." The Abbé Liszt took holy orders but not so many as to prevent him pursuing his previous lifestyle, and his diabolically erotic Mephisto Waltz was no doubt influenced, in part, by his own psychological tension. The program of the work is in fact based on a poem by Nikolaus Lenau, which leaves little to the imagination: The Devil plays his violin in a village inn, causing the villagers to start dancing with increasing abandon:

> Die liebenden beiden umklammern sich selig,
> Im Doppelgetön die verschmolzenen Stimmen
> Auf rasend die Leiter der Lust erklimmen.
> Und feuriger, brausender, stürmischer immer,
> Wie Männergejauchze, Jungferngewimmer,
> Erschallen der Geige verführende Weisen,
> Und alle verschlingt ein bacchantisches Kreisen.
>
> (Both lovers are hugging each other in joy,
> Their voices entwined in impassioned duet
> Are climbing the ladder of pleasures like mad.
> And ever more ardent, more stormy, more gusty
> As men when aroused, or as maidens when lusty,
> The violin's melodies temptingly sound,
> Till all in the temple of Bacchus are drowned.)

When Miles-Duncan appears after the ceremony, it is once again to Liszt's work that he greets Roxane, with whom Duncan had been having an incestuous relationship. Now, thanks to his new body, it can be continued with renewed vigor. Miles, once a third-rate pianist, suddenly becomes the world's greatest—as well as another person. He performs the Mephisto Waltz at a concert (Alda mimes convincingly) and receives standing ovations, much to his wife's despair, for she has lost her husband and gained a Satanist. The remainder of the film concerns her revenge, and as such has little to do with pianos. (She in fact murders Roxane and repeats the process to which Miles was subjected, transferring her own soul into Roxane's body.)

The demonic connotations of the piano in both the film and the score may have inspired Goldsmith to begin his famous main title music for Richard Donner's *The Omen* (1976) with the piano's sinister rumination on a minor seventh, ushering in the vocal chant of "Sanguis bibimus, corpus edimus." Here, the piano punctuates the first and second statements of Goldsmith's demonic choral theme. All the pianist has to do is play a single line played on the upper registers, the instrument's all-too-familiar timbre in this context sounding alienated and unsettling.

The inherent power and authority of the grand piano made it the obvious instrument of choice for Buxton, the evil cat in Serge Danot's *Dougal and the Blue Cat* (1970). Far better known in the English-language version scripted and performed by Eric Thompson, Buxton was actually named after composer Buxton Orr, who happened to be a family relative of Thompson's wife Phillida Law. Thompson thought Buxton—the name of a Yorkshire town—an absurd name to give anyone, so decided to give it to the cat, who consequently acquired a Yorkshire accent. When Buxton is eventually crowned king after a series of tests, he celebrates with a kind of piano concerto, composed for the film by Joss Baselli. This calls to mind *Dangerous Moonlight* as well as *The Cat Concerto* in Buxton's use of forefeet, back feet and tail at the keyboard. Also like Tom the Cat, Buxton segues from Lisztian pyrotechnics to more syncopated popular style, which causes one of his blue minions to start dancing, much to the disapproval of his comrades.

And the piano continues to exert its status and authority as a symbol of *power*. Even though millennial audiences may no longer be particularly interested in classical music, they are still responsive to the piano's image, and just as much attracted to the idea of power as anyone has ever been. Zu Quirke's teen drama *Nocturne* (2020) grafts sibling rivalry onto the hothouse world of Juilliard Academy music students, mixes it with echoes of Faustian diabolism and—hey presto-prestissimo—we have a *Mephisto Waltz* for the modern world in which greed, competition and status are prized rather more than the music itself, which has become truly incidental. "Music is a blood sport," says Ivan Shaw's ruthless tutor Dr. Henry Cask. "If you really want that spotlight, you won't let anything get in you way. Not even your sister." Accordingly, Juliet (Syndey Sweeney) invokes supernatural aid, via a former student's magical musical score, in an attempt to triumph over her more talented sister Vivien (Madison Iseman). No one is really interested in music here, still less the piano. It is what the piano symbolizes that is the point, for in an age when so few people still play it, that is really all that the piano has.

Finale

What do all these cinematic pianos tell us? There are surely reasons for their ubiquity. As well as charting the decline and fall of this particular instrument during the decadence of a specific (Western) culture, they also reveal something perhaps more significant about the human need for transformative art. Humanity, like nature, abhors a vacuum. While many people find the lack of meaning in their lives intolerable, a great many *more* find the lack of their own significance horrific. This is, after all, the reason for religion. After religion, Art comes to the rescue, which is why religions have so often commissioned Art, on which they so largely rely; and central to religion is our psychosexual reality, a reality we can only comes to terms with symbolically. What drives it remains a mystery...

I hope I have explained some of the reasons in my analysis of how the cinema has presented the piano as an icon of a particular cultural tradition. I have demonstrated that the piano is erotic and redemptive, and that the pianist is its presiding priest. Liszt certainly saw himself in this way—the Abbé Liszt who confessed his sins to the keyboard and absolved them in so doing. In this, he was indebted to the ideas of the Abbé Lamennais, who had inspired him in his youth. For Lamennais, Art was God made manifest and the Artist was indeed a priest preaching to his flock. This is a particularly Romantic ideal. No one worshipped Mozart in this way in his own day, but that was because God still existed at that time. The social structure in which Mozart found himself would anyway have prevented this (Mozart, like all musicians, was technically a servant); but God was growing moribund when Liszt appeared on the scene. Alternative gods—pantheistic, pagan and pianistic—were usurping His position. Whereas the conduit of music was once used to worship God, the conduit itself was now the object of veneration. Liszt was indeed a kind of god (even though he fervently believed in the Christian deity). When we watch composers and performers at the piano, we are really engaging in a form of communion. That is why Elizabeth Taylor weeps when listening to Rachmaninoff's

Second Piano Concerto in *Rhapsody*, and why Liberace performs "miracles" in *Sincerely Yours*. Audiences watch the divine prestidigitations of actors impersonating Gershwin or Liszt or Chopin—even Elton John—as they would a priest administering the blood and body of Christ. We are in the presence of mystical, godlike genius—musicians who open the way to our innermost desires of sex and power, ecstasy and possession. Geoffrey Rush as David Helfgott is shown as Christ keyboardified for our sins in *Shine*. At the beginning of the film, a man in a café laughs at the idea of this down-and-out (as Helfgott, in his mental illness, has become) being able to play the piano. The man's laughter is like that of Kundry in Wagner's *Parsifal*, who laughed at "Him" on his way to Calvary. But David soon slays this philistine Goliath, with a staggering rendition of "The Flight of the Bumblebee," thus absolving any feelings we might have shared with such a sinner.

The piano still has a high cultural status and continues to appear in films as signifier of cultural aspirations, romance and sophistication in contexts vastly remote from its own history. It even appears in science fiction. In Morten Tyldum's 2016 space epic *Passengers*, set on a luxurious spaceship on its way to colonize a distant planet, one of the crew, Jim Preston (Chris Pratt) wakes up from his sleep capsule 99 years before he should and in need of company decides to wake up the beautiful Aurora (Jennifer Lawrence). Their romance is celebrated in a variety of ways, one of which involves Jim serenading her on the grand piano in the spaceship's bar. A grand piano on a spaceship is the ultimate accolade of the instrument's power as an icon, but the musical culture it helped create is not really part of the equation. Even in films which use standard piano classics, the connotation of sophistication brought to the proceedings by the connotations of the music seems more important than the music itself, which isn't really on the same wavelength as the film's target audience. Similarly, in Len Wiseman's 2012 remake of *Total Recall*, the piano finds itself transplanted into a future world that has left the culture it represents far behind. Colin Farrell's Douglas Quaid has someone else's memory implanted into his consciousness by a kind of virtual reality corporation. In one scene, exhausted by his fruitless search, he sits at a shiny black grand piano and like so many others before him, starts to play (rather badly) the "Moonlight" Sonata. After a few bars, he gives up and tries instead part of the finale to Beethoven's "Tempest" Sonata. This goes well until he discovers that one of the black keys (C-sharp/D-flat) isn't working; and then he remembers that he has a black piano key in his pocket. He removes the faulty key and clips on the hi-tech replacement, which activates a hologram that explains who Jim is and what lies ahead for humanity in the dystopian world of the film. Farrell learned to play this fragment of Beethoven for his role, but again the music and the instrument have by this stage in cinematic history become mere symbols of something left behind. In both the context of the film as well as among its fans, who refer to the Beethoven sonata as a "song" when discussing it online, the music is no longer an integral part of cultural life. It is "special," added on, "extra," unusual, remote.

Nothing demonstrates the danger facing classical music in the real world better than the recent CD *Piano*, released in 2020 by Benny Andersson (of Abba fame). On this recording, he plays his own piano arrangements of Abba's hits on a finely tuned, closely miked Fazioli grand. This might not be worth mentioning but for one thing: Andersson is a highly accomplished, technically astute musician, and Abba created masterpieces of pop music, but the CD is released by Deutsche Grammophon. Even though it is now owned by Universal Music, DG is still the pre-eminent recording platform for the Western classical tradition; but 20 years ago, the thought of DG releasing an album of pop music would have been unthinkable. To present Abba's "Thank You for the Music" as if it were a Beethoven Sonata suggests that the post-modern understanding of esthetics and musical history has reached a critical stage.

No doubt we would all like to be able to play the piano, but a film like *Twilight* (dir. Catherine Hardwick, 2008), with its vampire pianist Edward, suggests that it is a skill reserved for "special" people, and anyway, in apparently much busier times, it requires too much time. (Edward has immortality on his side.) However, this is a modern problem of piano perception. In the past, as we have seen, the piano was common property, and no one had to be "special" to take it up.

Even though it may have lost its previous position of pre-eminence, the piano is still with us, and like the participation of initiates in Hellenistic *mysteria*, the experience of music gives us "the opportunity for a better life through direct contact with a transcendent realm of gods."[1] What seems to be impossible is shown, miraculously, to be true. If there are no real miracles in the world, a piano recital is certainly like a miracle. When combined with the experience of the cinema, the transcendental effect can be even more powerful. When Richard Noll writes, "In the words of an individual who had seen the mysteries of Eleusis, 'I came out of the Mystery Hall feeling like a stranger to myself,'"[2] he might also be describing what it feels like to emerge from the dark enchantment of a cinema. Disoriented, overwhelmed and purged of one's emotions, one returns to the traffic-roaring, pedestrian-pulsating reality of London's sunlit Leicester Square. This is the transformative power of light and music.

Chapter Notes

Introduction

1. Kenneth Clarke, *Civilisation* (London: Folio Society, 1999), 33.
2. Luigi Magnani (trans. Isabel Quigly), *Beethoven's Nephew* (London: W. H. Allen, 1997), viii.
3. Thomas Mann (trans. H. T. Lowe-Porter), *Doctor Faustus* (London: Secker & Warburg, 1976), 54.

Chapter One

1. Amy Fay, *Music-Study in Germany* (London: Macmillan, 1911), 195–196.
2. Arthur Loesser, *Men, Women and Pianos* (London: Victor Gollancz, 1955), 229.
3. D. H. Lawrence, "Nottingham and the Mining Country," http://www.spokesmanbooks.com/Spokesman/PDF/135Lawrence.pdf.
4. Peter Conradi, *Hitler's Piano Player—The Rise and Fall of Ernst Hanfstaengl, Confidant of Hitler, Ally of FDR* (London: Duckworth, 2006), 89–90.
5. Alan Walker, *Franz Liszt—The Virtuoso Years 1811–1847* (London: Faber and Faber, 1983), 304.
6. Dieter Hildebrandt, *Pianoforte—A Social History of the Piano* (New York: George Braziller, 1988), 179.
7. *Ibid.*, 3.
8. Sophy Roberts, *The Lost Pianos of Siberia* (London: Doubleday, 2020), 65.
9. Roland Barthes (trans. Stephen Heath), *Image Music Text* (London: Fontana, 1977), 147 ("Musica practica").
10. Sir Charles Hallé (ed. C. E. and Marie Hallé), *Life and Letters of Sir Charles Hallé* (London: Smith, Elder, & Co., 1896), 37–38.
11. Hector Berlioz (trans. David Cairns), *A Life of Love and Music—The Memoirs of Hector Berlioz 1803–1865* (London: Folio Society, 1987), 228.
12. Friedrich Nietzsche (trans. R. J. Hollingdale), *Ecce Homo* (Harmondsworth: Penguin, 1979), 61.
13. Thomas Mann (ed. H. T. Lowe-Porter), *Buddenbrooks* (London: Secker & Warburg, 1956), 407.
14. Thomas Mann (trans. H. T. Lowe-Porter), *Stories of Three Decades* (London: Martin Secker & Warburg, 1946), 153 ("Tristan").
15. Marcel Proust (trans. C. K. Scott Moncrieff and Terence Kilmartin), *Remembrance of Things Past*, Vol. 1 (New York: Vintage, 1982), 227–228 ("Swann in Love").
16. *Ibid.*, 231.
17. Anthony Burgess, *The Pianoplayers* (London: Hutchinson,1986), 127.
18. David Rowland, ed., *The Cambridge Companion to the Piano* (Cambridge: Cambridge University Press, 1998), 110–111.
19. Anthony Wilkinson, *Liszt* (London: Macmillan 1975), 49.
20. Paul Metzner, *The Crescendo of the Virtuoso—Spectacle, and Self-Promotion in Paris During the Age of Revolution* (Berkeley: University of California Press, 1998), 145.
21. *Ibid.*, 264.
22. Sophy Roberts, *The Lost Pianos of Siberia* (London: Doubleday, 2020), 155.
23. *Ibid.*, 199.
24. Martin Harrison and Bill Water, *Burne-Jones* (London: Barrie & Jenkins, 1973), 129.

25. Charles Rosen, *Piano Notes—The Hidden World of the Pianist* (London: Allen Lane, 2002), 64.
26. "Piano burning," https://en.wikipedia.org/wiki/Piano_burning.

Chapter Two

1. Tim Heard and Priscilla Ridgway, eds., *Great Stories of Crime and Detection*, Vol. 2 (London: Folio Society, 2002), 420–421 (Graham Greene, "A Little Place Off the Edgware Road").
2. John Huntley, *British Film Music* (London: Skelton Robinson, 1947), 26.
3. Michael Oliver, ed., *Settling the Score—A Journey Through the Music of the 20th Century* (London: Faber and Faber, 1999), 156.
4. Burgess, *The Pianoplayers*, 28.
5. George Burt, *The Art of Film Music* (Boston: Northeastern University Press, 1994), 181.
6. *Ibid.*, 182.
7. Oliver, *Settling the Score*, 155.
8. Huntley, *British Film Music*, 53.
9. *Ibid.*, 55.
10. Oliver, *Settling the Score*, 161–162.
11. Huntley, *British Film Music*, 55.
12. Anthony Burgess, *This Man and Music* (New York: Applause, 2001), 32.
13. Huntley, *British Film Music*, 190.
14. "The Myra Hess Concerts," National Gallery (London), https://www.nationalgallery.org.uk/about-us/history/the-myra-hess-concerts/how-the-concerts-started?viewPage=3.
15. Huntley, *British Film Music*, 86.
16. *Ibid.*, 69–70.
17. Oliver, *Settling the Score*, 161.
18. Huntley, *British Film Music*, 82.
19. Kevin Brownlow, *David Lean—A Biography* (London: Richard Cohen Books, 1996), 202–203.
20. *Ibid.*, 197.
21. Dmitri Shostakovitch (ed. Solomon Volkoff), *Testimony* (London: Hamish Hamilton, 1979), 196.
22. *Ibid.*, 113.
23. *Ibid.*, 194.
24. Geoffrey Norris, *Rakhmaninov—The Master Musicians* (London: Dent, 1976), 112.
25. *Ibid.*, 121.

Chapter Three

1. Charles Rosen, *The Romantic Generation* (London: HarperCollins, 1995), 594.
2. Friedrich Nietzsche (trans. R.J. Hollingdale), *Untimely Meditations* (Cambridge: University of Cambridge Press, 1995), 83 ("On the uses & disadvantages of history for life").
3. Michael Steen, *The Lives and Times of the Great Composers* (London: Icon Books, 2011).
4. Liberace, *Autobiography* (London: Star Books/W. H. Allen, 1974), 53.
5. *Ibid.*, 69.
6. Huntley, *British Film Music*, 51–52.
7. Henry C. Lahee, *Famous Pianists of Today and Yesterday* (Boston: L. C. Page, 1920), 230–231.
8. *Ibid.*, 224–225.
9. *Ibid.*, 223.
10. *Ibid.*
11. Harold C. Schonberg, *The Great Pianists* (London: Victor Gollancz, 1964), 285.
12. *Ibid.*, 291.
13. *Ibid.*, 290.
14. *Ibid.*, 285.
15. Darden Asbury Pyron, *Liberace—An American Boy* (Chicago: University of Chicago Press, 2000), 143.
16. *Ibid.*, 143–144.
17. *Ibid.*, 152–153.
18. Frederick Niecks, *Frederick Chopin as a Man and Musician* (Norderstedt, Germany: Books on Demand, 2018), 409–410.
19. Thomas Mann (trans. H. T. Lowe-Porter), *Doctor Faustus* (London: Secker & Warburg, 1976), 143.
20. Pyron, *Liberace*, 94.
21. *Ibid.*, ix.

Chapter Four

1. Alan Walker, *Franz Liszt—The Virtuoso Years 1811–1847* (London: Faber and Faber, 1983), 296.
2. Anthony Wilkinson, *Liszt* (London: Macmillan, 1975), 69.
3. Thomas Mann (trans. Allan Blunden), *Pro and Contra Wagner* (London: Faber and Faber, 1985), 92–93 ("The Sorrows and Grandeur of Richard Wagner").
4. Wilkinson, *Liszt*, 69.
5. Henry C. Lahee, *Famous Pianists of Today and Yesterday* (Boston: L. C. Page, 1920), 140.

6. Walker, *Liszt*, 303–304.
7. Wilkinson, *Liszt*, 54.
8. Marissa Silverman, *Gregory Haimovsky, A Pianist's Odyssey to Freedom* (Rochester: University of Rochester Press, 2018), 32.
9. Ken Russell, *A British Picture—An Autobiography* (London: Southbank Publishing 2008), 143.
10. *Ibid.*
11. Dirk Bogarde, *Snakes and Ladders* (London: Chatto & Windus. 1978), 178.
12. *Ibid.*, 181.
13. Dirk Bogarde, *A Postillion Struck by Lightning* (London: Chatto & Windus. 1977), 260.
14. Walker, *Liszt*, 321.

Chapter Five

1. Burgess, *The Pianoplayers*, 26–27.
2. Murray Shaffer, *British Composers in Interview* (London: Faber and Faber, 1963), 25.
3. Romain Rolland (trans. Gilbert Cannan), *Jean-Christophe* (New York: Random House, no date), 181–183.
4. George Eliot, *Daniel Deronda* (Ware, England: Wordsworth, 1996), 211.
5. George Bernard Shaw, *Music in London*, Vol. 2 (New York: Vienna House, 1973), 236 ("11 January 1893").
6. Gustave Flaubert (trans. W. Blaydes), *Madame Bovary* (London: Heron, no date), 953–954.
7. Dieter Hildebrandt, *Pianoforte—A Social History of the Piano* (New York: George Braziller, 1988), 123.
8. Henry James, *The Portrait of a Lady* (London: Heron Books, no date), 166–167.
9. Hildebrandt, *Pianoforte*, 124.
10. Louisa M. Alcott, *Little Women* (London: Dean & Son, no date), 15.
11. *Ibid.*, 41.
12. *Ibid.*, 60.
13. Hildebrandt, *Pianoforte*, 173.
14. Jane Austen, *Pride and Prejudice* (London: Heron Books, no date), 102.
15. Hildebrandt, *Pianoforte*, 173.
16. Henry Handel Richardson, *The Getting of Wisdom*, http://www.gutenberg.org/files/3728/3728-h/3728-h.htm#chap09.
17. Anthony Trollope, *North America*, Vol. 1, http://www.gutenberg.org/files/1865/1865-h/1865-h.htm.
18. Wilkie Collins, *The Woman in White* (London: Heron Books, no date), 292.
19. John Golby, ed., *Culture & Society in Britain 1850-1890—A Source Book of Contemporary Writings* (Oxford: Oxford University Press/The Open University, 1986), 104–105.
20. Flaubert, *Madame Bovary*, 52.

Chapter Six

1. Sophy Roberts, *The Lost Pianos of Siberia* (London: Doubleday, 2020), 218.
2. Thomas Mann (trans. H. T. Lowe-Porter), *Doctor Faustus* (London: Secker & Warburg, 1976), 373.
3. Rolland, *Jean-Christophe*, Book 1, 62–63.
4. Georgiana Burne-Jones, *Memorials of Edward Burne-Jones* (New York: Macmillan, 1904), 111.
5. George Du Maurier, *Novels of George Du Maurier—Trilby, The Martians, Peter Ibbetson* (London: Pilot Press & Peter Davis, 1947), 248 ("Trilby").
6. Gaston Leroux, *The Phantom of the Opera* (London: Michael O'Mara. 1987), 114.
7. *Ibid.*, 114.
8. *Ibid.*, 116.
9. *Ibid.*, 111.
10. John Gray, *Black Mass—Apocalyptic Religion and the Death of Utopia* (London: Penguin, 2008), 56.
11. Gabrielle D'Annunzio (trans. Georgina Harding), *The Child of Pleasure* (Sawtry, England: Dedalus, 1991), 259.
12. Geoffrey Norris, *Rakhmaninov—The Master Musicians* (London: Dent, 1976), 42.
13. Harold Schonberg, *The Great Pianists* (London: Gollancz, 1964), 369.
14. Thomas Mann (trans. H. T. Lowe-Porter), *Stories of Three Decades* (London: Martin Secker & Warburg, 1946), 105 ("Tonio Kröger").
15. David Whitaker in conversation with the author.
16. Hector Berlioz (trans. David Cairns), *A Life of Love and Music—The Memoirs of Hector Berlioz 1803-1865* (London: Folio Society, 1987), 13.
17. Igor Stravinsky (ed. Robert Craft), *Expositions and Developments* (London: Faber & Faber), 1981, 47.
18. Richard Wagner (trans. William

Ashton Ellis), *The Art-Work of the Future and Other Works* (Lincoln: University of Nebraska Press, 1993), 19 ("Autobiographical Sketch").

Chapter Seven

1. Harpo Marx (with Rowland Barber), *Harpo Speaks!* (Milwaukee, WI: Hal Leonard Corp., 2004), 284–285.
2. Charles Rosen, *Piano Notes—The Hidden World of the Pianist* (London: Allen Lane, 2002), 19.
3. Gabrielle D'Annunzio, (trans. Raymond Rosenthal), *Nocturne and Five Tales of Love and Death* (London: Quartet, 1988), 163–164 ("Leda Without Swan").
4. George Moore, *Evelyn Innes* (London: T. Fisher Unwin, 1898), 72–73.

Chapter Eight

1. Wilkinson, *Liszt*, 31.
2. Ralph Waldo Emerson, *The Complete Works* Vol. VII Society and Solitude (Boston: Houghton, Mifflin, 1904), p. 23 ("Civilization").
3. L. P. Hartley, *The Go-Between* (London: Guild Publishing, 1986), 140.
4. Henry James, "Lady Barbarina," https://www.gutenberg.org/files/37627/37627-h/37627-h.htm (section IV).
5. Leo Tolstoy, *The Kreutzer Sonata and Other Short Stories* (New York: Dover, 1993), 117 ("The Kreutzer Sonata").
6. *Ibid.*, 122 ("The Kreutzer Sonata").
7. Michael Sims ed., *Dracula's Guest—A Connoisseur's Collection of Victorian Vampire Stories* (London: Bloomsbury, 2010), 319–321 (Eric, Count Stenbock, "A True Story of a Vampire").
8. Marcus Hearn and Alan Barnes, *The Hammer Story* (London: Titan Books, 1997), 77.
9. Mike Murphy, *Dark Terrors*, Issue 24 (St. Ives: Mike Murphy, 1997), 16 ("The Kiss of the Vampire").
10. Charles Rosen, *The Romantic Generation* (London: HarperCollins, 1996), 351.
11. E. F. Benson, *Mapp and Lucia* (London: Black Swan, 1989), 138.
12. Maurice Renard, *The Hands of Orlac* (London: Souvenir Press, 1981), 83.
13. *Ibid.*, 84.
14. Eric Ambler, *Epitaph for a Spy* (London: Penguin, 2009), 192–193.
15. Antoine de Baecque and Serge Toubiana (trans. Catherine Temerson), *Truffaut—A Biography* (Berkeley: University of California Press, 1999), 159.
16. Samuel Taylor Coleridge (ed. Stephen Potter), *Select Poetry and Prose* (London: Nonesuch Press, 1971), 388 ("Othello")
17. Oscar Wilde (ed. Merlin Holland), *Letters and Essays* (London: Folio, 1993), 249 ("The Critic as Artist").
18. Fred Mustard Stewart, *The Mephisto Waltz* (London: Michael Joseph, 1969), 23.

Finale

1. Richard Noll, *The Aryan Christ—The Secret Life of Carl Gustav Jung* (London: Macmillan, 1997), 129.
2. *Ibid.*, 130.

Bibliography

Alcott, Louisa M. *Little Women*. London: Dean & Son, no date.

Austen, Jane. *Pride and Prejudice*. London: Heron Books, no date.

Baecque, Antoine de, and Serge Toubiana, (trans. Catherine Temerson). *Truffaut—A Biography*. Berkeley: University of California Press, 1999.

Barthes, Roland (trans. Stephen Heath). *Image Music Text*. London: Fontana, 1977.

Benson, E. F. *Mapp and Lucia*. London: Black Swan, 1989.

Berlioz, Hector (trans. David Cairns). *A Life of Love and Music—The Memoirs of Hector Berlioz 1803-1865*. London: Folio Society, 1987.

Bogarde, Dirk. *A Postillion Struck by Lightning*. London: Chatto & Windus, 1977.

Bogarde, Dirk. *Snakes and Ladders*. London: Chatto & Windus, 1978.

Brownlow, Kevin. *David Lean—A Biography*. London: Richard Cohen Books, 1996.

Burgess, Anthony. *The Pianoplayers*. London: Hutchinson, 1986.

Burgess, Anthony. *This Man and Music*. New York: Applause, 2001.

Burne-Jones, Georgiana. *Memorials of Edward Burne-Jones*. New York: Macmillan, 1904.

Burt, George. *The Art of Film Music*. Boston: Northeastern University Press, 1994.

Clarke, Kenneth. *Civilisation*. London: Folio Society, 1999.

Coleridge, Samuel Taylor (ed. Stephen Potter). *Select Poetry and Prose*. London: Nonesuch Press, 1971.

Collins, Wilkie. *The Woman in White*. London: Heron Books, no date).

Conradi, Peter. *Hitler's Piano Player—The Rise and Fall of Ernst Hanfstaengl, Confidant of Hitler, Ally of FDR*. London: Duckworth, 2006.

D'Annunzio, Gabrielle (trans. Georgina Harding). *The Child of Pleasure*. Sawtry, England: Dedalus, 1991.

D'Annunzio, Gabrielle (trans. Raymond Rosenthal). *Nocturne and Five Tales of Love and Death*. London: Quartet, 1988.

Du Maurier, George. *Novels of George Du Maurier—Trilby, The Martians, Peter Ibbetson*. London: Pilot Press & Peter Davis, 1947.

Eliot, George. *Daniel Deronda*. Ware, England: Wordsworth, 1996.

Emerson, Ralph Waldo. *The Complete Works*. Boston: Houghton Mifflin, 1904.

Fay, Amy. *Music-Study in Germany*. London: Macmillan, 1911.

Flaubert, Gustave (trans. W. Blaydes). *Madame Bovary*. London: Heron, no date.

Golby, John, ed. *Culture & Society in Britain 1850-1890—A Source Book of Contemporary Writings*. Oxford: Oxford University Press/The Open University, 1986.

Gray, John. *Black Mass—Apocalyptic Religion and the Death of Utopia*. London: Penguin, 2008.

Hallé, Charles (ed. C. E. and Marie Hallé). *Life and Letters of Sir Charles Hallé*. London: Smith, Elder, & Co., 1896.

Harrison, Martin, and Bill Water. *Burne-Jones*. London: Barrie & Jenkins, 1973.

Hartley, L. P. *The Go-Between*. London: Guild Publishing, 1986.

Heard, Tim, and Priscilla Ridgway, eds. *Great Stories of Crime and Detection* Vol. 2. London: Folio Society, 2002.

Hearn, Marcus, and Alan Barnes. *The Hammer Story*. London: Titan Books, 1997.

Hildebrandt, Dieter. *Pianoforte—A Social History of the Piano*. New York: George Braziller, 1988.
Huntley, John. *British Film Music*. London: Skelton Robinson, 1947.
James, Henry. "Lady Barbarina." https://www.gutenberg.org/files/37627/37627-h/37627-h.htm.
James, Henry. *The Portrait of a Lady*. London: Heron Books, no date.
Lahee, Henry C. *Famous Pianists of Today and Yesterday*. Boston: L. C. Page, 1920.
Lawrence, D. H. "Nottingham and the Mining Country." http://www.spokesmanbooks.com/Spokesman/PDF/135 Lawrence.pdf.
Leroux, Gaston. *The Phantom of the Opera*. London: Michael O'Mara, 1987.
Liberace. *Autobiography*. London: Star Books/W. H. Allen, 1974.
Loesser, Arthur. *Men, Women and Pianos*. London: Victor Gollancz, 1955.
Magnani, Luigi (trans. Isabel Quigly). *Beethoven's Nephew*. London: W. H. Allen, 1997.
Mann, Thomas (ed. H. T. Lowe-Porter), *Buddenbrooks*. London: Secker & Warburg, 1956.
Mann, Thomas (trans. H. T. Lowe-Porter). *Doctor Faustus*. London: Secker & Warburg, 1976.
Mann, Thomas (trans. Allan Blunden). *Pro and Contra Wagner*. London: Faber & Faber, 1985.
Mann, Thomas (trans. H. T. Lowe-Porter). *Stories of Three Decades*. London: Martin Secker & Warburg, 1946.
Marx, Harpo, with Rowland Barber. *Harpo Speaks!* Milwaukee, WI: Hal Leonard Corp., 2004.
Metzner, Paul. *The Crescendo of the Virtuoso—Spectacle, and Self-Promotion in Paris During the Age of Revolution*. Berkeley: University of California Press, 1998.
Moore, George. *Evelyn Innes*. London: T. Fisher Unwin, 1898.
Murphy, Mike, ed. *Dark Terrors*. Issue 24 St. Ives: Mike Murphy, 1997.
"The Myra Hess Concerts: The First Concert." *The National Gallery* (London). https://www.nationalgallery.org.uk/about-us/history/the-myra-hess-concerts/how-the-concerts-started?viewPage=3.
Niecks, Frederick, *Frederick Chopin as a Man and Musician*. Norderstedt, Germany: Books on Demand, 2018.

Nietzsche, Friedrich (trans. R. J. Hollingdale). *Ecce Homo*. Harmondsworth: Penguin, 1979.
Nietzsche, Friedrich (trans. R.J. Hollingdale). *Untimely Meditations*. Cambridge: University of Cambridge Press, 1995.
Noll, Richard. *The Aryan Christ—The Secret Life of Carl Gustav Jung*. London: Macmillan, 1997.
Norris, Geoffrey. *Rakhmaninov—The Master Musicians*. London: Dent, 1976.
Oliver, Michael, ed. *Settling the Score—A Journey Through the Music of the 20th Century*. London: Faber & Faber, 1999.
Proust, Marcel (trans. C. K. Scott Moncrieff and Terence Kilmartin). *Remembrance of Things Past*, Vol.1. New York: Vintage, 1982.
Pyron, Darden Asbury. *Liberace—An American Boy*. Chicago: University of Chicago Press, 2000.
Renard, Maurice. *The Hands of Orlac*. London: Souvenir Press, 1981.
Richardson, Henry Handel. *The Getting of Wisdom*. http://www.gutenberg.org/files/3728/3728-h/3728-h.htm#chap09.
Roberts, Sophy. *The Lost Pianos of Siberia*. London: Doubleday, 2020.
Rolland, Romain (trans. Gilbert Cannan). *Jean-Christophe*. New York: Random House, no date.
Rosen, Charles. *Piano Notes—The Hidden World of the Pianist*. London: Allen Lane, 2002.
Rosen, Charles. *The Romantic Generation*. London: HarperCollins, 1995.
Rowland, David, ed. *The Cambridge Companion to the Piano*. Cambridge: Cambridge University Press, 1998.
Russell, Ken. *A British Picture—An Autobiography*. London: Southbank Publishing 2008.
Schonberg, Harold C. *The Great Pianists*. London: Victor Gollancz, 1964.
Shaffer, Murray. *British Composers in Interview*. London: Faber & Faber, 1963.
Shaw, George Bernard. *Music in London*, Vol. 2. New York: Vienna House, 1973.
Shostakovitch, Dmitri (ed. Solomon Volkoff). *Testimony*. London: Hamish Hamilton, 1979.
Silverman, Marissa. *Gregory Haimovsky, A Pianist's Odyssey to Freedom*. Rochester: University of Rochester Press, 2018.
Steen, Michael. *The Lives and Times of the Great Composers*. London: Icon Books, 2011.

Stewart, Fred Mustard. *The Mephisto Waltz*. London: Michael Joseph, 1969.
Stravinsky, Igor (ed. Robert Craft) *Expositions and Developments*. London: Faber & Faber, 1981.
Tolstoy, Leo. *The Kreutzer Sonata and Other Short Stories*. New York: Dover, 1993.
Trollope, Anthony, *North America*, Vol. 1, http://www.gutenberg.org/files/1865/1865-h/1865-h.htm.
Wagner, Richard (trans. William Ashton Ellis). *The Art-Work of the Future and Other Works*. Lincoln: University of Nebraska Press, 1993.
Walker, Alan. *Franz Liszt—The Virtuoso Years 1811–1847*. London: Faber & Faber, 1983.
Wilde, Oscar (ed. Merlin Holland). *Letters and Essays*. London: Folio, 1993.
Wilkinson, Anthony. *Liszt*. London: Macmillan 1975.

Filmography

The Abominable Dr. Phibes (dir. Robert Fuest, 1971).
All About Eve (dir. Joseph L. Mankiewicz, 1950).
All Night Long (dir. Basil Dearden, 1962).
Amadeus (dir. Miloš Forman, 1984).
An American in Paris (dir. Vincente Minnelli, 1951).
The Angel Who Pawned Her Harp (dir. Alan Bromly, 1954).
Appointment in London (dir. Philip Leacock, 1953).
Autumn Sonata (dir. Ingmar Bergman, 1978).
Ballot-Box Bunny (dir. Fritz Freleng, 1951).
De Battre mon cœur s'est arrêté (*The Beat That My Heart Skipped*) (dir. Jacques Audiard, 2005).
The Beast with Five Fingers (dir. Robert Florey, 1946).
Behind the Candelabra (dir. Stephen Soderbergh, 2019).
Big (dir. Penny Marshall, 1988).
The Big Store (dir. Charles Reisner, 1941).
Billion Dollar Brain (dir. Ken Russell, 1968).
The Bishop's Wife (dir. Henry Costa, 1947).
Black Sunday (dir. Mario Bava, 1960).
Blazing Saddles (dir. Mel Brooks, 1974).
Booby Traps (dir. Robert Clampett, 1944).
The Boy Friend (dir. Ken Russell, 1972).
Brief Encounter (dir. David Lean, 1945).
Broadway Melody of 1940 (dir. Norman Taurog, 1940).
California Suite (dir. Herbert Ross, 1978)
Carry On Cowboy (dir. Gerald Thomas, 1965).
Casablanca (dir. Michael Curtis, 1942).
The Cat Concerto (dirs. William Hanna & Joseph Barbera, 1947).
Chopin: A Desire for Love (dir. Jerzy Antczak, 2002).
The Composer Glinka (dir. Grigoriy Aleksandrov, 1952).
The Constant Nymph (dir. Edmund Golding, 1943).
Crescendo (dir. Alan Gibson, 1970).
Cruel Intentions (dir. Roger Kumble, 1999).
Dangerous Moonlight (dir. Brian Desmond Hurst, 1941).
Dark Shadows (dir. Tim Burton, 2012).
A Day at the Races (dir. Sam Wood, 1937).
Death in Venice (dir. Luchino Visconti, 1971).
Deception (dir. Irving Rapper, 1946).
Doctor Faustus (dir. Franz Seitz, 1982).
Dr. Jekyll and Mr. Hyde (dir. Rouben Mamoullian, 1931).
Dr. Jekyll and Sister Hyde (dir. Roy Ward Baker, 1971).
Dr. Phibes Rises Again (dir. Robert Fuest, 1972).
A Doll's House (dir. Joseph Losey. 1973).
A Doll's House (dir. Patrick Garland, 1973).
Don't Look Now (dir. Nicolas Roeg, 1973).
Dougal and the Blue Cat (dir. Serge Danot, 1970).
Dragonwyk (dir. Joseph L. Mankiewicz, 1946).
Dream of Love (dir. José Bohr, 1935).
Dreams of Love (dir. Christian Stengel, 1947).
Easter Parade (dir. Charles Walters, 1948).
The Eddie Duchen Story (dir. George Sidney, 1956).
Eye of the Devil (dir. J. Lee Thompson, 1967).
The Fabulous Baker Boys (dir. Steve Kloves, 1989).
Fantasia (dir. Wilfred Jackson, et al, 1940).
Fantasia 2000 (dir. James Algar, et al, 1999).
Fingers (dir. James Toback, 1978).
Five Easy Pieces (dir. Bob Rafelson, 1971).

Florence Foster Jenkins (dir. Stephen Frears, 2016).
Follow the Fleet (dir. Mark Sandrich, 1936).
Gaslight (dir. Charles Vidor, 1944).
Gaslight (dir. Thorold Dickinson, 1940).
The Getting of Wisdom (dir. Bruce Beresford, 1977).
Girl in the Headlines (dir. Michael Truman, 1963).
The Glass Mountain (dir. Henry Cass, 1949).
The Go-Between (dir. Joseph Losey, 1971).
Go West (dir. Edward Buzzell, 1941).
Gosford Park (dir. Robert Altman, 2002).
Grand Piano (dir. Eugenio Mira, 2013).
Hammerhead (dir. David Miller, 1968).
Hands of a Stranger (dir. Newt Arnold, 1962).
The Hands of Orlac (dir. Edmond T. Greville, 1960).
The Hands of Orlac (dir. Robert Wiene, 1924).
Hangover Square (dir. John Brahm, 1945).
The Harpist (dir. Hansjörg Thurn, 1999).
Harry Potter and the Deathly Hallows (dir. David Yates, 2010).
The Haunted House of Horror (dir. Michael Armstrong, 1969).
The Hideous Sun Demon (dir. Robert Clarke, 1958).
His Musical Career (dir. Charles Chaplin, 1914).
El Hombre y el Monstro (*The Man and the Monster*) (dir. Raphael Baledón, 1959).
Horsefeathers (dir. Norman Z. McCleod, 1932).
Howards End (dir. James Ivory, 1992).
Humoresque (dir. Jean Negulesco, 1946).
I Walked with a Zombie (dir Jacques Tourneur, 1943).
If (dir. Lindsay Anderson, 1968).
Immortal Beloved (dir. Bernard Rose, 1995).
Intermezzo (dir. Gregory Ratoff, 1939).
I've Always Loved You (dir. Frank Borzage, 1946).
Jagged Edge (dir. Richard Marquand, 1985).
Jane Eyre (dir. Orson Welles, 1943).
The Kiss of the Vampire (dir. Don Sharp, 1963).
Laura (dir. Otto Preminger, 1944).
The Legend of 1900 (dir. Guiseppe Tornatore, 1998).
Leise Flehen meine Lieder (*Love Divine*) (dir. Will Forst, 1933).
Let's Dance (dir. Norman Z. McLeod, 1950).
Lisztomania (dir. Ken Russell, 1975).
Little Women (dir. Gillian Armstrong, 1994).
Little Women (dir. Mervyn LeRoy, 1948).
Love Happy (dir. David Miller, 1950).
Love Story (dir. Arthur Hiller, 1970).
Love Story (dir. Leslie Arliss, 1945).
Low Down (dir. Jeff Preiss, 2014).
Ludwig (dir. Luchino Visconti, 1973).
Mad Love (dir. Karl Freund, 1935).
Madame Sousatska (dir. John Schlesinger, 1988).
Magic Fire (dir. William Dieterle, 1956).
Mahler (dir. Ken Russell, 1974).
Man of Music (see *The Composer Glinka*).
The Man Who Knew Too Much (dir. Alfred Hitchcock, 1956).
The Man Who Played God (dir. John D. Adolfi, 1932).
The Mark of Cain (dir. Brian Desmond Hurst, 1947).
Men of Two Worlds (dir. Thorold Dickinson, 1946).
The Mephisto Waltz (dir. Paul Wendkos, 1970).
Mr. Soft Touch (dirs. Gordon Douglas and Henry Levin, 1945).
Monkey Business (dir. Norman Z. McCleod, 1932).
The Monster Maker (dir. Sam Newfield, 1944).
Monty Python's The Meaning of Life (dir. Terry Jones, 1983).
Moonlight Sonata (dir. Lothar Mendes, 1937).
Moonraker (dir. Lewis Gilbert, 1979).
Murder on the Orient Express (dir. Sydney Lumet, 1974).
The Music Box (dir. James Parrot, 1932).
The Music Lovers (dir. Ken Russell, 1971).
A Night at the Opera (dir. Sam Wood, 1931).
A Night in Casablanca (dir. Archie Mayo, 1946).
Nijinsky (dir. Herbert Ross, 1980).
The Omen (dir. Richard Donner, 1976).
The Opry House (dirs. Ub Iwerks and Walt Disney, 1929).
The Page Turner (dir. Denis Dercourt, 2006).
Pal Joey (dir. George Sidney, 1957)
Passengers (dir. Morgen Tyldum, 2016).
Peeping Tom (dir. Michael Powell, 1960).
The Perfection (dir. Richard Shepard, 2019).
The Phantom of the Opera (dir. Arthur Lubin, 1943).
The Phantom of the Opera (dir. Rupert Julian, 1925).
The Phantom of the Opera (dir. Terence Fisher, 1962).
The Philadelphia Story (dir. George Cukor, 1940).

The Pianist (dir. Roman Polanski, 2002).
The Piano (dir. Jane Campion, 1993).
The Piano Teacher (dir. Michael Haenke, 2001).
The Picture of Dorian Gray (dir. Albert Lewin, 1945).
Playing for Time (dir. Daniel Mann, 1980).
Pride and Prejudice (dir. Joe Wright, 2005).
Quartet (dir. Harold French, et al., 1958).
The Red Shoes (dir. Michael Powell, 1948).
Reefer Madness (dir. Louis Gassnier, 1936).
The Return of the Pink Panther (dir. Blake Edwards, 1975).
The Revenge of the Pink Panther (dir. Blake Edwards, 1978).
Rhapsody (dir. Charles Vidor, 1954).
Rhapsody in Blue (dir. Irving Rapper, 1945).
Rhapsody Rabbit (dir. Fritz Freleng, 1946).
Roberta (dir. William A. Seiter, 1935).
Rocket Man (dir. Dexter Fletcher, 2019).
A Room with a View (dir. James Ivory, 1985).
Rope (dir. Alfred Hitchcock, 1948).
Rushing Roulette (dir. Robert McKimson, 1965).
Scott Joplin—The Movie (dir. Jeremy Kagen, 1977).
Secret (dir. Jay Chou, 2007).
September Affair (dir. William Dieterle, 1950).
The Seven Year Itch (dir. Billy Wilder, 1955).
The Seventh Veil (dir. Compton Bennett, 1945).
The Seventh Victim (dir. Mark Robson, 1943).
Shine (dir. Scott Hicks, 1996).
Show-Biz Bugs (dir. Fritz Freleng, 1957).
Sincerely Yours (dir. Gordon Douglas, 1955).
The Smallest Show on Earth (dir. Basil Dearden, 1957).
Somewhere in Time (dir. Jeannot Szwarc, 1980).
Song of Love (dir. Clarence Brown, 1947).
Song of Summer (dir. Ken Russell, 1968).
A Song to Remember (dir. George Cukor, 1945).
Song Without End (dirs. Charles Vidor/George Cukor, 1960).
Sparky's Magic Piano (dir. Lee Mishkin, 1987).
Spellbound (dir. Alfred Hitchcock, 1946).
Spielzeugland (dir. Jochen Alexander Freydank, 2007).
Spione (dir. Fritz Lang, 1928).
The Spiral Staircase (dir. Robert Siodmak, 1946).

The Sting (dir. George Roy Hill, 1973).
Stolen Face (dir. Terence Fisher, 1952).
Stormy Weather (dir. Andrew L. Stone, 1943).
The Story of Three Loves (dirs. Gottfried Reinhardt and Vincente Minnelli, 1953).
Summer of '42 (dir. Robert Mulligan, 1971).
Sunset Boulevard (dir. Billy Wilder, 1950).
Superman Returns (dir. Bryan Singer, 2006).
Swing Time (dir. George Stevens, 1936).
Szerelmi álmok (dir. Heinz Hille, 1935).
Szerelmi álmok (dir. Márton Keleti, 1970).
Taste the Blood of Dracula (dir. Peter Sadsy, 1970).
The Tender Trap (dir. Charles Walters, 1955).
Testimony (dir. Tony Palmer, 1988).
The Thomas Crown Affair (dir. Norman Jewison, 1968).
The Three Amigos (dir. John Landis, 1987).
Tirez sur le pianist (*Shoot the Piano Player*) (dir. François Truffaut, 1960).
Total Recall (dir. Len Wiseman, 2012).
Träumerei (dir. Harald Braun, 1944).
Trio (dir. Ken Annakin, 1950).
Twilight (dir. Catherine Hardwick, 2008).
Twins of Evil (dir. John Hough, 1971).
The Unforgettable Year 1919 (dir. Mikheil Chiaureli, 1951).
Vier Minuten (dir. Chris Kraus, 2006).
Village of the Damned (dir. Wolf Rilla, 1960).
Vitus (dir. Fredi M. Murer, 2006).
Wagner (dir. Tony Palmer, 1983).
The Walking Dead (dir. Michael Curtiz, 1936).
Watch on the Rhine (dir. Herman Schumlin, 1943).
When the Cat's Away (dir. Walt Disney, 1929).
While I Live (dir. John Harlow, 1947).
Whispering City (dir. Fedor Ozep, 1947).
Who Framed Roger Rabbit? (dir. Robert Zemeckis, 1988).
Why Stop Now? (dirs. Phil Dorling & Ron Nyswaner, 2012).
The Wicker Man (dir. Robin Hardy, 1973).
Wideo Rabbit (dir. Robert McKimson, 1956).
Will You Be Mine? (dir. Sophy Laloy, 2009).
The World of Henry Orient (dir. George Ray Hill, 1964).
Your Lie in April (dir. Takehiko Shinjō, 2015).

Index

Numbers in **_bold italics_** indicate pages with illustrations.

Abba 68, 189
The Abominable Dr. Phibes (dir. Robert Fuest, 1971) 16, 123, 149–151, ***150***
Abraham, F. Murray 90
Adamczyk, Piotr 81
Adams, Robert 46
Addinsell, Richard 9, 42, 44; *Warsaw Concerto* 41, 42, 43, 44, 45, 51, 52, 61, 85
Adolfi, John D. 79
Adrian, Max 12, 144
Alcott, Louisa May 107–108; *Little Women* 107–108
Alda, Alan 183
Alda, Robert 12, 13, ***13***, 183
Alexander, Jane 119
Alexandrov, Grigoriy 99
All About Eve (dir. Joseph L. Mankiewicz, 1950) 29
All Night Long (dir. Basil Dearden, 1962) 173–174, ***174***, 175
Aller, Victor 96
Altman, Robert 10
Altschhul, Rudolf 24
Amadeus (dir. Miloš Forman, 1984) 90
Amadeus (Peter Shaffer) 79
Ambler, Eric 170; *Epitaph for a Spy* 170–171
An American in Paris (dir. Vincente Minelli, 1951) 12, 24
Anderson, Benny 189
Anderson, Lindsay 151
Andresen, Björn 113, ***114***
Andrews, Dana 40, 56
The Angel Who Pawned Her Harp (dir. Alan Bromly, 1954) 29, 154
Anholt, Christien 155
Annakin, Ken 29
Antczak, Jerzy 81
Antonelli, Laura 162

Appointment in London (dir. Philip Leacock, 1953) 30
Aristotle 129
Arliss, George 79
Armstrong, Gillian 108
Armstrong, Michael 30
Arnold, Newt 170
Arrau, Claudio 97
The Arrival of a Train at La Ciotat Station (dirs. Auguste & Louis Lumière, 1896) 35
Artemis 81 (dir. Alastair Reid, 1981) 26
Astaire, Fred 28, 141–142
Astley, Edwin 156
Astor, Mary 46
Attenborough, Richard 174
Atwell, Winifred 14, 59, 68, 92
Audiard, Jacques 175
Audley, Maxine 36
Austen, Jane 110; *Pride and Prejudice* 110
Autumn Sonata (dir. Ingmar Bergman, 1978) 182–183
Aylmer, Felix 154
Aznavour, Charles 173

Bach, Carl Philip Emmanuel 18
Bach, Johann Sebastian 11, 14, 24, 25, 45, 53, 65, 66, 109, 148, 149, 150, 155, 170, 175, 176, 178, 181, 188; Toccata and Fugue in D minor 53, 109, 149, 150, 154, 176
Badel, Alan 100
Baecque, Antoine de 173
Bains, Bill 32
Baker, Roy Ward 139
Baledón, Raphael 179, 181
Balfe, Michael 28
Ballot-Box Bunny (dir. Fritz Freleng, 1951) 137
Barbera, Joseph 83, 128

201

Barry, John 42
Barrymore, John 123
Barthes, Roland 20
Bartók, Bela 31
Baselli, Joss 186
Basie, Count 30
Bates, Alan 160
Bates, Michael 138
Bath, Hubert 46, 47; *Cornish Rhapsody* 46, 47
De battre mon cœur s'est arrêté (aka *The Beat That My Heart Skipped*, dir. Jacques Audiard, 2005) 175
Bava, Mario 109
Baxter, John 47
Beacham, Sir Thomas 15, 155
The Beast with Five Fingers (dir. Robert Florey, 1946) 131, 181
The Beat That My Heart Skipped (aka *De Battre Mon Cœur S'est Arrêté*, dir. Jacques Audiard, 2005) 175
Becce, Giuseppe 37–38
Beckett, Scotty 103
"The Beer Barrel Polka" 72, 73, 76, 92
Beethoven, Ludwig van 3, 4, 9, 20, 22, 24, 28, 29, 33, 35, 44, 45, 53, 67, 68, 70, 79, 86, 103, 108, 111, 113, 126, 129, 143, 163, 167, 176, 190; "Appassionata" Piano Sonata 45, 53, 143; "Emperor" Piano Concerto 44; "Für Elise" 113; "Kreutzer" Violin Sonata 163; "Moonlight" Piano Sonata 4, 27, 33, 70, 86, 129, 167, 170, 188; "Pathètique" Piano Sonata 9, 30, 35, 126, 129; "Tempest Piano Sonata 188; "Waldstein" Piano Sonata 111
Behind the Candelabra (dir. Stephen Soderbergh, 2019) 67
Beljiojoso, Princess Cristina Trivulzio 87
Benjamin, Arthur 138
Bennett, Compton 46
Bennett, Hywel 26
Bennett, Richard Rodney 40–41
Bennett, Tony 28
Benson, E.F. 167
Bergman, Ingmar 182
Bergman, Ingrid 9, 16, 182, 183
Berkassy, Stephen 74
Berkeley, Busby 142
Berlin, Irving 11, 72, 141
Berlioz, Hector 18, 20, 24, 27, 144, 176; *Symphonie Fantastique* 20
Bernard, James 164, 165
Bernhardt, Sarah 124
Bernstein, Elmer 61
Big (dir. Penny Marshall, 1988) 86
The Big Store (dir. Charles Reisner, 1941) 153

Billion Dollar Brain (dir. Ken Russell, 1968) 40–41
The Bishop's Wife (dir. Henry Koster, 1947) 153
Bisset, Jacqueline 184
Black Sunday (dir. Mario Bava, 1960) 109–10
Blackman, Honor 116
Blair, Betsy 174
Blanc, Mel 128
Blazing Saddles (dir. Mel Brooks, 1974) 30
Bleibtreu, Monica 135
Blind Corner (dir. Lance Comfort, 1964) 57
Bliss, Sir Arthur 46; *Baraza* 46
Bloom, Claire 140
Boeme, Carl 36
Bogarde, Dirk 30, 57, 88, 95–97, **95**, 98, 101, 113, 115, 147, 165
Bohr, José 97
Bolling, Claude 41, 42
Bonham-Carter, Helena 111
Booby Traps (dir. Robert Clampett, 1944) 137
Bordeau, Isild 134
Born of Fire (dir. Jamil Dehlavi, 1987) 17
Borsani, Fabrizio 135
Borzage, Frank 53
The Boy Friend (dir. Ken Russell, 1972) 142
Boyer, Charles 9, 10, 144
Bradley, Dorothy 111
Brady, James 45
Brahm, John 123, 171
Brahms, Johannes 10, 29, 45, 79, 95, 99, 129, 183; Waltz in A-Flat 29, 129
Braun, Harald 97
Brent, George 46
Bressart, Felix **54**
Bridges, Beau 174
Bridges, Jeff 42, 174
Brief Encounter (dir. Alan Bridges, 1974) 62
Brief Encounter (dir. David Lean, 1945) 35, 48–51, 52, 55, 62, 150
Broadway Melody of 1940 (dir. Norman Taurig. 1940) 141
Brontë, Charlotte 106
Brooks, Mel 30
Brown, Clarence 8
Browne, Corale 128
Browning, Logan 136
Brownlow, Kevin 48
Brubeck, Dave 174, **174**
Buck, Dudley 24
Bülow, Hans von 22
Burgess, Anthony 4, 25, 38, 44, 103; *A Clockwork Orange* 4; *The Pianoplayers* 25, 38, 103

Index

Burne-Jones, Sir Edward 31, 121
Burns, Mark *102*, 113, 147
Burt, George 40
Burton, Humphrey 122
Burton, Richard 62, 101, 140, 146
Burton, Tim 161, 181
Bury, Sean 150
Busch, Wilhelm 90, *91*, 92, 131
Byron, Lord George Gordon 23
Byron, Kathleen 138

Cage, John 31
Caine, Michael 41
California Suite (dir. Herbert Ross, 1978) 42
Callow, Simon 24, 111
Campion, Jane 159
Capucine 96
Carlei, Carlo 42
Carmen, Eric 62, 65
Carradine, John 167
Carry On Cowboy (dir. Gerald Thomas, 1965) 30
Carry On Up the Khyber (dir. Gerald Thomas, 1968) 43
Carter, Bill 53
Casablanca (dir. Michael Curtiz, 1942) 183
Cass, Henry 51
Castle, Roy 17
The Cat Concerto (dirs. Willam Hanna & Joseph Barbera, 1947) 83–84, *84*, 85–87, 137, 186
Cavallaro, Carmen 80
Chamberlain, Richard 12
Chaney, Lon 124, *125*, 127, 133, 149
Chaplin, Charles 39, 94, 146
Chekhov, Michael 58
Chiaureli, Mikheil 52
Chopin, Frédéric 9, 11, 16, 25, 26, 29, 31, 33, 35, 45, 46, 54, 55, 65, 67, 68, 70, 72, 74–76, 77, 78, 79, 80, 81, 85, 90, 96, 116, 122, 125, 129, 160, 162, 164, 165, 166, 167, 169, 170, 171, 176–181, 183, 188; Ballades 9, 169, 170; Études 16, 26, 29, 76, 129, 169, 176; Fantasie-Impromptu 129, 169; Marche funèbre 179; Mazurkas 65; Nocturnes 25, 45, 76, 165, 170; Piano Concerti 54; Polonaises 70, 75, 176; Preludes 8, 33, 65, 122, 125, 166, 177, 178, 179, 180–181, 183; Sonatas 169; Waltzes 16, 35, 45, 46, 65, 80, 116, 129, 162, 180
Chopin: A Desire for Love (dir. Jerzy Antczac, 2002) 81
"Chopsticks," 2, 72, 76, 80, 82, 86, 88, 94, 118
Chou, Jay 90
Choudhry, Navin 121
Christie, Agatha 41
Christie, Julie 160
Cilento, Diane 10, 154
Clampett, Robert 137
Clarke, Alan 154
Clarke, Cuthbert 28
Clarke, Kenneth 3, 45
Clarke, Robert 43
Cliffe, Frederick 104
Clive, Colin 169
Close, Glenn 42
Clouzot, Henri-Georges 135
Coburn, Charles 10
Coleridge, Samuel Taylor 173
Collins, Wilkie 112; *The Woman in White* 112
Comfort, Lance 57
The Common Touch (dir. John Baxter, 1941) 47
Conreid, Hans 116, *117*
The Constant Nymph (dir. Edmund Goulding, 1943) 10, 144
Conway, Russ 14, 30, 68, 92
Conway, Tom 29
Conyngham, Barry 33
Cooper, Gladys 153
Corelli, Arcangelo 24
Corlan, Anthony 109, 114
The Corpse Bride (dir. Tim Burton, 2005) 181
Cortesa, Valentina 51
Cotton, Joseph 57, *58*, 150
Coulouris, George 28–29
Coward, Noël 10, 48, 49
Cowell, Henry 136, 170
Crawford, Joan 16
Cregar, Laird 171, *172*
Crescendo (dir. Alan Gibson, 1970) 122, 123
Cristofori, Bartolomeo 19
Cromwell, John 56
Cruel Intentions (dir. Roger Kumble, 1999) 86
Cukor, George 40, 74, 88, 95, 96
Curtis, Tony 128
Curtiz, Michael 169, 176, 183
Cushing, Peter 109
Czerny, Carl 3, 84

d'Agoult, Countess Marie 94, 146, 158
Dahl, Nikolai 61–62
Daltry, Roger 16, 92, *93*, 94, 96, 155
Damon, Matt 67
Dangerous Moonlight (dir. Brian Desmond Hurst, 1941) 42–44, 46, 85, 123, 125, 186
Daniel, Jennifer 165
Daniell, Henry 97, *98*
Daniels, Paul 32

Index

D'Annunzio, Gabrielle 131, 156, 162; *L'Innocente* 162; "Leda Without Swan" 154; *Il Piacere* 131–132
Danot, Serge 185
Dantine, Helmut 47
Dark Shadows (dir. Tim Burton, 2012) 162
Darnell, Linda 171
Davis, Bette 28, 29, 46, 143, *143*
Davis, Carl 32
Davis, Judith 134
Day, Doris 138
A Day at the Races (dir. Sam Wood, 1937) 151–152
Dearden, Basil 35, 173
Death in Venice (dir. Luchino Visconti, 1971) 113, *114*, 115, 147–148
Debussy, Claude 53, 167
Deception (dir. Irving Rapper, 1946) 16–17, 31, 142–143, *143*
Dehlavi, Jamil 17
Delibes, Leo 92
Delius, Frederick 38, 144–146
DeMille, Cecil B. 38
Dench, Dame Judi 110
Dennison, Michael 51
Depp, Johnny 162
Dercourt, Denis 135
Dexter, Colin 29
Les diaboliques (dir. Henri-Georges Clouzot, 1955) 135
Diaghilev, Serge 75, 143–144
Diamant, Otto 120
Dickinson, Thorold 9, 43, 45
Dieterle, William 57, 100
Disney, Walt 18, 82, 86, 154
Doctor Faustus (dir. Franz Seitz, 1982) 114, 115
Doctor Faustus (Thomas Mann) 4–5, 114
Dr. Jekyll and Mr. Hyde (dir. Rouben Mamoulian, 1931) 108–109
Dr. Jekyll and Sister Hyde (dir. Roy Ward Baker, 1971) 139
Dr. Terror's House of Horrors (dir. Freddie Francis, 1965) 17
Dr. Phibes Rises Again (dir. Robert Fuest, 1972) 16, 123, 149
A Doll's House (dir. Joseph Losey, 1973) 140
A Doll's House (dir. Patrick Garland, 1973) 140
Donner, Richard 185
Don't Look Now (dir. Nicolas Roeg, 1973) 115
Dorling, Phil 135
Dorn, Philip 53, *54*
Dors, Diana 138
Dougal and the Blue Cat (dir. Serge Danot, 1970) 185–186

Douglas, Gordon 35, 69, 72
Dragonwyck (dir. Joseph L. Mankiewicz, 1946) 27–28, **28**
Drake, Francis 169
Dream of Love (dir. José Bohr, 1935) 97
Dreams of Love (aka *Rêves d'amour*, dir. Christian Stengel, 1947) 99
Dreyfuss, Richard 148
Dreyschock, Alexander 26–27
Duchin, Eddie 80
Duris, Romain 175
Dvořák, Antonín 16, 65

Easedale, Brian 36
Easter Parade (dir. Charles Walters, 1948) 72, 141
Eatwell, Brian 150
Eden, Mark 57
The Eddie Duchin Story (dir. George Sidney, 1956) 80
Edwards, Blake 41
Egerton, Taron 5, 93
Eggerth, Màrtha 161
Eich, Cedric 120
Elgar, Sir Edward 163
Eliot, George 104; *Daniel Deronda* 104–105
Ellis, Antonia 142
Elvira Madigan (dir. Bo Widerberg, 1967) 2–3
Emerson, Keith 94
Emerson, Ralph Waldo 108, 159
The Entertainer (dir. George Roy Hill, 1973) 90
Érard, Sébastien 19, 26, 152
Ericson, John 58
Evans, Edward 29
Ewell, Tom 60, **60**
Ewing, Barbara 179
Eye of the Devil (dir. J. Lee Thompson, 1967) 153–154

The Fabulous Baker Boys (dir. Steve Kloves, 1989) 161, 174–175
Fain, Sammy 76
Fairchild, Edgar 167
Fantasia (dir. Samuel Armstrong, James Algar, Bill Roberts, *et al.*, 1941) 17–18, 82, 154
Fantasia 2000 (dir. James Algar *et al.*, 1999) 130
Farrell, Charles 70
Farrell, Colin 188
Fauré, Gabriel 2
Fay, Amy 7
Fedderson, Don 73
Fenby, Eric 38, 145–146
Fénelon, Fania 119

Index 205

Ferber, Albert 50–51
Ferrer, Mel 169
Finch, Jon 114
Fingers (dir. James Toback, 1978) 175
Firth, Peter 17
Fisher, Terence 30
Five Easy Pieces (dir. Bob Rafelson, 1971) 180
The 5,000 Fingers of Dr. T. (dir. Roy Rowland, 1953) 116–118, *117*, 128, 129
Flaubert, Gustave 105, 113; *Madame Bovary* 105–106, 113
Fleming, Ian 33
Fletcher, Dexter 5
Florence Foster Jenkins (dir. Stephen Frears, 2016) 180–181
Florey, Robert 131, 181
Follow the Fleet (dir. Mark Sandrich, 1936) 141
Fontaine, Joan 57, *58*, 59, 106, 144
Ford, Glenn 72
Forman, Miloš 90
Forst, Willi 161
Forster, E.M. 24
Forward, Anthony 96
Foster, Stephen 153
Fowle, Susannah 110
Fox, James 130
Francen, Victor 181
Francis, Freddie 17, 179
François, Déborah 135
Frankenstein's Monster 2, 18, 38, 67, 95, 167, 176
Franz Joseph, Emperor 8
Frazer, Sir James 154
Frears, Stephen 180
Freleng, Fritz 83, 137
French, Harold 57, 97
Freund, Karl 169
Freydank, Alexander 119–120
Friedrich, Caspar David 23
Fröhlich, Carl 38
Frot, Catherine 135
Fuest, Robert 150

Gable, Christopher 144
Gallu, Sam 169
Gamley, Douglas 165
Gann, Rita 101
Garfield, John 16
Garland, Judy 141
Garland, Patrick 140
Gaslight (dir. Charles Vidor, 1944) 9–10
Gaslight (dir. Thorold Dickinson, 1940) 9, 43
Gasnier, Louis J. 43
Gassman, Vittorio 58

Gellar, Sarah Michelle 86
Gershwin, George 12–13, *13*, 16, 24, 76, 130, 144, 188; Concerto in F 12, 24; *Rhapsody in Blue* 13, 130
The Getting of Wisdom (dir. Bruce Beresford, 1977) 110–112
Gheorghiu, Ted 135
Gianni, Giancarlo 162
Gibson, Alan 122
Gielgud, John 130–131, 133
Gilbert, Lewis 33
Gilbert, William Schwenck 160
Gimby, Bobby 72
Gimpel, Jakob 9, 184
Girl in the Headlines (dir. Michael Truman, 1963) 29
The Glass Mountain (dir. Henry Cass, 1949) 51–52, 57
Glinka, Mikhail 99–100
Gluck, Christoph Willibald 121
The Go-Between (dir. Joseph Losey, 1971) 160
Go West (dir. Charles Reisner, 1941) 92, 153
Gobbi, Tito 51
Goethe, Johann Wolfgang von 129
Golden Boy (dir. Rouben Mamoulian, 1939) 109
Golding, Edmund 46
Goldsmith, Jerry 183–185
Gonino, Valeria 4
Goodis, David 173
Gordon, Douglas 34
Goring, Marius 143
Gosford Park (dir. Robert Altman, 2002) 10
Gottschalk, Louis 85–86, 129, 136
Gough, Michael 160
Goulding, Edmund 10
Gounod, Charles 24, 65
Grand Piano (dir. Eugenio Mira, 2013) 137–138
Granger, Farley 36–37, *37*
Granger, Stewart 16, 47
Grant, Cary 153
Gray, John 129
Gray, Sally 43, 50
The Great Lie (dir. Edmund Golding, 1941) 46
Green, Eva 162
Greene, Barbara 70
Greene, Graham 35
Greenwell, Peter 142
Gregg, Everley 49
Gréville, Edmond T. 169
Grieg, Edvard 11, 128, 129, 182; Piano Concerto in A minor 128, 129, 182
Grint, Rupert 113
Guard, Dominic 161

206 Index

Guicciardi, Countess Giulietta 4
Gwenn, Edmund 17

Hadfield, Hurd 165, *177*, 178
Haenke, Michael 133
Haimovsky, Gregory 89
Hallé, Charles 20
Hambourg, Mark 47
Hamilton, Patrick 9, 171
Hammerhead (dir. David Miller, 1968) 138
Handel, George Frideric 24, 25, 39
Hands of a Stranger (dir. Newt Arnold, 1962) 170
The Hands of Orlac (dir. Edmond T. Gréville, 1960) 169–170
The Hands of Orlac (dir. Robert Wiene, 1924) 123, 166, 168–169
Hanfstaengl, Ernst "Putzi," 11, 12
Hangover Square (dir. John Brahm, 1945) 123, 134, 135, 171–173, *172*
Hanks, Tom 86
Hanna, William 83, 128
Hannan, Michael 33
Hardwick, Catherine 189
Hardy, Oliver 39
Hardy, Robin 10
Harlow, John 47
The Harpist (dir. Hansjörg Thurn, 1999) 154–155
Harris, Paul 173
Harrison, Philip 94
Harry Potter and the Deathly Hallows (dir. David Yates, 2010) 113–114
Hartley, L.P. 161
Haskin, Byron 8
Hatton, Rondo 176
The Haunted House of Horror (dir. Michael Armstrong, 1969) 30
Hawkes, John 175
Hayes, Frank 39
Hayes, J. Milton 28
Hayes, Peter Lind 117
Haynes, Battison 24
Heine, Heinrich 26
Helberg, Simon 180
Helfgott, David 130–133, 188
Helfgott, Peter 130
Hemmings, David 154
Hendry, Ian 29
Henreid, Paul 16, 97, 143
Hepburn, Katharine 8, 97–99, *98*
Herek, Stephen 148
Herrmann, Bernard 16, 138, 171, 172
Herzsprung, Hannah 135
Hess, Myra 45, 51, 53
Hess, Rudolf 45
Heston, Charlton 8

Hickox, Douglas 121
Hicks, Scott 130
The Hideous Sun Demon (dir. Robert Clarke, 1958) 43
Hilary and Jackie (dir. Annand Tucker, 1998) 17
Hildebrandt, Dieter 19, 106, 107, 110, 112
Hill, George Ray 61
Hill, George Roy 90
Hille, Heinz 97
Hiller, Arthur 41
Hindley, Myra 45
His Musical Career (dir. Charles Chaplin, 1914) 39
Hitchcock, Alfred 36, 37, 52, 138, 182
Hitler, Adolf 11, 32, 45, 118, 130, 137
Hobart, Rose 108
Hoffmann, E.T.A. 121
Hoffmann, Peter 140
Holden, William 109, 149
Hollingsworth, John 50–51, 165
Holt, Seth 179
El Hombre y el Monstro (aka *The Man and the Monster*, dir. Raphael Baledón, 1959) 179, 181–182
Hopkins, Anthony 140
Hopkins, Miriam 109
Horse Feathers (dir. Norman Z. McLeod, 1932) 90, 92
Hoskins, Bob 89
Hough, John 109
House of Dracula (dir. Erle C. Kenton, 1945) 167
House of Wax (dir. Andre de Toth, 1953) 169
Howard, Leslie 16
Howard, Trevor 49, 102, *102*
Howard's End (dir. James Ivory, 1992) 24
Hulse, Tom 89
Humoresque (dir. Jean Negulesco, 1946) 16, 55
Humphries, Barry 112
Hunt, Leigh 151
Hunt, William Holman 112–113
Hunter, Holly 159, *160*
Huntley, John 38, 44, 45, 46, 47, 48, 69
Huppert, Isabelle 133, *134*
Hurst, Brian Desmond 42, 50

I Walked with a Zombie (dir. Jacques Tourneur, 1943) 29
Ibsen, Henrik 139, 141; *A Doll's House* 139–140
Idle, Eric 10
If (dir. Lindsay Anderson, 1968) 151
Immortal Beloved (dir. Bernard Rose, 1995) 3–4
Intermezzo (dir. Gregory Ratoff, 1939) 16

Ireland, John 103–104, 118
Iseman, Madison 186
It's a Knockout (BBC TV series) 32–33
I've Always Loved You (dir. Frank Borzage, 1946) 53–56, **54**, 57, 58, 60, 63, 175
Ivory, James 24, 111
Iwerks, Ub 82

Jacoby, Siegfried 24
Jäger, Julia 120
Jagged Edge (dir. Richard Marquand, 1985) 42
James, Henry 106, 161; "Lady Barbarina" 161; *Portrait of a Lady* 106–107
James, Rian 48
James, Sid 30, 43
Jane Eyre (dir. Orson Welles, 1943) 106, 180
Janina, Olga 158–159
Jaray, Hans 161
Je Te Mangerais (aka *You Will Be Mine*, dir. Sophy Laloy, 2009) 134–135
Jewison, Norman 41
Jhabvala, Ruth Prawer 24
Jones, Gwyneth 140
Jones, Terry 10
Jones, Tom 16
John, Elton 3, 5, 16, 68, 92–93, 130, 188
Johnson, Celia 49, 59
Joplin, Scott 90
Joyce, Eileen 46, 47, 48
Jurgens, Curt 183

Kagen, Jeremy 90
Karajan, Herbert von 17–18
Karloff, Boris 67, 176
Kaun, Bernhard 176
Keaton, Buster 38
Keitel, Harvey 159, 175
Keleti, Márton 97, 100
Kentner, Louis 44, 45, 85
Kern, Jerome 28, 141
Kestelman, Sara 96
King, Oliver 24
Kings Row (dir. Sam Wood, 1942) 53, 103
Kingsley, Ben 147
Kingston, Shirley 94
The Kiss of the Vampire (dir. Don Sharp, 1963) 123, 164–167, **165**, 168, 169
Klein-Rogge, Rudolf 139
Klic, Karel 55, **56**
Klinger, Max 131, 168
Kloves, Steve 161, 174
Knightley, Keira 110
Knowles, Bernard 16
Konarski, Michel 81
Korngold, Erich Wolfgang 10, 31, 100, 143
Koster, Henry 153

Kraus, Chris 135
Kumble, Roger 86
Kunz, Charlie 93
Kusevitsky, Sergey 132

Lahee, Henry 71
Lai, Francis 41
Laloy, Sophy 134
Lammenais, Félicité Robert, Abbé 187
Landis, John 30
Lang, Fritz 139
Lanner, Joseph 9
Lansbury, Angela 166, **177**, 178
LaShelle, Joseph 172
Laura (dir. Otto Preminger, 1944) 40
Laurel, Stan 39
Law, Phillida 185
Lawrence, D.H. 11; *A Collier's Friday Night* 11
Lawrence, Jennifer 188
Leabu, Tristan Lake 39
Leacock, Philip 30
Lean, David 35, 48, 49, 51
Lee, Sir Christopher 10, 169
Lee, Leonard 48
LeFanu, J. Sheridan 164
The Legend of 1900 (dir. Guiseppe Tornatore, 1998) 90
Legrande, Michel 41
Lehrer, Tom 31
Leighton, Margaret 160
Leise Flehen Meine Lieder (aka *Lover Divine*, dir. Willi Forst, 1933) 161
Lenau, Nikolaus 184
Lennon, John 159
Leonard, Harry 40
LeRoy, Mervyn 108
Leroux, Gaston 123, 124, 127, 150; *The Phantom of the Opera* 77, 94, 109, 123, 124, 133, 134, 136, 138, 149, 150, 166, 169, 171, 181
Let's Dance (dir. Normal Z. McLeod, 1950) 141–142
Levant, Oscar 12, 13, 16, 24, 61
Levin, Henry 35, 72
Lewes, George Henry 105
Lewin, Albert 166, 178
Lewis, Fiona 94
Lewton, Val 29
Liberace 5, 8, 12, 13, 14, 16, 18, 67–80, 81, 84, 87, 88, 89, 92, 93, 94, 95, 96, 101, 106, 109, 117, 118, 130, 153, 159, 172, 174, 182, 188
Ligeti, György 189
Linnane, Joe 154
L'Innocente (dir. Luchino Visconti, 1976) 162–163
Liszt, Franz 2, 7, 8, 9, 10, 13, 14, 16, 17, 18,

19, 21, 26–27, 28, 29, 39, 44, 55, **56**, 58, 64, 65, 67, 68, 70, 71, 72, 74, 75, 76, 77, 81–82, **83**, 84–89, 92–102, 104, 111, 116, 131, 133, 146, 155, 158–159, 162, 166, 169, 181, 183–184, 185, 186, 187, 188; *Années de Pèlerinage* 19; *La Campanella* 86; *Consolations* 170; First Piano Concerto in E-flat major 96; "Funerailles" 94; *Grand Galop Chromatique* 81–82; *Hungarian Fantasy* 170; *Liebestraum No. 3*, 29, 44, 58, 94, 97; *Mephisto Waltz No. 1*, 97, 101, 166, 183–185; Second Hungarian Rhapsody 70, 76, 81, 82, 87, 88, 89, 92, 153; *Totentanz* 94
Lisztomania (dir. Ken Russell, 1975) 16, 87, 92–95, **93**, 101, 146, 155, 158
Little Women (dir. Gillian Armstrong, 1994) 108
Little Women (dir. Mervyn LeRoy, 1948) 108
Lockwood, Annea 33
Lockwood, Margaret 47
The Lodger (dir. John Brahm, 1944) 171
Loggia, Robert 86
Lohkamp, Emil 97
Lom, Herbert 124, 125
Lonsdale, Michael 33
Loos, Adolf 8
Loren, Sophia 62
Lorre, Peter 169, 181
Losey, Joseph 140, 160
Love, Geoff 51
Love Happy (dir. David Miller, 1950) 153
Love Story (dir. Arthur Hiller, 1970) 41, 133
Love Story (dir. Leslie Arliss, 1944) 46, 47
The Loved One (dir. Tony Richardson, 1965) 67, 159
Lover Divine (aka *Leise Flehen Meine Lieder*, dir Willi Forst, 1933) 161
Low Down (dir. Jeff Preiss, 2014) 175
Lubin, Arthur 51
Ludwig (dir. Luchino Visconti, 1973) 102, **102**
Ludwig II of Bavaria 66, 67, 102
Lukas, Paul 28
Lumet, Sidney 41

MacLaine, Shirley 121
Mad Love (dir. Karl Freund, 1935) 169
Madame Sousatzka (dir. John Schlesinger, 1988) 121–123
Magic Fire (dir. William Dieterle, 1956 100–101
Magimel, Benôit 133, **134**
Magnani, Luigi 4
Mahler (dir. Ken Russell, 1974) 120
Mahler, Gustav 119, 120, 145, 148
Malone, Dorothy 77

Mamoulian, Rouben 108, 109
The Man and the Monster (aka *El Hombre Y El Monstro*, dir. Raphael Baledón, 1959) 179, 181–182
Man of Music (aka *The Composer Glinka*, dir. Grigoriy Aleksandrov, 1952) 99–100
The Man Who Knew Too Much (dir. Alfred Hitchcock, 1956) 138
The Man Who Played God (dir. John D. Adolfi, 1932) 79
Mancini, Henry 41
Manilow, Barry 65
Mankiewicz, Joseph L. 27, 29
Mann, Daniel 118
Mann, Thomas 4, 22, 75–76, 84–85, 113, 114, 119, 135, 156; *Buddenbrooks* 22; "Death in Venice" 113; *Doctor Faustus* 113; "Tonio Kröger" 135–136; "Tristan" 22–23, 156
Mantovani 51
The Mark of Cain (dir. Brian Desmond Hurst, 1947) 50–51
Marlowe, Fay 171
Marshall, Penny 86
Marquand, Richard 42
Marx, Adolf Bernhard 107
Marx, Chico 86, 87, 90, 92, 152
Marx, Harpo 92, 152, 153
Marx, Karl 129
Mason, James 59, 125, **126**
Mason, Dr. William 70
"Master Class" (*Midsummer Murders* episode, dir. Renny Rye, 2010) 130
Mathieson, Muir 44, 46, 48, 49, 50
Mathieu, André 47; *Concerto De Québec* 47–48
Maugham, W. Somerset 29, 97
Maurier, George du 121
Mayakovsky, Vladimir 31
Mayo, Archie 92, 123
McFarland, Gary 154
McGann, Stephen 154
McGoohan, Patrick 173
McKay, Wanda 176
McKimson, Robert 83, 137
McLeod, Catherine 53, **54**
McLeod, Norman Z. 90, 92, 141
Meck, Nadezhda von 12
Men of Two Worlds (dir. Thorold Dickinson, 1946) 45–46
Mendelssohn, Felix 8, 24, 25, 29, 36, 53, 65, 66, 106, 122, 150; *Lieder Ohne Worte* 25, 36, 106, 122
Mendes, Lothar 69
Mengele, Dr. Josef 119
The Mephisto Waltz (dir. Paul Wendkos, 1970) 9, 123, 183–185, 186

Index

Merchant, Ismail 24
Messiaen, Olivier 89
Metzner, Paul 27
Meyerbeer, Giacomo 100
Meyerhold, Vsevolod 147
Michell, Keith 174
Midsommer Murders TV series 130
Miles, Lilian 43
Miller, Annie 112
Miller, David 138, 153
Miller, George 163
Miller, Martin 36
Mills, Mrs. 68
Mingus, Charles *174*
Minnelli, Vincente 59
Mira, Eugenio 137
Mishkin, Lee 128
Mr. Holland's Opus (dir. Stephen Herek, 1995) 148
Mr. Soft Touch (dirs. Gordon Douglas & Henry Levin, 1949) 35, 72
Monkey Business (dir. Norman Z. McLeod, 1931) 92
Monroe, Marilyn 60, *60*
The Monster Maker (dir. Sam Newfield, 1944) 176, 178
Monty Python's the Meaning of Life (dir. Terry Jones, 1983) 10
Moonlight Sonata (dir. Lothar Mendes, 1937) 69-70, *69*
Moonraker (dir. Lewis Gilbert, 1979) 33
Moore, Dudley 1, 180
Moore, George 156; *Evelyn Innes* 156
Moorhead, Agnes 59
Morgan, Ralph 176
Morrison, Angus 9
Morton, Jelly Roll 90
Mozart, Leopold 129, 130
Mozart, Wolfgang Amadeus 3, 25, 66, 77, 78, 90, 112, 125, 129, 131, 153, 162, 187; "Elvira Madigan" Concerto 3; "Facile" Sonata 125, 129, 153
Mueller-Stahl, Armin 130
Mulligan, Robert 41
Murder on the Orient Express (dir. Sidney Lumet, 1974) 41
Murer, Fredi M. 135
The Music Box (dir. James Parrott, 1932) 39
The Music Lovers (dir. Ken Russell, 1971) 12, 76
Mystery of the Wax Museum (dir. Michael Curtiz, 1933) 169

Naish, J. Carrol 176
The Naked Jungle (dir. Byron Haskin, 1954) 8
Napoleon Bonaparte 19

Negulesco, Jean 16, 55
Neill, Sam 159
Newfield, Sam 176
Newman, Alfred 72
Nicholson, Jack 163, 180
Nicol, Alex 76
Niecks, Frederick 75
Nietzsche, Friedrich 22, 66, 113
A Night at the Opera (dir. Sam Wood, 1935) 153
A Night in Casablanca (dir. Archie Mayo, 1946) 92, 153
Night Song (dir. John Cromwell, 1948) 56-57
Nijinsky (dir. Herbert Ross, 1980) 142
Niven, David 153
Nocturne (dir. Zu Quirke, 2020) 186
Noll, Richard 189
Norris, Geoffrey 62
Northam, Jeremy 10
Novak, Kim 80
Novello, Ivor 10
Nyman, Lena 182
Nyman, Michael 159
Nyswaner, Ron 135

Oberon, Merle 56, 57, 74
O'Brien, Dave 43
Ogden, John 124
O'Herlihy, Dan 26
Oldman, Gary 3
The Omen (dir. Richard Donner, 1976) 185
The Opry House (dirs. Ub Ewers & Walt Disney, 1929) 82
O'Rawe, Geraldine 155
Ormandy, Eugene 56
Orr, Buxton 185
Osborne, Vivienne 27
Ouspenskaya, Maria 53, 103
Ozep, Fedor 47, 48
Özvatan, Tamay Bulut 120

Paderewski, Ignaz 14, 25, 68-72, *69*, 77, 81, 97, 117
Paganini, Niccolò 8, 16, 84, 85, 86
Page, Genevieve *95*
The Page Turner (dir. Denis Dercourt, 2006) 135
Pal Joey (dir. George Sidney, 1957) 8, 142
Palmer, Tony 8, 101, 140, 146, 147
Paquin, Anna 159, *160*
Paranoiac (dir. Freddie Francis, 1963) 155
Parker, Eleanor 8
Parrott, James 39
Parton, Dolly 180
Passengers (dir. Morton Tyldum, 2016) 188
Pattinson 189

Peeping Tom (dir. Michael Powell, 1960) 36
Penda's Fen (dir. Alan Clarke, 1974) 154
Penderecki, Krzysztof 189
The Perfection (dir. Richard Shepard, 2019) 136
Peterson, Nan 43
Pfeiffer, Michelle 161, 174
The Phantom of the Opera (dir. Arthur Lubin, 1943) 51, 124
The Phantom of the Opera (dir. Rupert Julian, 1925) 124, **125**, 127, 133
The Phantom of the Opera (dir. Terence Fisher, 1962) 124
The Philadelphia Story (dir. George Cukor, 1940) 40, 41
Phillipe, Ryan 86
The Pianist (dir. Roman Polanski, 2002) 119
The Piano (dir. Jane Campion, 1993) 159–161, **160**, 162, 168
The Piano Teacher (dir. Michael Haenke, 2001) 133–134, **134**
The Picture of Dorian Gray (dir. Albert Lewin, 1945) 166, **177**, 178–179
Pinter, Harold 161
Piranesi, Giovanni Battista 117
Playing for Time (dir. Daniel Mann, 1980) 118–119
Poe, Edgar Allan 149
Polanski, Roman 119, 135
Porter, Cole 61, 141
Portman, Eric 50, 70
Poulenc, Francis 36
Powell, Eleanor 141
Powell, Michael 36
Powell, Robert 144
Power, Tyrone 80
Pratt, Chris 188
Pré, Jacqueline du 17
Preiss, Jeff 175
Preminger, Otto 40
Presley, Elvis 16
Previn, André 53
Price, Vincent 16, 27, **28**, 121, 123, 128, 149
Pride and Prejudice (dir. Joe Wright, 2005) 110
Prokofiev, Sergei 147
Proust, Marcel 23; *À La Recherche Du Temps Perdu* 23
Pryor, Richard 30
Psycho (dir. Alfred Hitchcock, 1960) 182
Puccini, Giacomo 108, 119, 121
Putnam, David 93
Pyron, Darden Asbury 76, 78

Quartet (dir. Harold French, *et al.*, 1948) 57, 97, 115–116
Quirke, Zu 186

Rabinowitz, Max 10
Rachmaninoff, Sergei 11, 35, 42, 44, 47, 48, 49–51, 52–53, 57, 58, 59–63, 72, 76, 82, 127, 129, 130, 132–133, 138, 152, 184, 187; First Piano Concerto in F-sharp minor 50–51; Prelude in C-sharp minor 53, 82, 129, 132, 152; *Rhapsody on a Theme of Paganini* 59, 62, 129; Second Piano Concerto in C minor 11, 35, 48–51, 52–55, 57, 58, 60–63, 127, 188; Third Piano Concerto in D minor 130
Radcliffe, Ann 179; *The Mysteries of Udolpho* 179
Rafelson, Bob 180
Ragghianti, Ippolito 24
Rains, Claude 124, 142
Raksin, David 40
Rambal, Enrique 181
Rapper, Irving 17
Ravel, Maurice 144
Rear Window (dir. Alfred Hitchcock, 1954) 36
Redgrave, Vanessa 18
The Red Shoes (dirs. Michael Powell & Emeric Pressburger, 1948) 143–144
Reefer Madness (dir. Louis Gasnier, 1936) 43
Reeve, Christopher 62
Regnier, Charles 100
Reid, Alastair 26
Reinhardt, Gottfried 59
Reisner, Charles 92, 153
Renard, Maurice 168, 169, 170
Repulsion (dir. Roman Polanski, 1965) 135
Rettig, Tommy 116, **117**
Return of the Ape Man (dir. Phil Rosen, 1944) 167
The Return of the Pink Panther (dir. Blake Edwards, 1975) 41–42
The Revenge of the Pink Panther (dir. Blake Edwards, 1978) 41–42
Rêves D'amour (aka *Dreams Of Love*, dir. Christian Stengel, 1947) 99
Reynolds, Debbie 142
Rhapsody (dir. Charles Vidor, 1954) 57–59, 63, 188
Rhapsody in Blue (dir. Irving Rapper, 1945) 12, **13**, 183
Rhapsody Rabbit (dir. Fritz Freleng, 1946) 83, 87–89, **88**
Rich, Gary 120
Richard, Cliff 95–96
Richard-Willm, Pierre 99
Richardson, Bernard 26
Richardson, Henry Handel 110–11; *The Getting of Wisdom* 110–111
Richardson, Ralph 140

Index

Richardson, Tony 67
Richter, Hans 100
Richter, Sviatoslav 99
Rilla, Wolf 29
Rimsky-Korsakoff, Nicolai 16, 29, 129; "Flight of the Bumblebee" 16, 86, 129, 188
Roberta (dir. William A. Seiter, 1935) 141
Roberts, Sophy 31
Robson, Mark 29
Rocketman (dir. Dexter Fletcher, 2019) 5, 93
Rodriguez, Maria Theresa 181–182
Roeg, Nicolas 115
Rogers, Ginger 28
Rolland, Romain 104, 120; *Jean-Christophe* 104, 120–121
Rollinat, Charles 75
Romeo and Juliet (dir. Carlo Carlei, 2013) 42
A Room with a View (dir. James Ivory, 1985) 111
Rope (dir. Alfred Hitchcock, 1948) 36–37, **37**
Rosay, Françoise 57, 116
Rosé, Alma 119
Rose, Bernard 3
Rosen, Charles 31, 65, 155, 157, 165
Rosen, Phil 167
Ross, Herbert 42, 142
Rota, Nino 51–52; *Legend of the Glass Mountain* 51–52
Roth, Martha 182
Roth, Tim 90
Rowland, Roy 116
Rózsa, Miklós 52, 59, 75; *Spellbound Concerto* 52
Rubinstein, Anton 12
Rubinstein, Artur 53, 56–57, 97
Rubinstein, Josef 11, 12
Rudkin, David 26, 154
Rush, Geoffrey 130, 188
Rushing Roulette (dir. Robert McKimson, 1965) 137
Ruskin, John 112
Russell, Ken 12, 16, 40, 41, 76, 87, 92–95, 96, 120, 142, 145, 146, 158
Rutherford, Margaret 35
Rye, Renny 130

Saint-Saëns, Camille 115
Saint-Simon, Lucile 170
Salieri, Antonio 90
Salmen, Hans 106
Sand, George 74, 75, 160, 178
Sanders, George 29
Sandrich, Mark 141
Sarandon, Susan 163

Sasdy, Peter 109
Satie, Eric 42
Sayn-Wittgenstein, Princess Caroline 96, 158
Scarlatti, Domenico 45, 156
Schade, Fritz 39
Schall, Ekkehard 101
Schlesinger, John 121, 122
Schoenberg, Arnold 64–65, 144
Schonberg, Harold 71
Schubert, Franz 22, 45, 65, 111–112, 135, 161, 176
Schumann, Clara 8, 97–99
Schumann, Robert 23, 28, 54, 97–99, 107, 108, 121, 124, 129, 136, 176, 183; *Fantasiestücke* 108, 129; Piano Concerto in A minor 54, 121, 136, 183
Schumlin, Herman 28
Scott, Lizabeth 30
Scott, Margaretta 122
Scott Joplin—The Movie (dir. Jeremy Kagen, 1977) 90
Scriabin, Alexander 17, 36, 94, 124, 166, 167, 169, 184
Secret (dir. Jay Chou, 2007) 90
Seitz, Franz 114, 115 ~Sellers Peter }
Sellers, Peter 61*September Affair* (dir. William Dieterle, 1950) 57, **58**, 63
The Seven Year Itch (dir. Billy Wilder, 1955) 60, **60**
The Seventh Veil (dir. Compton Bennett, 1944) 46, 59, 124–128, **126**, 131
The Seventh Victim (dir. Mark Robson, 1943) 29
Seymour, Jane 62
Shaffer, Peter 79
Shakespeare, William 173, 174
Sharp, Don 123, 164–165
Shaw, George Bernard 105
Shaw, Ivan 186
Shearer, Moira 59, 144
Shelley, Barbara 57
Shepard, Richard 136
Shine (dir. Scott Hicks, 1996) 130–133, 188
Shinjō, Takehiko 133
Shoot the Piano Player (dir. François Truffaut, 1960) 14, 30, 173
Shostakovitch, Dmitri 31, 38, 52, 131, 147; *The Assault on Beautiful Gorky* 52
Show-Biz Bugs (dir. Fritz Freleng, 1957) 137
Sibelius, Jean 94
Sidney, George 8, 80
Sigalvitch, Anna 134
Silverman, Marissa 89
Sims, Joan 30
Sinatra, Frank 8, 28, 142

212　Index

Sincerely Yours (dir. Gordon Douglas, 1955) 69, 70, 76–80, **77**, 159, 188
Sinding, Christian 182
Singer, Bryan 39
Sinkovits, Imre 97, 100
Siodmak, Robert 35
The Smallest Show on Earth (dir. Basil Dearden, 1957) 35
Smirnov, Boris 100
Smith, Dame Maggie 10
Soderbergh, Stephen 67
Somewhere in Time (dir. Jeannot Szwarc, 1980) 62
Song of Love (dir. Clarence Brown, 1947) 8, 97–99, **98**, 133
Song of Summer (dir. Ken Russell, 1968) 145–146
A Song to Remember (dir. George Cukor, 1945) 74–76, **74**, 96, 171–172
Song Without End (dirs. Charles Vidor & George Cukor, 1960) 75, 88, 95–97, **95**
Souza, Edward de 165, 166
Spaeth, Merrie 61
Sparky's Magic Piano (dir. Lee Mishkin, 1987) 128–129
Spellbound (dir. Alfred Hitchcock, 1946) 52
Spielzeugland (aka *Toyland*, dir. Alexander Freydank, 2007) 119–120
Spindler, Fritz 24
Spione (dir. Fritz Lang, 1928) 139
The Spiral Staircase (dir. Robert Siodmak, 1946) 35
Stabb, Dinah 26
Stalin, Joseph 52
Standing, John 179
Stapleton, James 170
Steele, Barbara 109
Steiner, Max 41, 46, 181
Steiner, Rudolf 70
Stenbock, Count Eric 164; "The True Story of a Vampire" 164
Stengel, Christian 99
Stevens, Bernard 50
Stevens, George 28
Stevens, Leith 56–57
Stevens, Marti 173
Stevens, Robert 147
Stewart, Fred Mustard 183, 184
Stewart, James 36, **37**, 40
Stewart, Rod 28
Stoker, Bram 164
Stokowski, Leopold 18, 53
Stolen Face (dir. Terence Fisher, 1952) 30
Stone, Andrew L. 14
The Story of Three Loves (dirs. Gottfried Reinhardt, & Vincent Minnelli, 1953) 59

Stormy Weather (dir. Andrew L. Stone, 1943) 14
Strauss, Johann 9, 18, 67
Stravinsky, Igor 128, 144, 145
Streep, Meryl 180
Stroheim, Erich von 149
Sullivan, Sir Arthur 160
Sullivan, Ed 79
The Summer of '42 (dir. Robert Mulligan, 1971) 41
Sunset Blvd. (dir. Billy Wilder, 1950) 149, 151
Superman Returns (dir. Bryan Singer, 2006) 39
Sutherland, Donald 115
Svengali (dir. Archie Mayo, 1931) 123
Swanson, Gloria 149
Sweeney, Sydney 186
Swing Time (dir. George Stevens, 1936) 28
Sylvester, William 57
Szerelmi álmok (aka *Song of Love*, dir. Heinz Hille, 1935) 97
Szerelmi álmok (aka *Song of Love*, dir. Márton Keleti, 1970) 97, 100
Szwarc, Jeannot 62

Taste of Fear (dir. Seth Holt, 1961) 179–180, 181
Taste the Blood of Dracula (dir. Peter Sasdy, 1970) 109, 114
Taupin, Bernie 68
Taurog, Norman 141
Taylor, Elizabeth 58–59, 187
Taylor, Noah 130
Tchaikovsky, Pyotr 11, 12, 16, 25, 29, 46, 47, 66, 73, 76, 78, 79, 124, 181; First Piano Concerto in B-flat minor 12, 16, 46, 47, 76, 78; Second Piano Concerto in G major 181
Telezynska, Izabella 12
The Tender Trap (dir. Charles Walters, 1955) 142
Testimony (dir. Tony Palmer, 1988) 147
Thackeray, William Makepeace 110; *Vanity Fair* 110
Thalberg, Sigismond 26–27, 87, 111
Theatre of Blood (dir. Douglas Hickox, 1973) 121
Theatre of Death (dir. Sam Gallu, 1967) 169
Thomas, Gerald 30, 43
The Thomas Crown Affair (dir. Norman Jewison, 1968) 41
Thompson, Carlos 100
Thompson, Eric 185
Thompson, J. Lee 153
The Three Amigos (dir. John Landis, 1986) 30

Thurn, Hansjörg 154
Tierney, Gene 27, *28*
Tiomkin, Dimitri 169
Tissot, James 9
Toback, James 175
Todd, Ann 125, *126*, 131, 133
Tolstoy, Leo 163; "The Kreutzer Sonata" 163
Tommy (dir. Ken Russell, 1975) 92
Tornatore, Guiseppe 90
Torture Garden (dir. Freddie Francis, 1967) 179, 181
Total Recall (dir. Len Wiseman, 2012) 188
Toth, Andre de 169
Toubiana, Serge 173
Tourneur, Jacques 29
Tours, Berthold 24
Toyland (aka *Spielzeugland*, dir. Alexander Freydank, 2007) 119-120
Träumerei (dir. Harald Braun, 1944) 97
Trio (dir. Ken Annakin, 1950) 29
Trollope, Anthony 111
Trotsky, Leon 129
Truffaut, François 14, 30, 173
Truman, Michael 29
Tucker, Annand 17
Twilight (dir. Catherine Hardwick, 2008) 189
Twins of Evil (dir. John Hough, 1971) 109
Tyldum, Morten 188

Ullmann, Liv 182
The Unforgettable Year 1919 (dir. Mikheil Chiaureli, 1951) 52

Vaughan, Peter 138
Veidt, Conrad 166, 168
Vidor, Charles 9, 57, 88, 96
Vier Minuten (dir. Chris Kraus, 2006) 135-136
Village of the Damned (dir. Wolf Rilla, 1960) 29
Visconti, Luchino 102, 113, 147, 162
Vitus (dir. Fredi M. Murer, 2006) 135

Waggner, George 55
Wagner (dir. Tony Palmer, 1983) 8, 11, 101, 140-141
Wagner, Richard 11, 16, 17, 18, 22, 38, 64, 67, 85, 93, 94, 95, 100-102, 120, 140-141, 146-147, 156, 169, 188; *Der Fliegender Holländer* 100, 147; *Die Meistersinger Von Nürnberg* 11; *Parsifal* 64, 100, 188; *Das Rheingold* 64; *Rienzi* 94; *Das Ring Des Nibelungen* 85, 100; *Siegfried* 101; *Siegfried Idyll* 169; *Tristan Und Isolde* 11, 16, 17, 22, 76, 140, 146, 156
Wakeman, Rick 94

Walbrook, Anton 9, 42, 44, 51, 143
Walker, Alan 19, 86-87
Walker, Kerry 162
Walker, Robert *98*, 99
Walker, Tippy 61
The Walking Dead (dir. Michael Curtiz, 1936) 176
Waller, Thomas "Fats," 14
Wallis, Jacquie *164*, 166
Walters, Charles 72, 142
Wang, Yuja 16
Warbeck, David 109
Ward, Edward 51; *Lullaby of the Bells* 51-52
Warren, Barry 165, *165*, 166, 168
Washbourne, Mona 32
Watch on the Rhine (dir. Herman Schumlin, 1943) 28-29
Watson, Emma 113
Waugh, Evelyn 67
Waxman, Franz 40, 41
Wayne, Johnny 72
Whatever Became of Jack and Jill? (dir. Bill Bains, 1972) 32-33
Why Stop Now? (dirs. Phil Dorling & Ron Nyswaner, 2012) 135
Weber, Carl Maria von 113
Weine, Robert 123, 168
Welles, Orson 106, 180
Wendkos, Paul 9, 183
West, Samuel 24
When the Cat's Away (dir. Walt Disney, 1939) 86
While I Live (dir. John Harlow, 1947) 47
Whispering City (dir. Fedor Ozep, 1947) 47-48
Whitaker, David 138-139
Who Killed Roger Rabbit? (dir. Robert Zemeckis, 1988) 89
The Wicker Man (dir. Robin Hardy, 1970) 10-11
Wideo Wabbit (dir. Robert McKimson, 1956) 83, 89
Widerberg, Bo 2
Widmark, Richard 41
Wiemann, Mathias 97
Wilde, Cornel 74, *74*, 96
Wilde, Oscar 30, 178
Wilder, Billy 60, 149
Wilkinson, Anthony 84
Williams, Alison 136
Williams, Charles 47; *The Dream of Olwen* 47
Williams, Clarence 90
Williams, Kenneth 30
Willman, Noel 165
Wilson, Dooley 183

Wiseman, Len 188
The Witches of Eastwick (dir. George Miller, 1987) 163
Wolf, Hugo 124
The Wolf Man (dir. George Waggner, 1941) 55
Wollenhaupt, Hermann 24
Wood, Elijah 137
Wood, Sam 103, 151, 153
Woodwood, Edward 10
The World of Henry Orient (dir. George Ray Hill, 1964) 60–61
Wright, Joe 110

Wyndham, John 29
Wynyard, Diana 9

Yates, David 113
You Will Be Mine (aka *Je Te Mangerais*, dir Sophy Laloy, 2009) 134–135
Young, Terence 42
Younger, Earl 138
Your Lie in April (dir. Takehiko Shinjō, 2015) 133

Zedong, Mao 31
Zemeckis, Robert 89

www.ingramcontent.com/pod-product-compliance
Lightning Source LLC
Chambersburg PA
CBHW020836020526
44114CB00040B/1221